Illustrated
AutoSketch 2.0

Paul L. Schlieve

Wordware Publishing, Inc.

Library of Congress Cataloging-in-Publication Data

Schlieve, Paul L.
    Illustrated AutoSketch 2.0 / Paul L. Schlieve.
        p.   cm.
    ISBN 1-55622-172-X
    1. AutoSketch (Computer program)   I. Title.

TS385.S286   1990
620'.00425'02855369--dc20   89-78485
                                                                   CIP

ISBN 1-55622-172-X
10 9 8 7 6 5 4 3 2 1
9002

AutoSketch and AutoCAD are trademarks of Autodesk, Inc.
IBM is a registered trademark of International Business Machines Corporation.
MS DOS is a registered trademark of Microsoft Corporation.
Ventura Publisher is a registered trademark of Ventura Software, Incorporated.
WordStar is a registered trademark of MicroPro International Corporation.
Xerox is a trademark of Xerox Corporation.

All inquiries for volume purchases of this book should be addressed to Wordware Publishing, Inc.,
at the above address. Telephone inquiries may be made by calling:

(214) 423-0090

Table of Contents

Table of Contents (Cont.)

Recommended Learning Sequence

Recommended Learning Sequence (Cont.)

Module 1
ABOUT THIS BOOK

INTRODUCTION

This book describes the AutoSketch computer-aided design system. This software system, a product of Autodesk, Inc., provides basic capabilities for drawing and computer aided drafting. This book presents detailed information about AutoSketch, and each command and technique is illustrated with examples. This book is designed for a broad range of users. It is designed for first-time users of CAD systems who need a sequential introduction to the system. The book is also designed for experienced AutoSketch users who need a reference manual with numerous examples from which to extract the full benefits of this software system. Finally, the book is for the classroom instructor in need of a concise, instructionally designed AutoSketch text.

A recommended learning sequence is provided to guide you through AutoSketch operations in a simple-to-complex fashion. It follows a computerized version of the paper-and-pencil procedures you would normally use to develop a drawing from selection of the paper size, pen width, and scale through production of finished drawings on paper.

ORGANIZATION

This book is not designed to be read in page-number order. If you are learning AutoSketch, follow the Recommended Learning Sequence printed in the front of the book.

After a brief introduction to AutoSketch in Modules 1 and 2, Modules 3 through 65 are arranged alphabetically by command. The alphabetical sequence is provided so that, in addition to serving as a guide for learning AutoSketch, the book can continue serving you as a convenient command reference.

If you are like most computer users, you are probably in a hurry to see your software in action. Does this description fit you? If so, then Module 2 is for you. Module 2 provides a step-by-step sample session in which you use AutoSketch to draw the walls of an office and then draw and position the office furniture. This experience gives you insight into the power of AutoSketch and lets you use many of its commands in a matter of minutes.

STYLE CONVENTIONS

Knowing a few practices followed in the book can make your understanding of its content clearer.

The discussion of AutoSketch features, procedures, and applications is presented in paragraph form. Steps which you perform in the Typical Operations are numbered.

KEYBOARD CONVENTIONS The following guidelines are used in working with the keyboard:

- Keys that are typed or pressed are indicated by bold type.
- Two-key combinations are indicated by a statement such as "Press **Ctrl-C** to cancel the operation." The word *press* is your clue that you must use a function key or key combination. The notation **Ctrl-C** means that you press and hold the key marked **Ctrl,** then press and release the key for typing the letter **c**, and finally release the **Ctrl** key.
- The notation **<CR>** stands for the "Carriage Return" key on your computer. The key cap notation used by computer manufacturers differ for this key. The key may be engraved with "Return" or "Enter." Some computers have both a **Return** key and an **Enter** key. Both are identical for AutoSketch applications and are used interchangably. Some IBM PC's use the symbol ↵ to designate the **Enter** or **Return** key and do not provide a printed legend.

MOUSE CONVENTIONS The following guidelines are used when working with a mouse or other digitizer. When you use the keyboard instead of a mouse, press the Ins key instead of the mouse button.

- Commands you pick from a screen menu with the mouse are printed in **bold** type.
- The word "pick" is used to describe the process of moving the mouse pointer to the required position, then pressing and releasing the left mouse button.
- The word "drag" is used to describe the process of moving the mouse pointer to the required position, pressing and holding the left mouse button while moving the mouse (and the object with it) into the desired location, then releasing the mouse button.

BEFORE YOU BEGIN

HARDWARE REQUIREMENTS First, you must install AutoSketch on your computer. You must have an IBM-compatible computer system with PC/MS-DOS 2.0 or later. You must have a graphics display and a minimum of 512K of RAM. You must have at least one floppy disk drive. A mouse or other pointing device is not required, but aids greatly in the drawing process. You need a graphics printer or a plotter if you want to produce paper output from the program.

There are several things that can add to AutoSketch's performance. Additional RAM, up to the 640K DOS maximum, allows you to work with more complex drawings. A math co-processor speeds up AutoSketch by a factor of three. A hard disk provides faster loading for the AutoSketch program and drawings. Because AutoSketch must refer to the program disk often, a hard disk also increases the speed of program operation. If you have a math co-processor, consider upgrading to enhanced AutoSketch. You get another three-times speed increase and decreased RAM requirements, allowing you to develop more complex drawings.

SOFTWARE INSTALLATION You can't run AutoSketch from the original diskettes. You must copy the diskettes either onto diskettes, or into a subdirectory of your hard disk.

Floppy-disk Systems You need the original AutoSketch disks and two blank, formatted disks.

1. Place the AutoSketch program disk in drive A: and the blank disk in drive B:.

2. Type **Copy A:*.* B:** and press **Enter**.

3. Remove the disks and label the copy. Do not write-protect the copy of the program disk.

4. Place the AutoSketch supplemental disk in drive A: and the blank disk in drive B:.

5. Type **Copy A:*.* B:** and press **Enter**.

6. Remove the disks and label the copy.

Hard-Disk Systems It is best to copy the files into a subdirectory, rather than placing them in the root directory.

1. Type **MD \SKETCH** and press **Enter**.

2. Type **CD \SKETCH** and press **Enter**.

3. Insert the program disk in drive A:, then type **COPY A:*.* C:\SKETCH**.

4. (Optional) Repeat step #3 with the supplemental disk to copy the sample drawings to the hard disk.

CONFIGURING AUTOSKETCH

The first time you start AutoSketch it inquires about your mouse, display, and printer or plotter. This information is written to a file named SKETCH.CFG on either your floppy disk or the SKETCH subdirectory of your hard disk. To change the configuration, if, for example, you purchase a new printer, erase the file SKETCH.CFG. AutoSketch then repeats the configuration dialog the next time you start the program.

START AUTOSKETCH

The procedure you use to start AutoSketch varies with your computer configuration.

FLOPPY DISK SYSTEM Place your working copy of the AutoSketch program disk in drive A: and a data disk in drive B:.

1. Type **floppy** and press **Enter** to cause AutoSketch to use drive B: for saving your drawing files.

2. Type **sketch** and press **Enter**.

HARD DISK SYSTEM Your screen should show the DOS prompt with the drive letter of the hard disk.

3. Type **cd\sketch** and press **Enter**.

4. Type **sketch** and press **Enter**.

AUTOSKETCH DRAWING SCREEN

When you start AutoSketch, the drawing screen appears, with the command menu bar at the top of the screen.

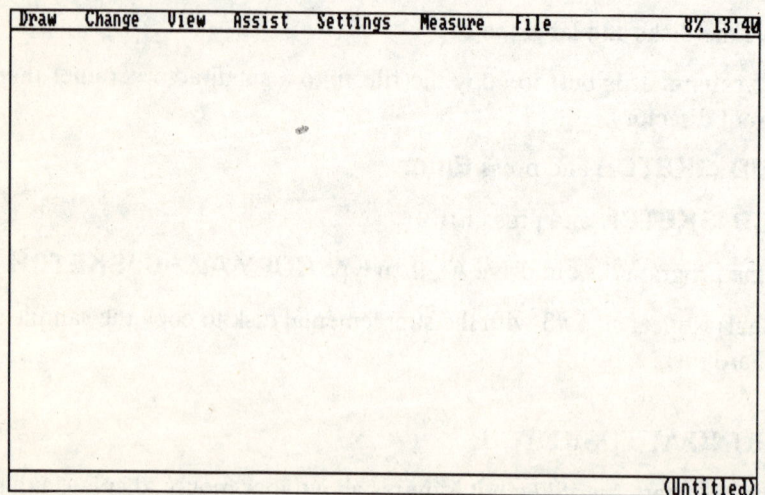

5. To quit AutoSketch, pick "File" in the menu bar. The File menu opens.

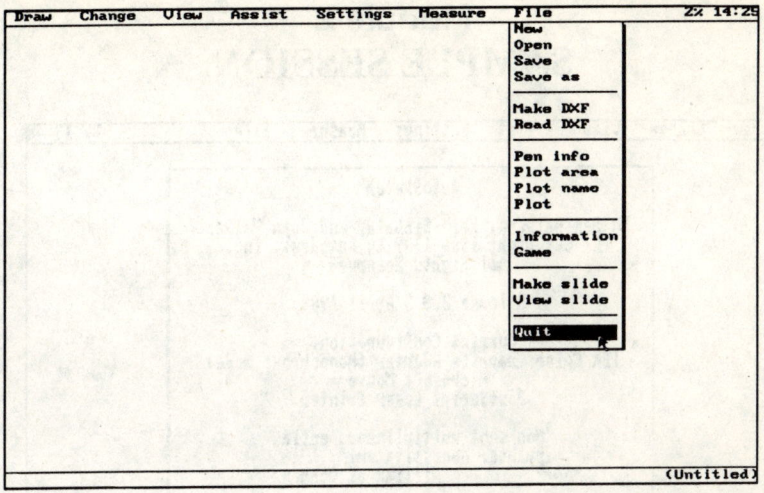

6. Pick **Quit** from the File menu.

7. Continue the learning sequence with Module 2, Sample Session.

Module 2
SAMPLE SESSION

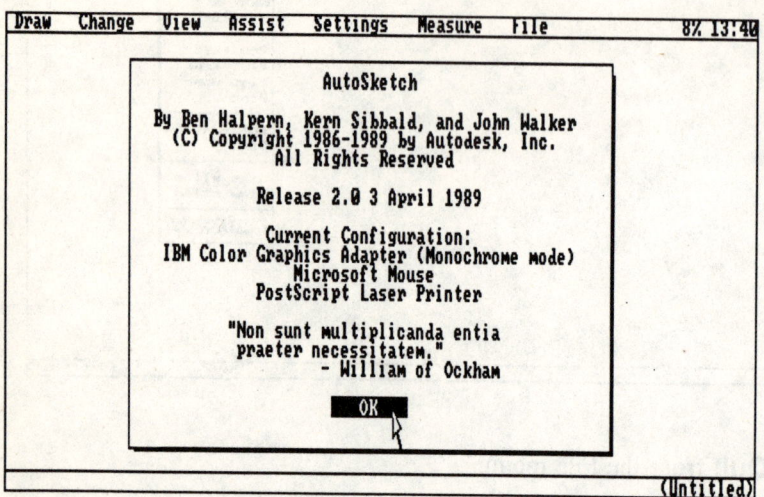

DESCRIPTION

This sample session guides you through the steps required to produce an AutoSketch drawing. This session introduces you to many of the most popular AutoSketch commands. The following commands are used to produce a typical office floor plan and are listed below in their order of appearance:

- Limits
- Grid
- Point
- Break
- Arc
- Rotate
- Text

- Snap
- Zoom
- Box
- Line
- Copy
- Group
- Redraw

TYPICAL OPERATION

Use AutoSketch to design the interior layout of an office. This module assumes that you have followed the instructions in your AutoSketch manual to start the program and get the drawing screen to appear on your computer's display. Begin with a new untitled drawing.

After AutoSketch has entered the drawing editor screen, the menus appear across the top of your computer screen. All you need do to start a new command is pick a menu by moving the screen pointer arrow until it highlights the menu name you want to use and then press the pick button on your input device (mouse) to get the pull down menu to appear under the menu name. After the menu pulls down, just move the screen pointer until the desired command is highlighted (do not hold the pick button down while doing this, AutoSketch does not mimic the Macintosh environment). After the desired command is highlighted, press the pick button and the command prompt (input request) appears at the bottom of the screen. In this activity, the command prompt (input request) is printed in regular type and the things you need to type or pick are printed in bold type.

Before beginning the first numbered steps on the office drawing, you must determine the size of your drawing sheet. One of the differences between AutoSketch and manual drafting is that you always work with full scale in AutoSketch. In the case of our office layout, the sheet of paper must be large enough for a drawing of 120 X 144 inches plus some border area. At the input request, type the bold letters (or follow the instructions) that follow.

NOTE

<CR> means to press Enter or Return (Carriage Return)

Take a look at the office illustration.

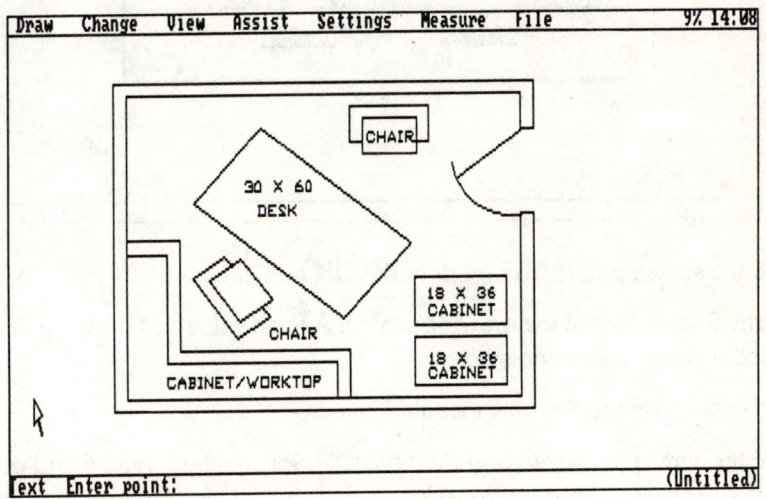

Set the size of the drawing sheet with the Limits command.

1. Pick **Limits** from the Settings menu.

Move the screen pointer to each box shown on the Drawing Limits dialogue box. Notice that some of the boxes change color as the screen pointer enters their boundary. This phenomenon is called "highlighting." When a box is highlighted, anything you type from the keyboard replaces what was originally in the box. The value zero in the "Left" and "Bottom" boxes are not changed.

2. Move the screen pointer to highlight the Right box. Type **192** and press **Enter**.

3. Move the screen pointer to highlight the "Top" box. Type **158** and press **Enter**.

The "Right" value is the setting for "X" (horizontal) size. The "Top" value is the setting for the "Y" (vertical) size.

The Drawing Limits dialogue box should now appear as shown in the following illustration.

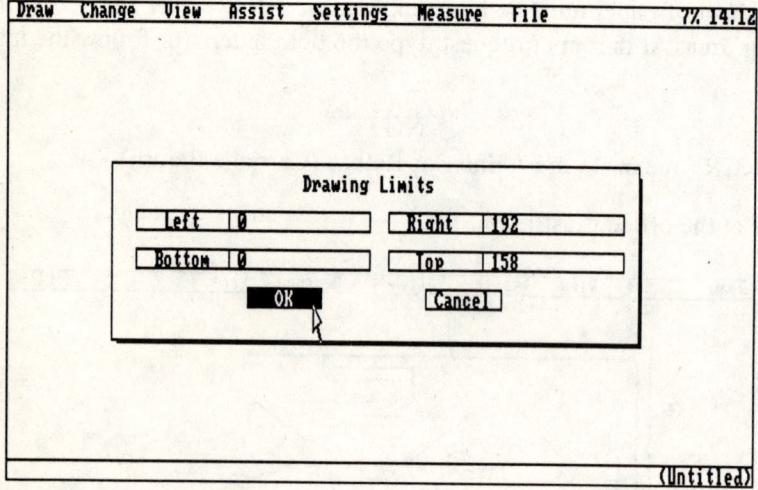

4. Move the screen pointer to highlight the **OK** box and pick it.

Designate the Snap value for the drawing screen. A Snap value of 4 drawing units (inches) is designated with the following steps.

5. Pick **Snap** from the Settings menu.

6. Move the screen pointer to highlight the "X" Spacing box, type **4** and press **Enter**.

The Snap dialogue box shows both the X and Y settings to be set to a value of 4.

7. Move the screen pointer to highlight the **Off** box and pick it.

The Snap dialogue box now shows the Snap as turned On.

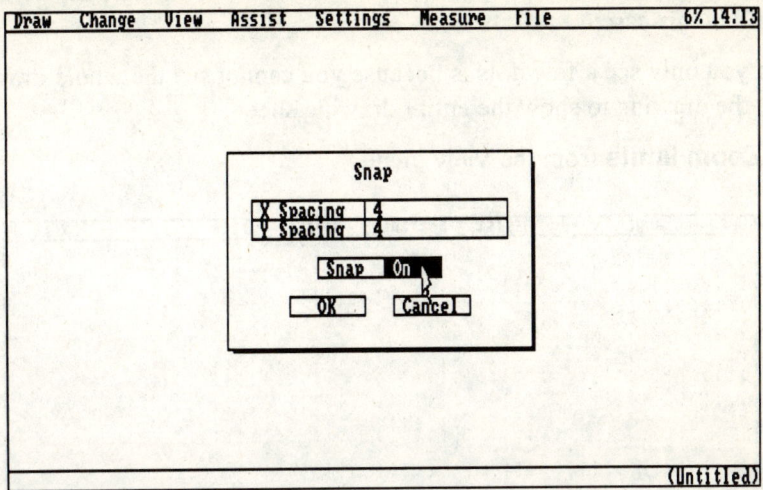

8. Move the screen pointer to highlight the **OK** box and pick it.

9. Select the **Assist** menu.

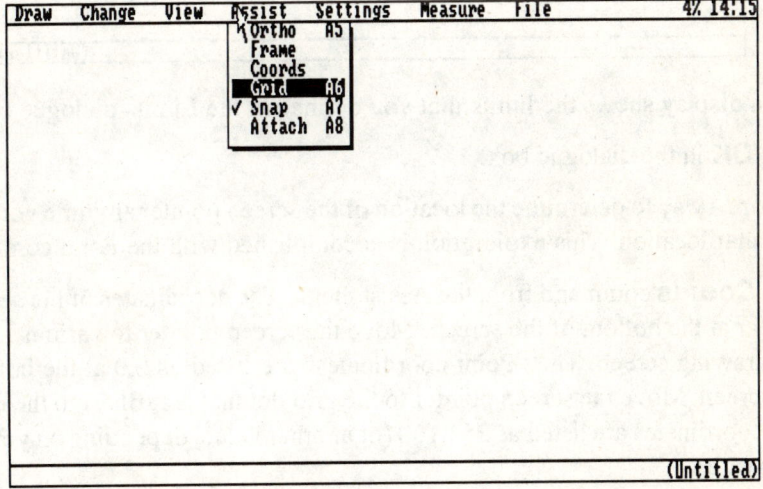

Notice that the Snap command listed on the Assist menu has a check beside it. This means that Snap is now On. Remember that you turned it on. You can also turn the Snap on and off from the Assist menu. As you can see, there is often more than one way to accomplish something in AutoSketch.

10. Pick the **Grid** command in the Assist menu.

Look at your screen closely, there are several widely spaced dots. The Grid command has a default value of zero. If you leave Grid set to zero, it follows the Snap setting. This is what you did in this case.

The reason you only see a few dots is because you cannot see the whole drawing sheet. Now zoom the drawing to show the entire drawing sheet.

11. Pick **Zoom limits** from the View menu.

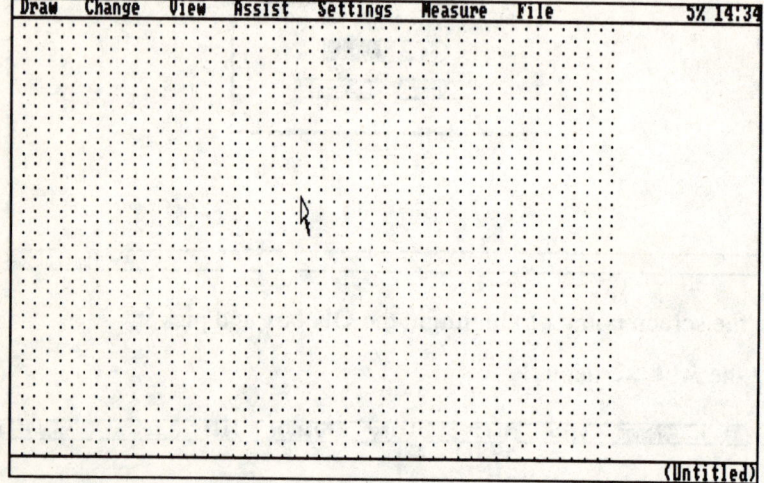

The screen display shows the limits that you defined in the Limits dialogue box.

12. Pick **OK** in the dialogue box.

Now explore a way to determine the location of the screen pointer anytime you are unsure of a particular location. This exploration is accomplished with the Point command.

13. Pick **Coords** command from the Assist menu. The coordinates of the screen cursor appear at the bottom of the screen. Move the screen pointer to various locations on the drawing screen. The "Point coordinates" are listed as 0,0 at the bottom left of the screen. Move the screen pointer to the grid dot that is furthest to the upper right. The coordinates are listed as 252,160 (or another value, depending on your graphics hardware).

14. Pick **Coords** from the Assist menu. The coordinate display disappears.

NOTE
As you perform the drawing activities in the book you may choose to activate the Coords display to provide a display of the current coordinate system. On a slower computer system, the screen cursor is less responsive with the coordinates displayed. On a faster

computer system, the coordinate display does not noticably affect the system response.

Sometimes after completing a drawing activity, it is a good idea to go back to each point entered at the keyboard and find out where that specific point is on the screen. This helps to develop deeper understanding of what is actually happening in each step of the example.

Draw a box to produce the outer wall of the office.

15. Pick **Box** from the Draw menu.

16. Type **24,28 <CR>** as the first corner point and **168,140 <CR>** as the second corner point.

Draw a box to produce the inner wall of the office.

17. Continue the box command. Type **28,32 <CR>** as the first corner and **164,136 <CR>** as the second corner.

Remove a section of the wall to form a door opening by using the Break command. When breaking out a portion of the box, the break occurs in a counterclockwise direction, so it matters which is the first and second break location.

18. Pick **Break** from the Change menu. Respond to the prompts as shown in the following list:

Break Select object: **168,132 <CR>**
Break First break point: **168,96 <CR>**
Break Second break point: **168,132 <CR>**
Break Select object: **164,132 <CR>**
Break First break point: **164,96 <CR>**
Break Second break point: **164,132 <CR>**

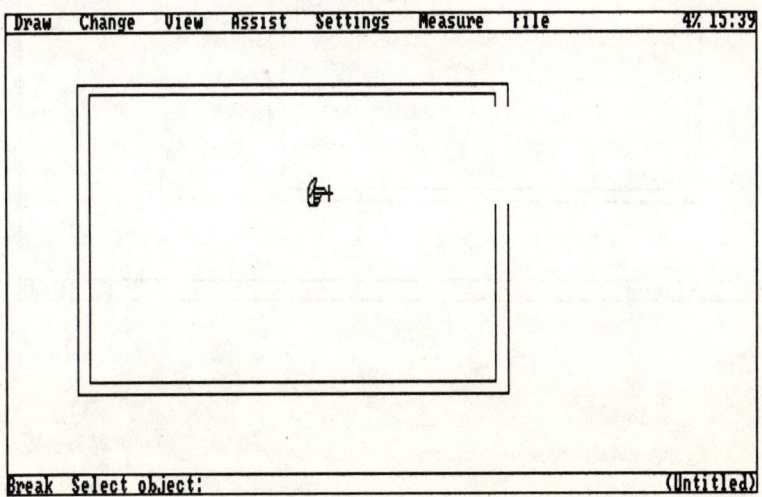

Use the Zoom box command to improve your view of the drawing. This lets you see the work area around the door opening more easily. Then add the two lines to close and complete the outer wall. Watch the screen closely to determine what each command entry is doing as it is entered.

19. Pick **Zoom box** from the View menu.

20. Type **132,88 <CR>** as the first corner and **180,148 <CR>** as the second corner.

21. Pick **Line** from the Draw menu. Respond to the following prompts as shown.

    Line Enter point: **164,132 <CR>**
    Line To point: **168,132 <CR>**
    Line Enter point: **168,96 <CR>**
    Line To point: **164,96 <CR>**
    Line Enter point: **164,132 <CR>**
    Line To point: **P(34.4093,234) <CR>**

Complete the schematic door symbol with the Arc command.

22. Pick **Arc** from the Draw menu. Type **164,96 <CR>** as the start point, **144,104 <CR>** as a point on the arc, and **140,108 <CR>** as the arc end point.

Zoom the screen back out to a full view of the entire drawing limits.

23. Pick **Zoom limits** from the View menu.

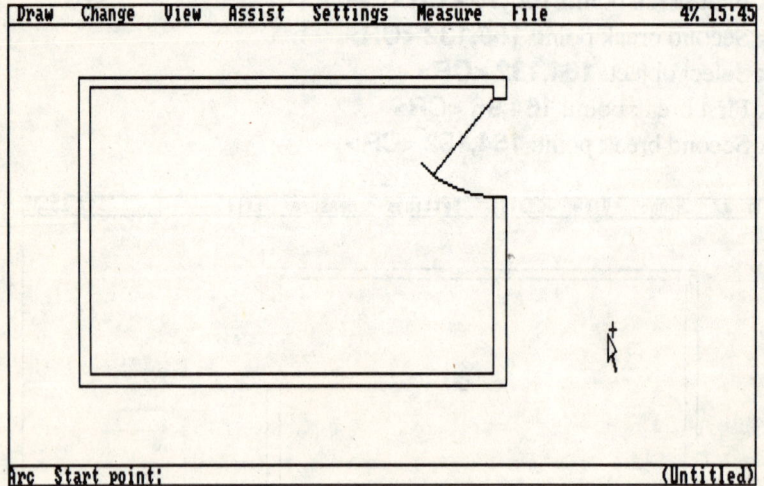

Draw an 18 X 36 file cabinet.

24. Pick **Line** from the Draw menu. Respond to the prompts as shown in the following list:

Line Enter point: **160,36 <CR>**
Line To point: **R(–36,0)**
Line Enter point: **/LPOINT <CR>**
Line To point: **R(0,18)**
Line Enter point: **/LPOINT <CR>**
Line To point: **P(36,0)**
Line Enter point: **/LPOINT <CR>**
Line To point: **P(18,270)**

Copy the file cabinet.

25. Pick **Copy** from the Change menu. Respond to the prompts as shown in the following list:

Copy Select object: **120,60 <CR>**
Copy Crosses/window corner: **164,32 <CR>**
Copy Enter point: **160,36 <CR>**
Copy Enter point: **160,56 <CR>**

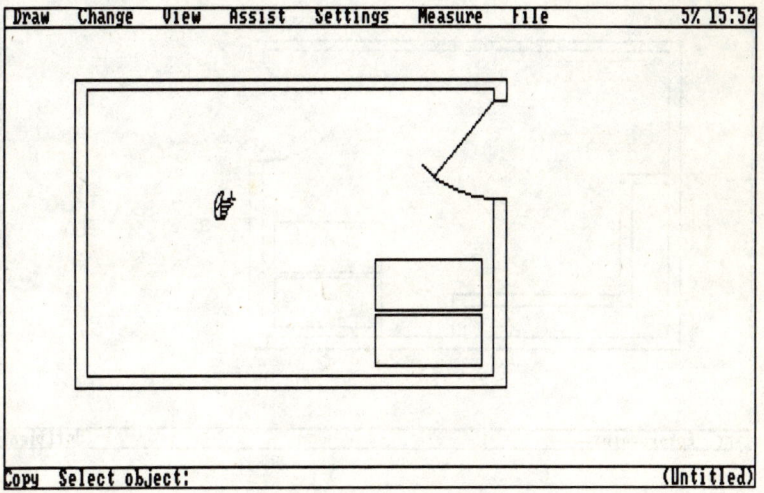

Draw built-in cabinets and worksurface.

26. Pick **Line** from the Draw menu. Respond to the prompts as shown.

> Line Enter point: **96,32 <CR>**
> Line To point: **96,44 <CR>**
> Line Enter point: **96,44 <CR>**
> Line To point: **40,44 <CR>**
> Line Enter point: **40,44 <CR>**
> Line To point: **40,88 <CR>**
> Line Enter point: **40,88 <CR>**
> Line To point: **28,88 <CR>**
> Line Enter point: **28,92 <CR>**
> Line To point: **R(16,0) <CR>**
> Line Enter point: **/LPOINT <CR>**
> Line To point: **44,48 <CR>**
> Line Enter point: **44,48 <CR>**
> Line To point: **100,48 <CR>**
> Line Enter point: **/LPOINT <CR>**
> Line To point: **100,32 <CR>**

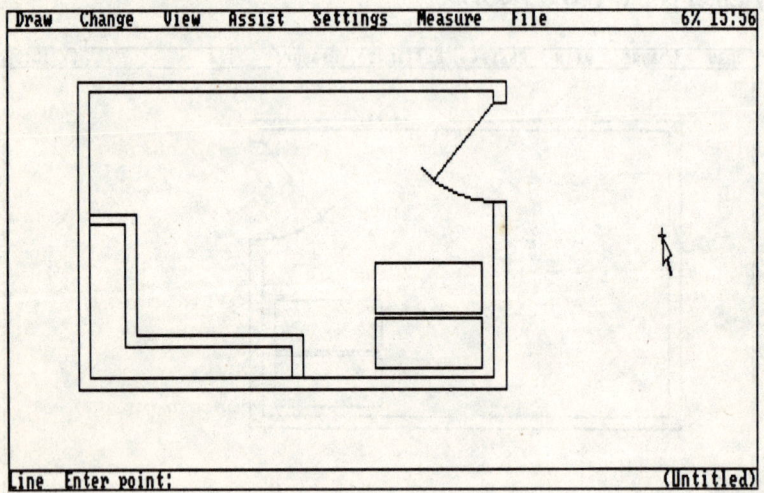

Draw a 30 X 60 Desk.

27. Pick **Box** from the Draw menu. Type **56,100 <CR>** as the first corner and **R(60,30)** as the second corner.

Rotate the desk to an appropriate position.

28. Pick **Rotate** from the Change menu. Respond to the prompts as shown:

    Rotate Select object: **52,96 <CR>**
    Rotate Crosses/window corner: **120,132 <CR>**
    Rotate Center of rotation: **56,108 <CR>**
    Rotate Second point: **P(60,323) <CR>**

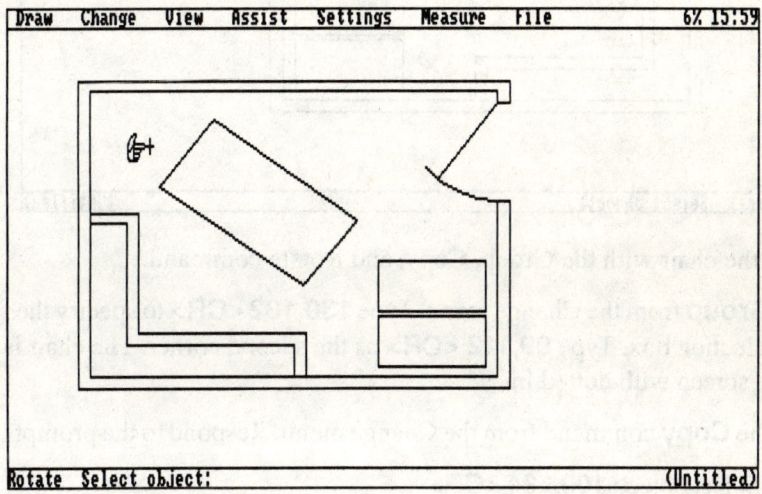

Draw an office chair.

29. Pick **Box** from the Draw menu. Respond to the prompts as shown:

    Box First corner: **104,112 <CR>**
    Box Second corner: **124,128 <CR>**
    Box First corner: **100,116 <CR>**
    Box Second corner: **128,132 <CR>**

Use the Break command to remove the extra line.

30. Pick **Break** from the Change menu. Respond to the prompts as shown:

    Break Select object: **112,116 <CR>**
    Break First break point: **104,116 <CR>**
    Break Second break point: **124,116 <CR>**

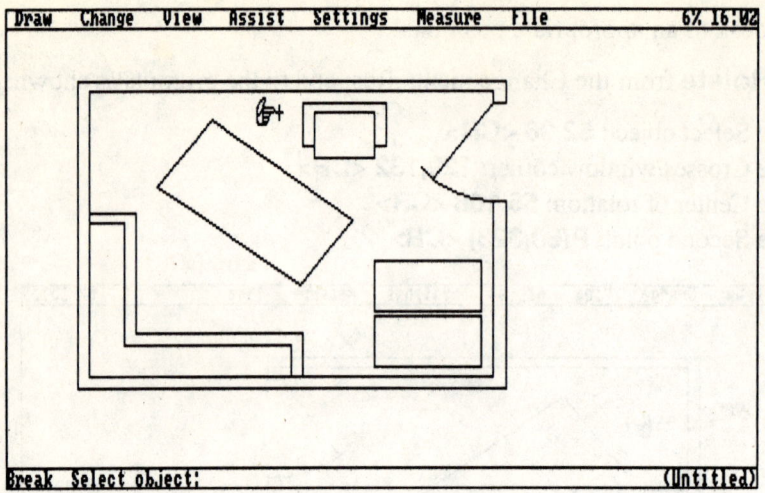

Reproduce the chair with the Group, Copy, and Rotate command.

31. Pick **Group** from the Change menu. Type **130,132 <CR>** to specify the first corner of a selection box. Type **99,112 <CR>** as the second corner. The chair is displayed on the screen with dotted lines.

32. Pick the **Copy** command from the Change menu. Respond to the prompts as shown:

    Copy Select object: **100,124 <CR>**
    Copy Enter point: **100,124 <CR>**
    Copy Enter point: **52,68 <CR>**

33. Pick the **Rotate** command from the **Change** menu. Type **52,68 <CR>** to select the object, type **64,68 <CR>** as the center of rotation, and type **P(12,123) <CR>** as the second rotation point.

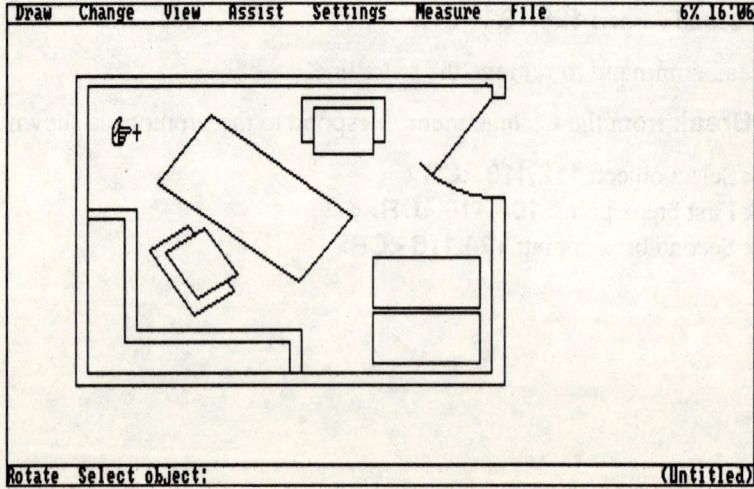

Change the Text height to 4 inches and add text to the office components.

34. Pick the **Text** command from the Settings menu. Move the cursor to highlight the Height value and type **4 <CR>**.

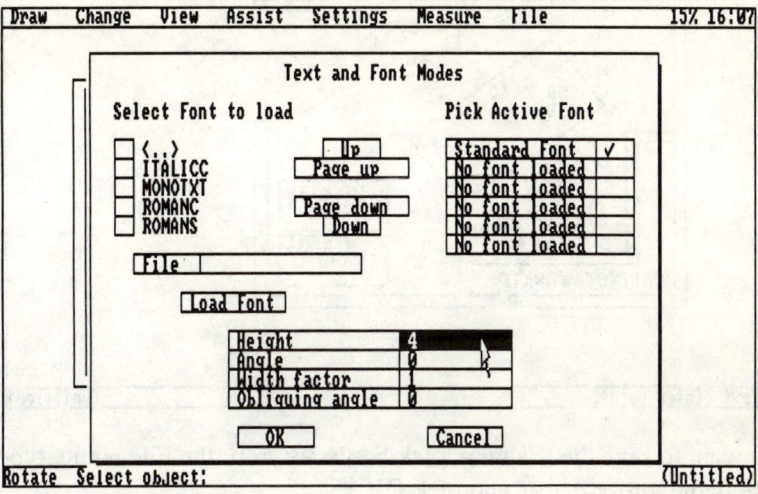

35. Pick **OK**.

36. Pick **Text** from the Draw menu. Respond to the prompts as shown:

Text Enter point: **32,36 <CR>**
Text Enter text: **CABINET/WORKTOP <CR>**
Text Enter point: **80,56 <CR>**
Text Enter text: **CHAIR <CR>**
Text Enter point: **64,104 <CR>**
Text Enter text: **30 X 60 <CR>**
Text Enter point: **68,98 <CR>**
Text Enter text: **DESK <CR>**
Text Enter point: **105,116 <CR>**
Text Enter text: **CHAIR <CR>**
Text Enter point: **132,68 <CR>**
Text Enter text: **18 X 36 <CR>**
Text Enter point: **132,63 <CR>**
Text Enter text: **CABINET <CR>**
Text Enter point: **132,48 <CR>**
Text Enter text: **18 X 36 <CR>**
Text Enter point: **132,43 <CR>**
Text Enter text: **CABINET <CR>**

37. Pick **Redraw** from the View menu. The completed drawing appears as follows.

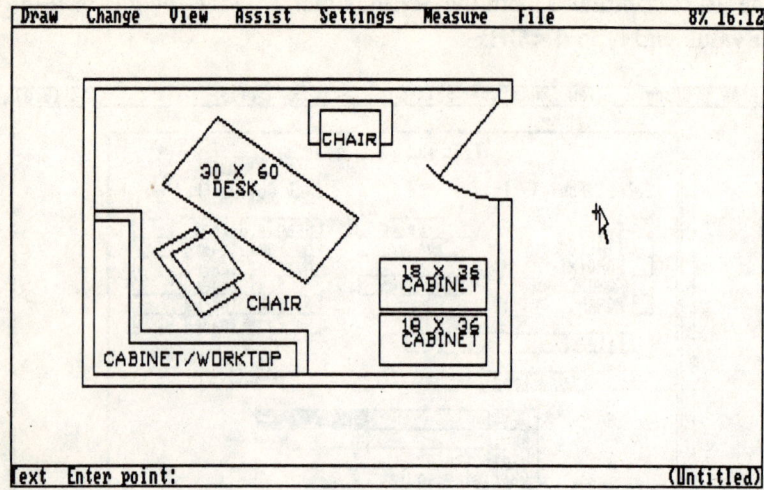

38. If you want to save the drawing, pick **Save as** from the File menu, type **Office** as the file name, press **Enter** and pick **OK**.

39. Pick **Quit** from the File menu.

40. Turn to Module 49, Quit, to continue the learning sequence.

Module 3
ANGLE

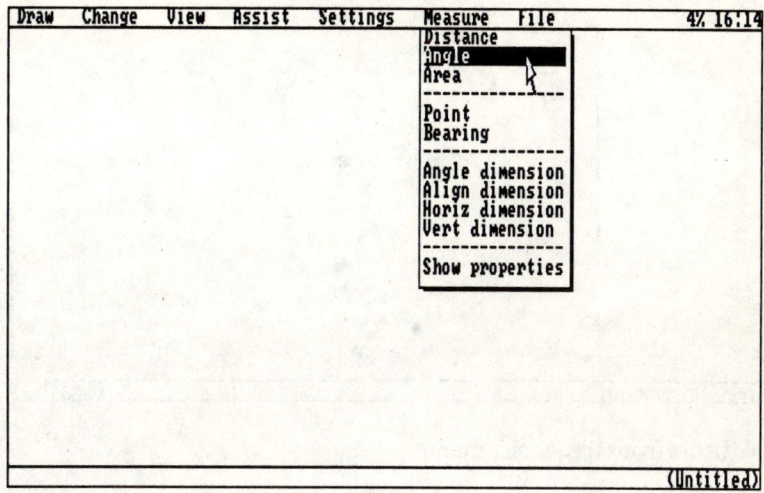

DESCRIPTION

Use the Angle command on the Measure menu to measure the angle between two bearings or directions. AutoSketch requests three points. The first entry is the vertex, or the base point. It then asks for two points or bearings from the base point. AutoSketch then calculates the angle between the two points using the base point as the vertex of the angle. The result is displayed in a dialogue box. The angle returned by the Angle command can be any angle between 0 and 180 degrees. AutoSketch uses variables to save information obtained when certain commands are used. The variable named "/LANGLE" is where the last result of the Angle command is saved.

APPLICATIONS

Many times in a drawing operation it is necessary to find the angle between two lines. The Angle command will return that information to the operator upon request.

TYPICAL OPERATION

In this operation you draw a horizontal and an angled line and then use the Angle command to find out what the angle is between the two lines. Begin with a new (Untitled) drawing.

1. Pick the **Line** command from the Draw menu. Pick three points, creating an angle as shown in the following illustration. The accuracy of your points is not important.

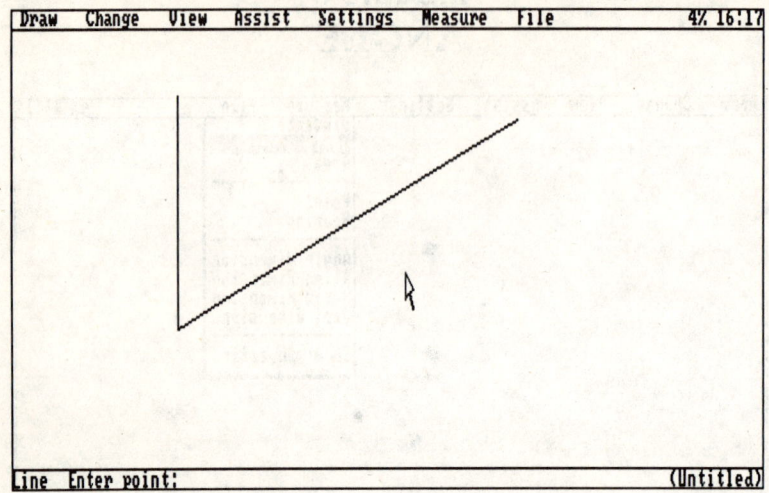

2. Pick **Attach** from the Assist menu.

Now, use the Angle command to find the angle measure between the two lines.

3. Pick **Angle** from the Measure menu. Notice the prompt at the bottom of the screen for the position of the vertex of the angle.

4. Pick the vertex. (Move the screen pointer to the vertex and pick the point.) Since Attach is active, all you need to do is get close to the left end of one of the lines and pick that point.

5. Pick the right end of the horizontal line by moving the screen cursor as close to the right end of the line as possible and then picking that point. Again, the Attach option takes care of the accuracy of your pick.

6. Pick the upper right end of the angled line by moving the screen pointer to that point and pressing the left mouse button.

AutoSketch displays the measure of your chosen angle in a dialogue box.

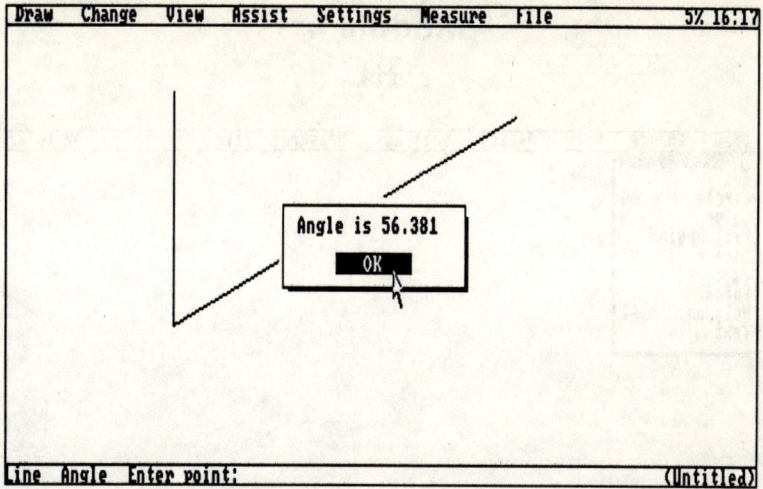

```
Draw   Change   View   Assist   Settings   Measure   File              5% 16:17
```

Angle is 56.381

OK

```
Line  Angle  Enter point:                                           (Untitled)
```

7. Pick **OK** in the dialogue box.

8. Quit AutoSketch, or turn to Module 7, Bearing, to continue the learning sequence.

Module 4
ARC

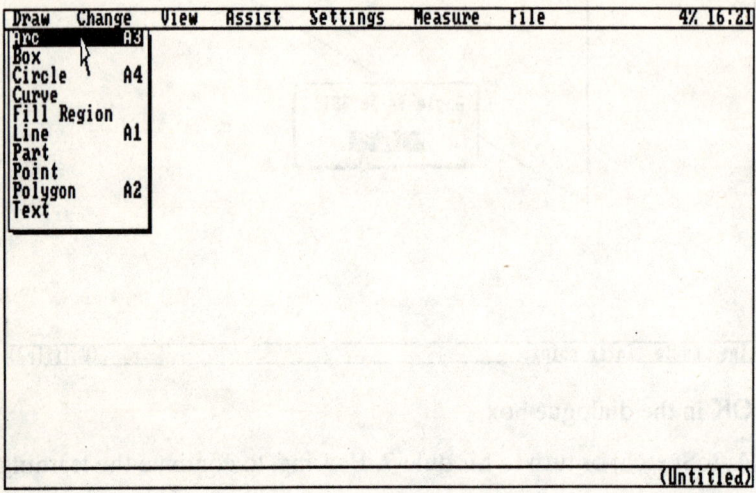

DESCRIPTION

The Arc command, located on the Draw menu, is used to create a portion of a circle. Either select the command from the menu, or press Alt-F3. AutoSketch prompts you to enter three points of the Arc: its starting point, a point on the Arc, and its endpoint. After you enter the first two points, move your pointer to drag a rough approximation of the Arc until it reaches the size you want. Then select the endpoint.

APPLICATIONS

Use the Arc command anytime you need to draw a portion of a circle. It is quicker and easier to draw an arc than to draw a circle and break it.

TYPICAL OPERATION

In this operation you draw a simple schematic of a suspension bridge. Some lines are drawn first to give reference points for the Arc command and to finish the schematic.

1. Begin a new AutoSketch drawing.

2. Pick **Snap** from the Settings menu. Pick the **1** corresponding to the X Spacing, type **.25**, and press **Enter**.

3. Pick **Off** as the Snap setting, toggling its setting to On.

4. Pick **OK** in the dialogue box, returning to the drawing editor.

5. Pick **Grid** from the Assist menu.

6. Draw a horizontal line pick. Pick **Line** from the Draw menu, type **1,3** and press **Enter**, then type **12,3** and press **Enter**.

7. Draw a short vertical line at the left side of the drawing by typing **2.375,3**, pressing **Enter**, then typing **2.375,3.50** and pressing **Enter**.

8. Type **10.625,3** and press **Enter**, then type **10.625,3.50** and press **Enter** to draw a second vertical line.

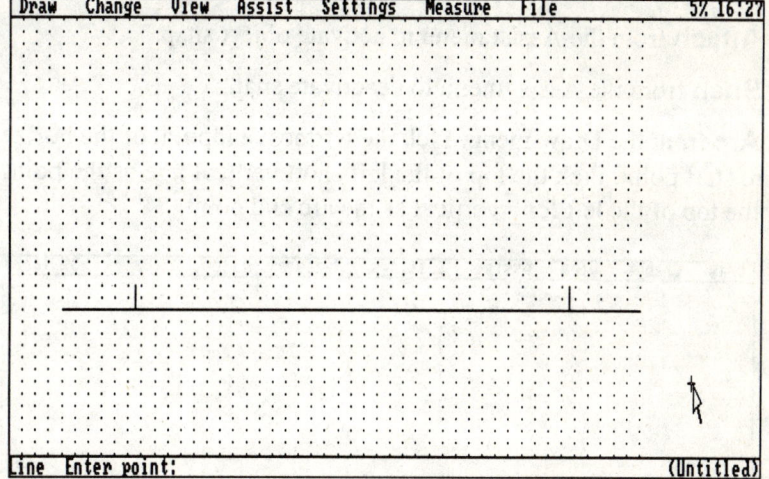

9. Draw the two long vertical lines by typing **3.75,2** and pressing **Enter**, typing **3.75,4.5** and pressing Enter, typing **9.25,2** and pressing **Enter**, then typing **9.25,4.5** and pressing **Enter**.

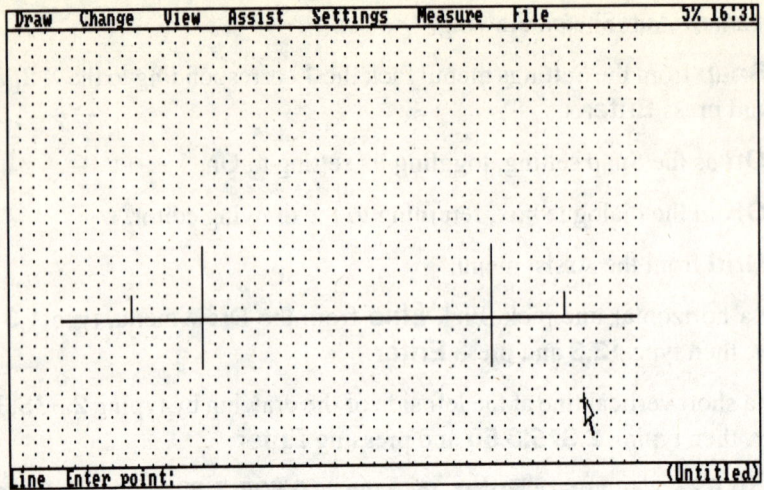

10. Select **Pick** from the Settings menu. Type **5** as the Pick interval and press **Enter**. Pick **OK** in the Pick dialogue box.

11. Pick **Attach** from the Assist menu to activate object snap.

12. Pick **Snap** from the Assist menu to deactivate snap.

13. Pick **Arc** from the Draw menu. Pick the leftmost endpoint of the horizontal line as the arc start point. Pick the top of the left short vertical line as the point on the arc. Pick the top of the left long vertical as the arc end point.

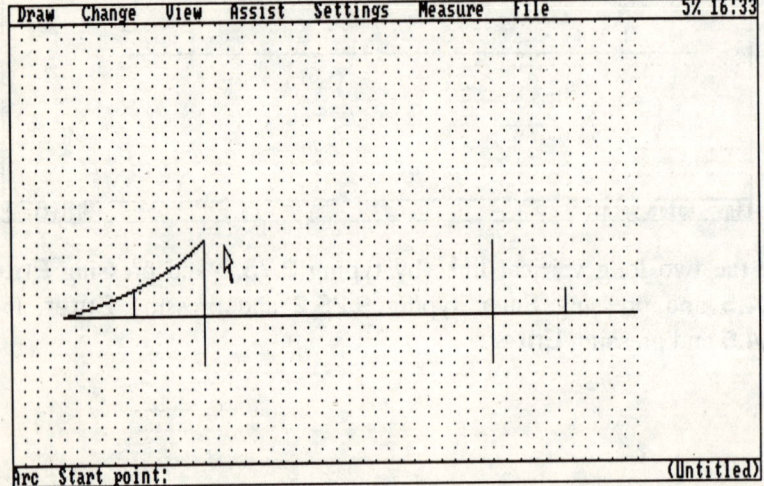

14. Draw the second arc by picking the top of the right tall vertical as the arc start point, the top of the right short vertical as a point on the arc, and the right end of the horizontal line as the arc end point.

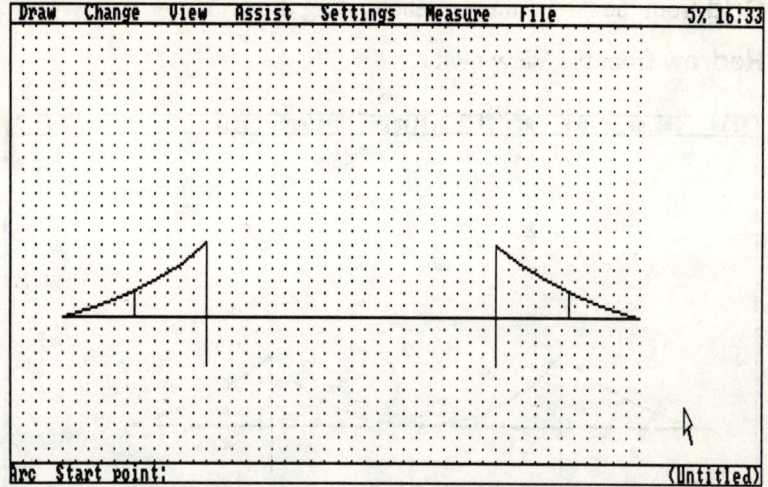

15. Draw the center arc by picking the top of the tall left vertical as the arc start point, the midpoint of the horizontal line as a point on the arc, and the top of the right tall vertical line as the arc end point.

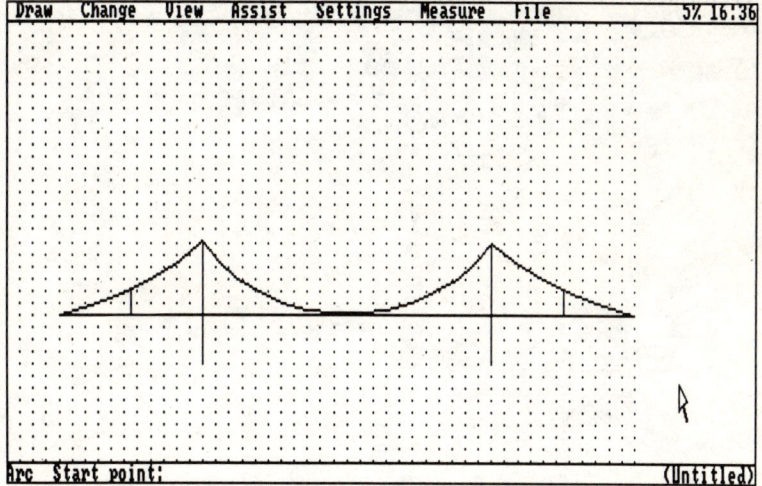

16. Pick **Erase** from the Change menu. The screen pointer now appears as a pointing finger. Position the end of the pointing finger so that it touches one of the short vertical lines and click the mouse button. Now pick the other short vertical line.

17. Pick **Grid** from the Assist menu, deactivating the grid.

18. Pick **Redraw** from the View menu.

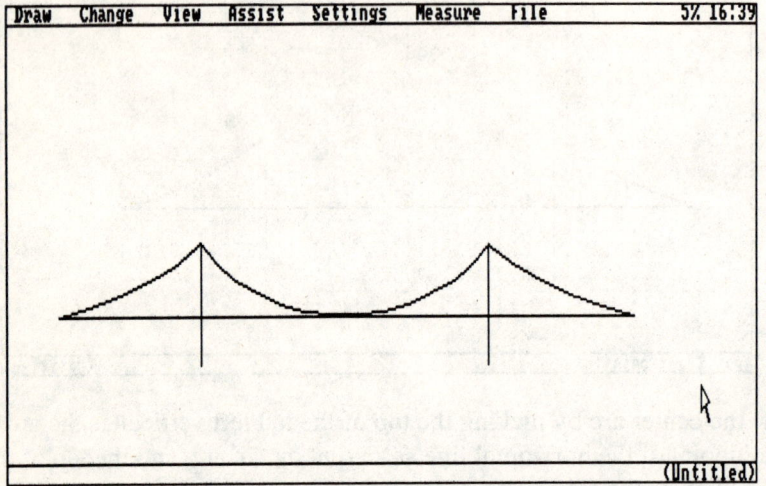

19. Quit AutoSketch, or turn to Module 19 to continue the learning sequence.

Module 5
AREA

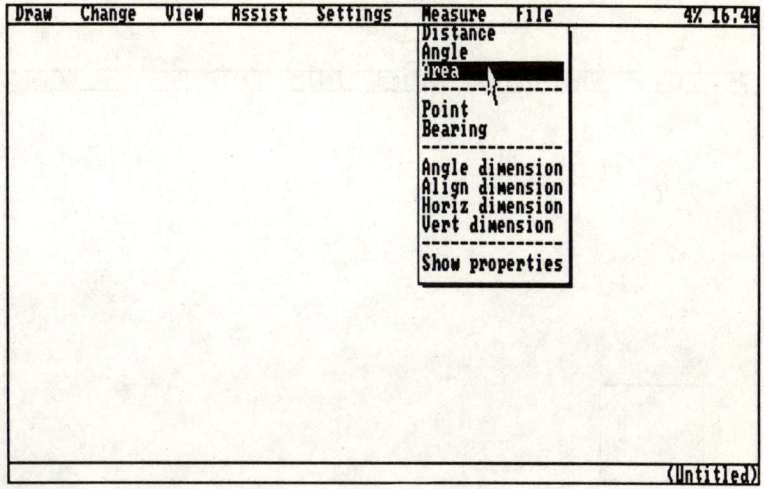

DESCRIPTION

The Area command, located on the Measure menu, determines the area and perimeter of a portion of the drawing (an enclosed figure). After selecting Area from the Measure menu, the first point picked on the screen produces a large "X" in that position. All consecutive points picked are marked with smaller "x's." After you have marked all the points describing the perimeter of the area you want calculated, pick the first point (marked by the large "X") again. A dialogue box appears containing three items: (1) Area = value, (2) Perimeter = value, and (3) a check box containing "OK." The value of Area and Perimeter is expressed in decimal units.

APPLICATIONS

There are many reasons to use the Area command. A designer of buildings and homes can use the Area command to quickly calculate the square footage of a room or building. The perimeter result can be helpful in calculating total amounts of materials required to build the structure. Real estate persons need to calculate odd totals concerning acreage. The Area command can be used to provide this information after the plot has been entered into AutoSketch. When parts are cut or machined from material of uniform thickness, the Area command provides an easy way to determine the weight of the finished product. (Multiply the area by the weight per square unit.)

TYPICAL OPERATION

In this session you compute the area of several regions.

1. Begin a new AutoSketch drawing.

2. Pick **Box** from the Draw menu. Type **1,1** and press **Enter**. Then type **3,3** and press **Enter**.

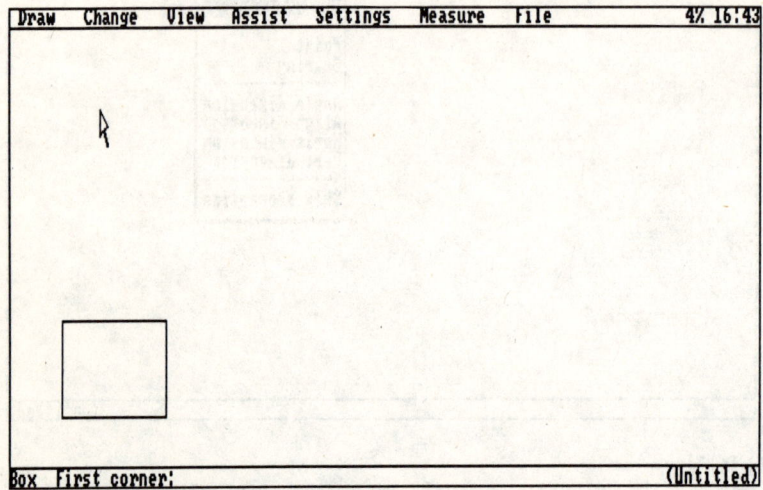

```
Draw   Change   View   Assist   Settings   Measure   File          4% 16:43
```
```
Box First corner:                                              (Untitled)
```

3. Pick **Polygon** from the Draw menu. Type **5,1 <CR>** as the first point, **5,3 <CR>** as the second point, **7,3 <CR>** as the third point, **7,4 <CR>** as the fourth point, **8,4 <CR>** as the fifth point, **8,3 <CR>** as the sixth point, **7.5,3 <CR>** as the seventh point, **7.5,1 <CR>** as the eighth point, **6.5,.75 <CR>** as the ninth point, and **5,1 <CR>** as the tenth point.

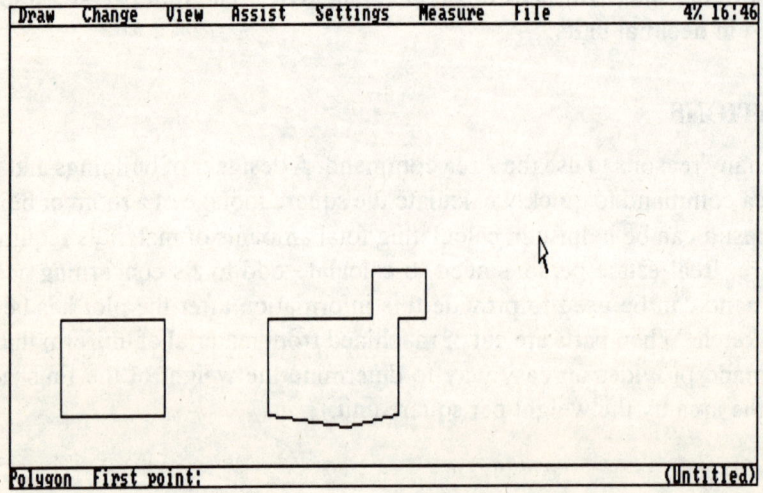

```
Draw   Change   View   Assist   Settings   Measure   File          4% 16:46
```
```
Polygon First point:                                           (Untitled)
```

4. Activate object snap by picking **Attach** from the Assist menu.

5. Pick **Area** from the Measure menu. Pick the four corners of the square, beginning at the top left corner. Pick the top left corner again to close the area.

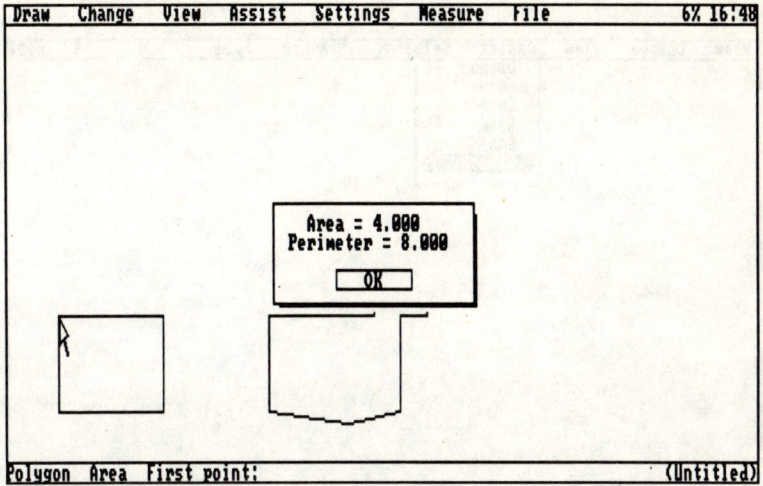

6. Pick **OK** in the dialogue box.

7. Compute the area and perimeter of the polygon. Pick a vertex of the polygon. Follow the perimiter of the polygon, picking each vertex in turn. Pick the starting vertex to close the area.

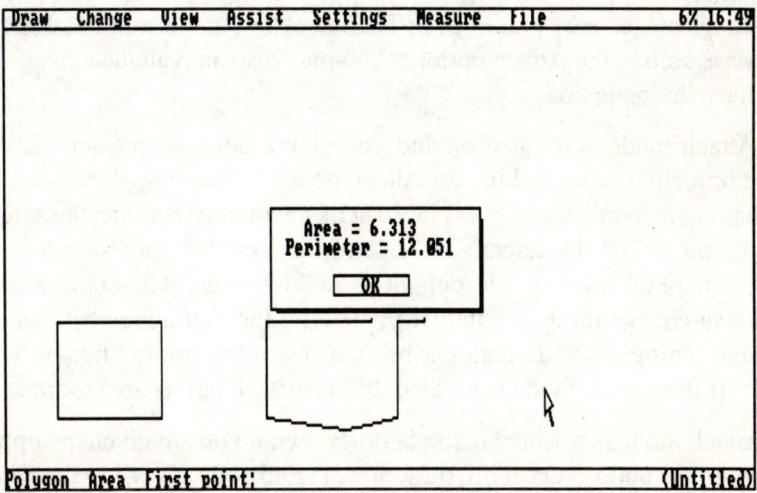

8. Pick **OK** in the dialogue box.

9. Quit AutoSketch, or turn to Module 3 to continue the learning sequence.

Module 6
ATTACH

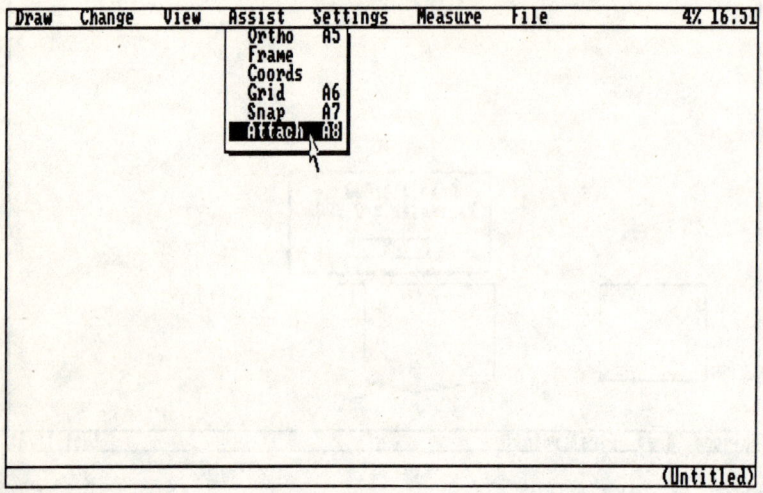

DESCRIPTION

The Attach command on the Assist menu activates AutoSketch's object snap mode, used when you want to make sure that an entity (such as a line) begins or ends at an exact point on an existing object in your drawing. You may either toggle this mode by picking Attach from the Settings menu, or by pressing Alt-F8. Select the Attach command on the Settings menu to choose among the Attach options. You may also activate/deactivate object snap from the Attach dialogue box.

When the Attach mode is toggled on and you pick a point on the screen, AutoSketch searches the immediate area looking for Attach points on existing objects in the drawing. If an Attach point is found, the pick is placed at its location rather than the actual physical point that you picked on the screen. The size of the area that AutoSketch will search is determined by the Pick interval. The default of the Pick interval is set to 1% of the screen height. You can change the Pick interval by picking the Settings menu and picking the Pick command. This gives you a dialogue box with complete information on how to adjust this variable. If the Attach mode is toggled off, all Attach points are ignored.

When the Attach mode is selected in the Settings menu, you are given the opportunity to toggle all the Attach options On or off, these are: (1) End point, (2) Midpoint, (3) Quadrant, (4) Center, and (5) Node point. The End point and Midpoint options deal with Lines and Arcs. The Quadrant (0, 90, 180, and 270-degree) and Center options deal with points on arcs and circles. The Node option attaches to a Point or to the Endpoints of Text object baselines.

APPLICATIONS

The Attach mode allows you to draw entities that are precisely attached to existing objects. As an example, a line could be drawn from the exact midpoint of an existing line to the exact center of an existing circle. The Attach mode is used anytime it is necessary to automatically locate the end of a line, the midpoint of a line, the center of a circle, the quadrant of a circle, or a point. The portion of the object you wish to attach to must be the closest Attach point to where you pick on the screen.

TYPICAL OPERATION

This activity illustrates the operation of the Attach command by letting you draw lines that are attached to specific attachment points on the drawing. You attach lines between the endpoints and midpoint of a line to parts of a circle and to points. Lines are also drawn between attachment points on arcs, circles, and points.

1. Begin a new AutoSketch drawing.

2. Pick **Circle** from the Draw menu. Type **6,4 <CR>** as the center point, and **6,6 <CR>** as the point on the circle.

3. Pick **Arc** from the Draw menu. Type **8,2 <CR>** as the arc start point, **9,4 <CR>** as a point on the arc, and **8,6 <CR>** as the arc endpoint.

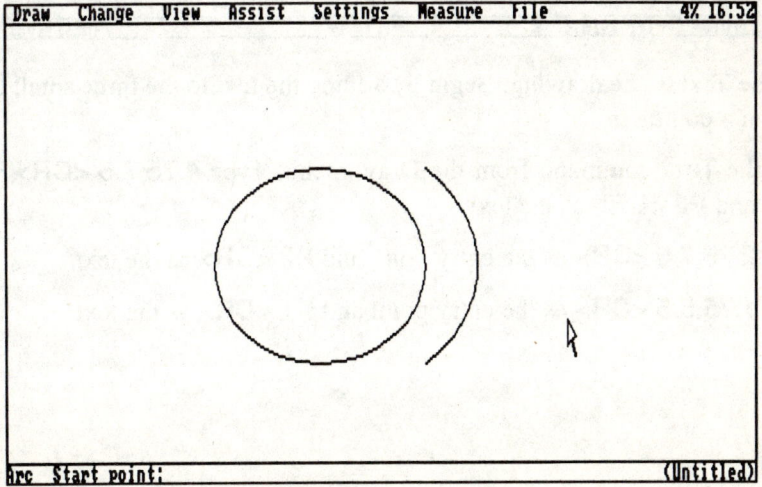

4. Pick **Line** from the Draw menu. Type **6,1 <CR>** as the first point and **2,3 <CR>** as the second point.

5. Pick **Circle** from the Draw menu. Type **2,5 <CR>** as the center point, and **2,5.25 <CR>** as the point on the first circle. Type **3,7 <CR>** as the center point and **3,7.25 <CR>** as the point on the second circle. Type **5,7 <CR>** as the center point and **5,7.25 <CR>** as the point on the circle.

6. Draw points in the center of the three small circles. Pick the **Point** command from the Draw menu. Type **2,5 <CR>**, **3,7 <CR>**, and **5,7 <CR>** as the points.

The points are now on the drawing at the center of the three small circles — look closely and you can see them.

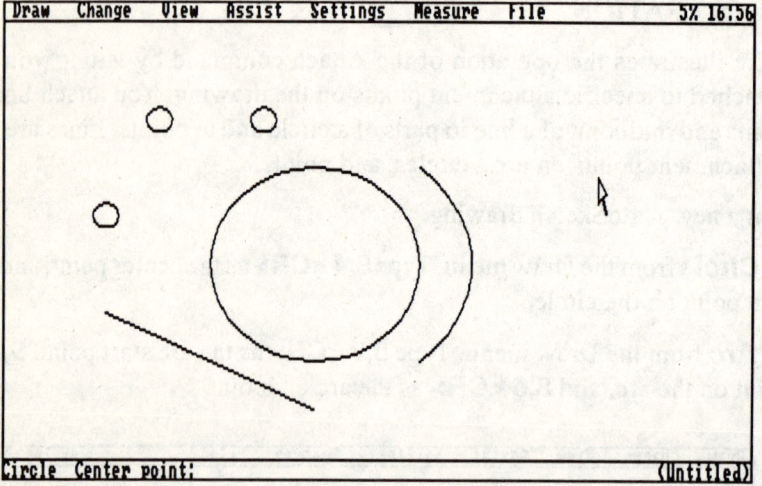

Now add the Text to the drawing. Begin by adding the text to the three small circles that each contain a point.

7. Pick the **Text** command from the Draw menu. Type **4.75,7.5 <CR>** as the first point and **P3 <CR>** as the text.

8. Type **2.75,7.5 <CR>** as the entry point and **P2 <CR>** as the text.

9. Type **1.75,5.5 <CR>** as the entry point and **P1 <CR>** as the text.

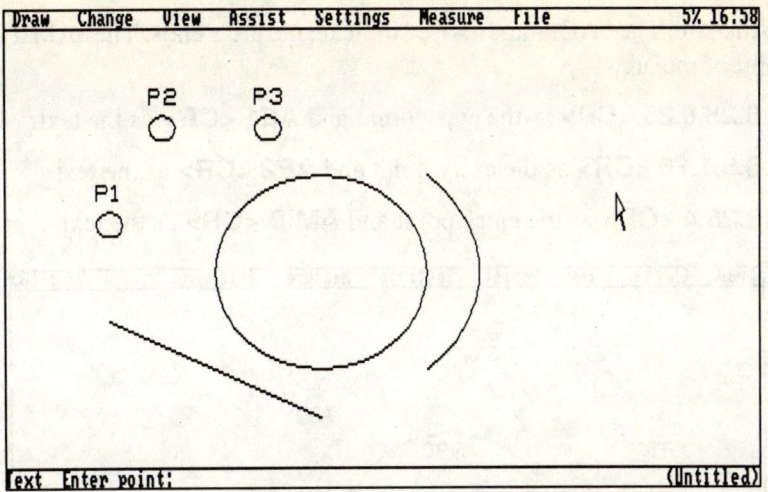

Add text to the large circle. The "Q" indicates the quadrant of the circle and "C" indicates the circle's center.

10. Type **5.75,5.5 <CR>** as the entry point and **Q90 <CR>** as the text.

11. Type **5.75,4 <CR>** as the entry point and **C <CR>** as the text.

12. Type **7.25,3.75 <CR>** as the entry point and **Q0 <CR>** as the text.

13. Type **6.25,1.5 <CR>** as the entry point and **Q270 <CR>** as the text.

14. Type **4.25,3.75 <CR>** as the entry point and **Q180 <CR>** as the text.

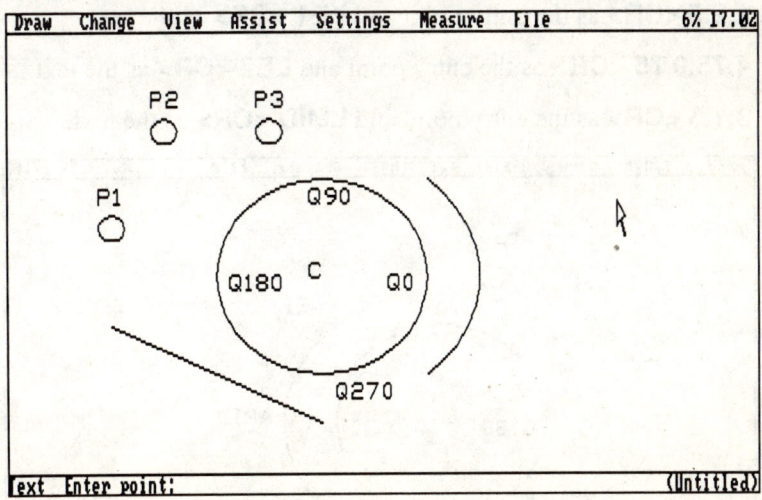

Add text to the Arc. The "AE1" and "AE2" indicate the arc's ends. The "AMID" indicates the mid point of the arc.

15. Type **8.25,6.25 <CR>** as the entry point and **AE1 <CR>** as the text.

16. Type **8.5,1.75 <CR>** as the entry point and **AE2 <CR>** as the text.

17. Type **9.25,4 <CR>** as the entry point and **AMID <CR>** as the text.

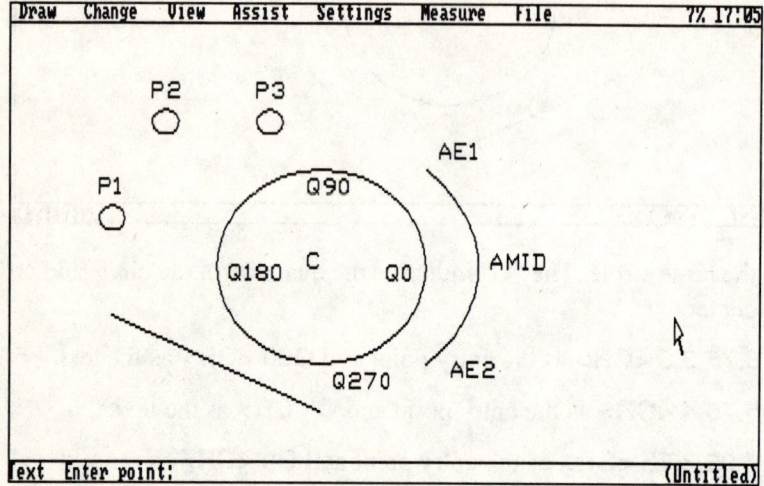

Add text to the line. The "LE1" and "LE2" indicate the line's ends. The "LMID" indicates the mid point of the line.

18. Type **1,2.5 <CR>** as the entry point and **LE1 <CR>** as the text.

19. Type **4.75,0.75 <CR>** as the entry point and **LE2 <CR>** as the text.

20. Type **3,1.5 <CR>** as the entry point and **LMID <CR>** as the text.

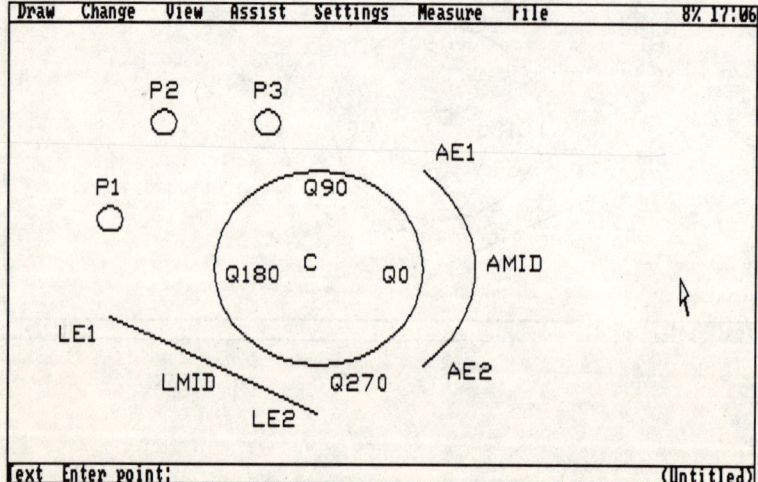

The reference text has all been added to the drawing. You are now ready to learn how the Attach mode works. As you go through the next part of the exercise it is very important that you watch the screen closely as you accomplish each step. If you watch closely, you should understand how the Attach mode works when you have finished all the steps.

21. Pick **Attach** from the Assist menu.

22. Pick **Line** from the Draw menu. Pick a point on the line near LE1 as the first point and a point near P1 as the second point.

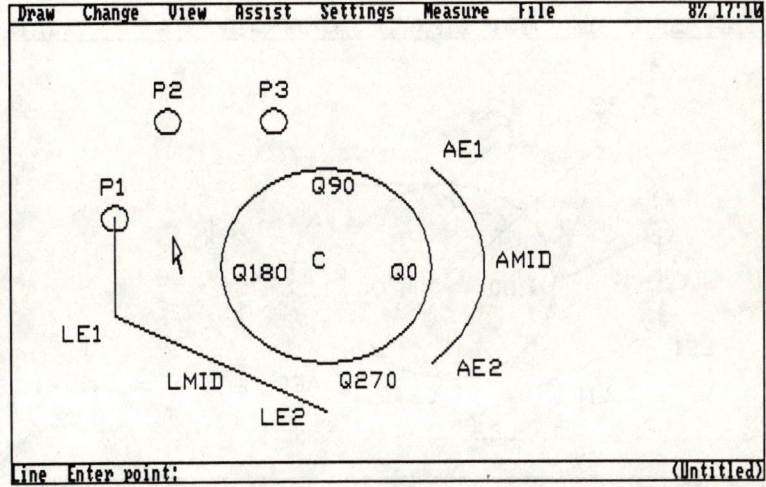

NOTE

If you miss any of the attach operations, pick Erase from the Change menu, erase the incorrect entity, and repeat the last drawing operation.

23. Pick a point closest to the point at **P1**, then pick a point closest on the circle at **Q180**.

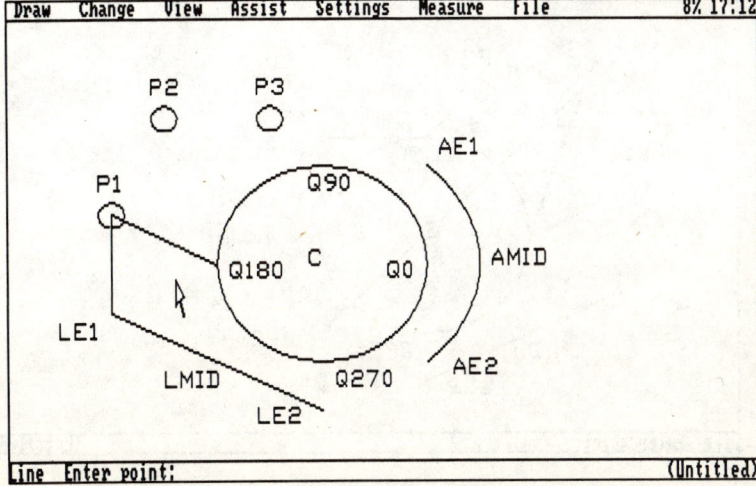

24. Type **/LPOINT <CR>** to continue the line from the last point, then pick a point closest to the point at P2.

25. Type **/LPOINT <CR>** to continue the line from the last point, then pick a point closest to the center of the circle at C.

26. Pick a point closest to the point at P3, then pick a point closest on the circle at Q90.

27. Continue the line by typing **/LPOINT <CR>** as the first point, then pick a point on the arc closest to AE1.

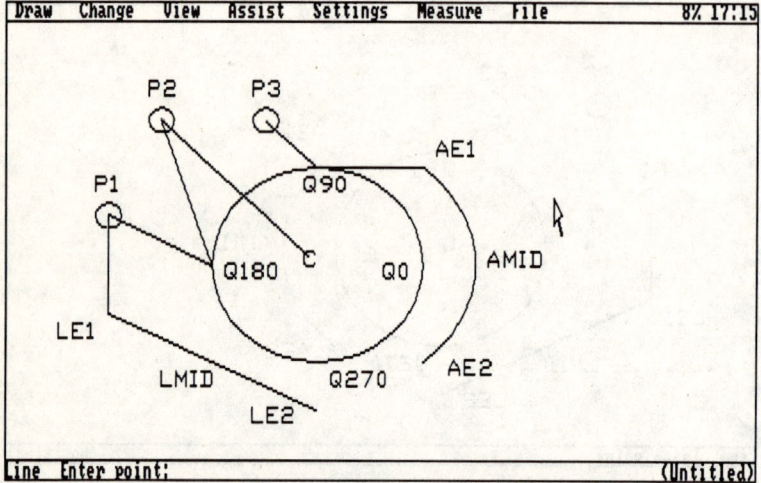

28. Continue the line by typing **/LPOINT <CR>** as the first point, then pick a point close to the C.

29. Continue the line by typing **/LPOINT <CR>** as the first point, then pick a point on the arc closest to AE2.

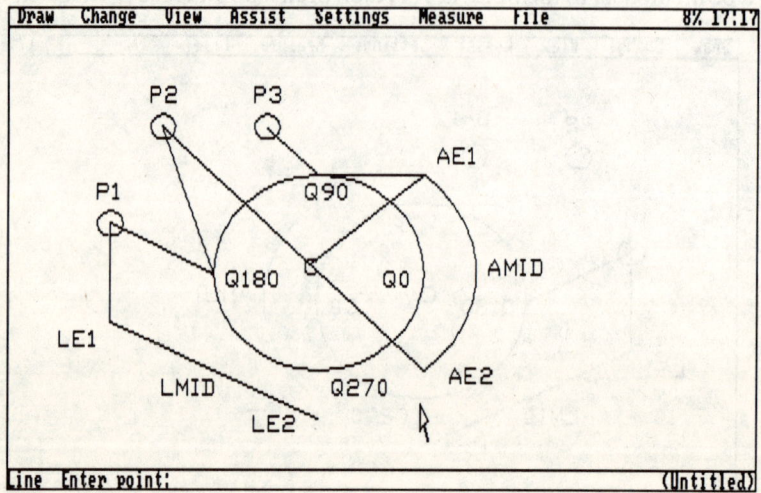

30. Pick a point closest to the C, then pick a point closest on the circle at Q270.

31. Type **/LPOINT <CR>** to continue the line, then pick a point on the line closest to LE2.

32. Pick a point on the circle closest to Q270, then pick a point on the line closest to LMID.

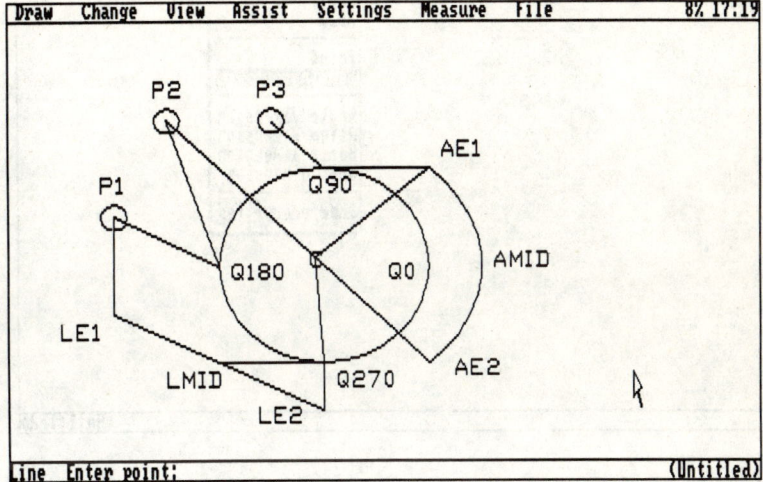

33. Pick a point on the circle closest to Q0, then pick a point on the arc closest to AMID.

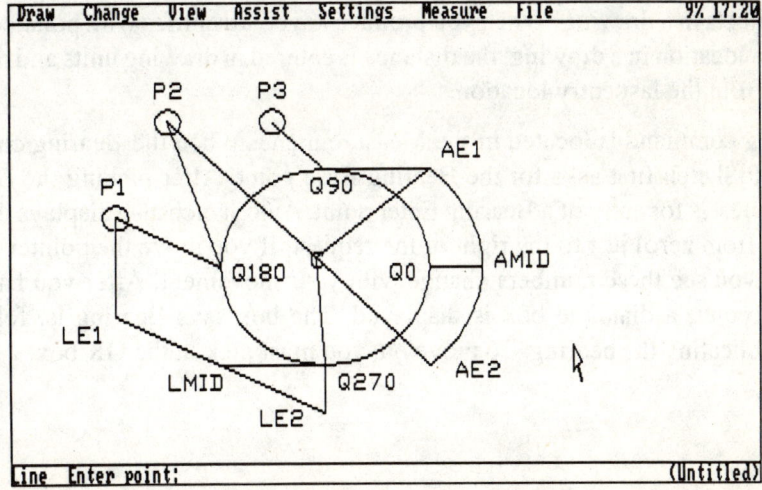

34. Quit AutoSketch, or turn to Module 43, Pick, to continue the learning sequence.

Module 7
BEARING

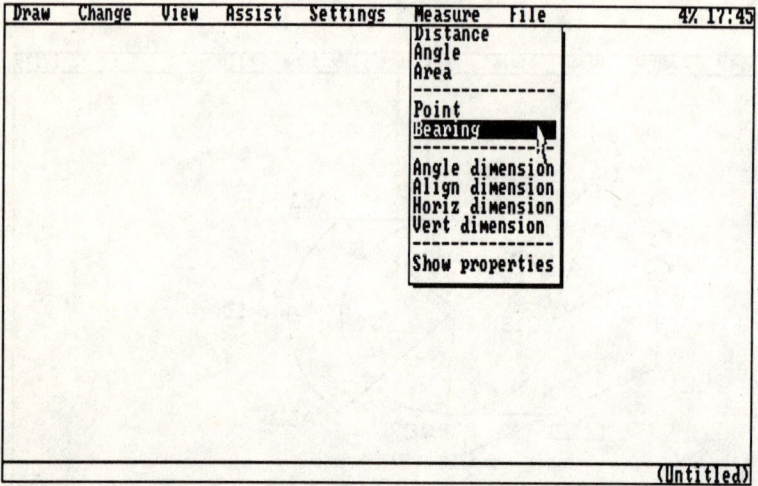

DESCRIPTION

In AutoSketch, a bearing is a direction measured in degrees. Bearings begin with 0 (zero) degrees at the far right and increase in a counterclockwise direction. Bearings can be used to locate objects in a drawing. When you produce keyboard entries with polar coordinates to indicate a location in a drawing, the distance is entered in drawing units and the bearing in degrees from the last entry location.

The Bearing command is located in the Measure menu. When the Bearing command is picked, AutoSketch first asks for the Bearing Base point. After picking the Base point, the next request is for entry of a Bearing Enter point. AutoSketch also displays the degrees (calculated from zero) just to the right of the request. If you move the pointer around on the screen, you see these numbers change with your movement. After you have picked the second point, a dialogue box is displayed. The box says Bearing is, followed by numerals indicating the bearing. To move on, you must pick in the OK box.

The following illustration is a picture of where the bearings in degrees are located in AutoSketch.

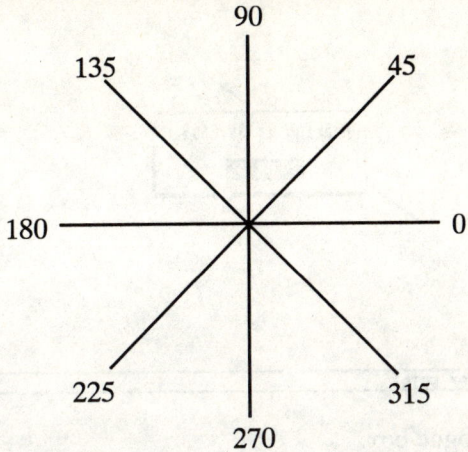

APPLICATIONS

The Bearing command is useful anytime you need to know the bearing of an entity. When dimensioning an angle, the Bearing command could be used to find the angle's value for listing on the drawing.

TYPICAL OPERATION

In this operation you draw a line and then use the Bearing command to find its bearing.

1. Begin a new drawing.

2. Pick the **Line** command from the Draw menu. Type **4,3 <CR>** as the first point and **8,6 <CR>** as the second point.

3. Pick **Attach** from the Settings menu.

4. To find the bearing of the line starting with the lower left end of the line, first pick **Bearing** from the Measure menu. Pick the left end of the line, then pick the right end of the line.

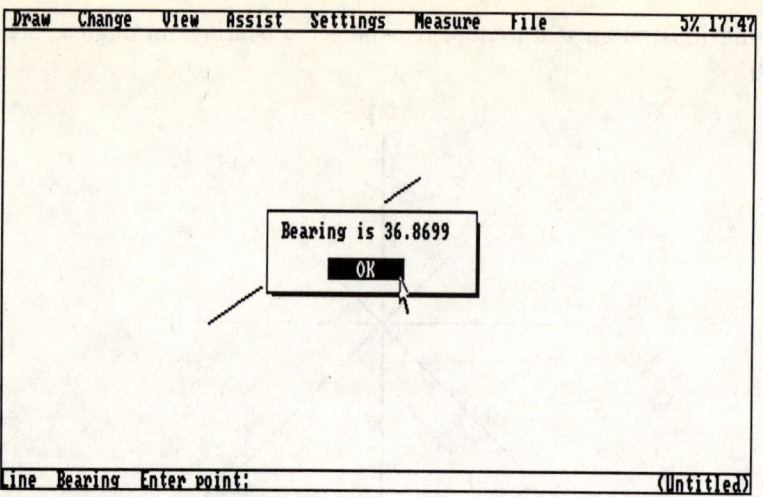

5. Pick **OK** in the dialogue box.

6. Pick **Bearing** from the Measure menu. Pick the right end of the line, then pick the left end.

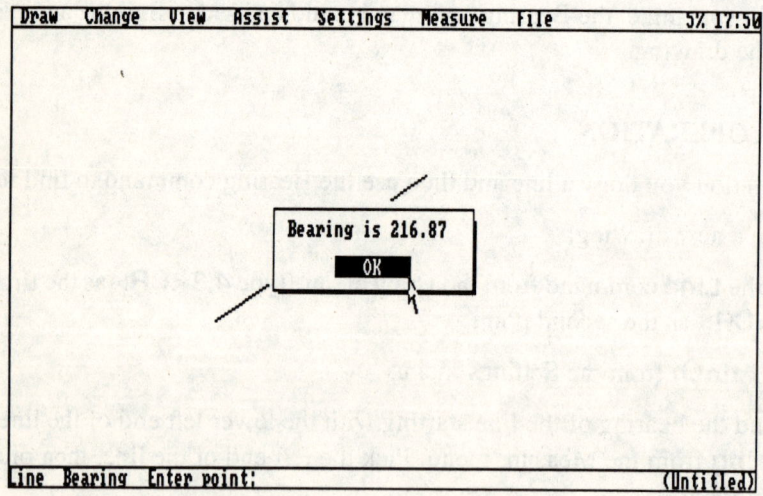

7. Quit AutoSketch, or turn to Module 20, Fill Region, to continue the learning sequence.

Module 8
BOX

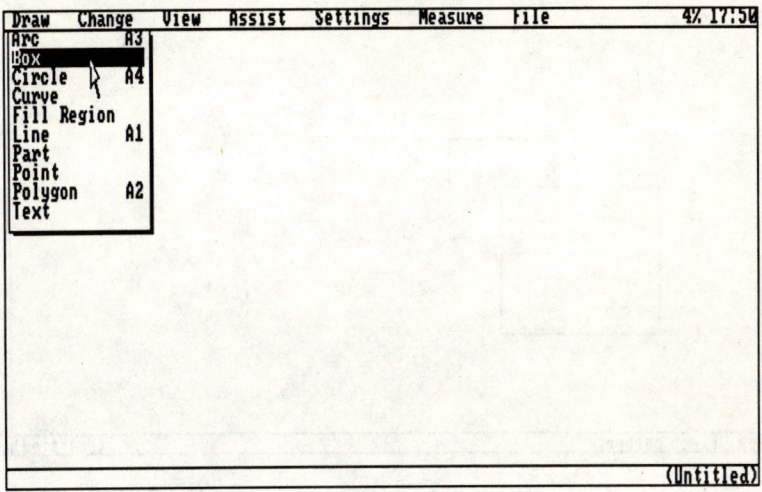

DESCRIPTION

The Box command is on the Draw menu. When you pick the Box command, AutoSketch asks for "Box First corner." Enter a point on the screen as one corner of the box. Then AutoSketch asks for "Box Second corner." Enter another point on the screen as the diagonal corner of the box. After entering the first point on the box, you can move the screen pointer until you get the box shape you want before picking the second point. The corner coordinates can also be entered from the keyboard.

APPLICATIONS

Anytime you need a rectangle, the Box command is the command to use. Although boxes may also be constructed with lines, the Box command provides a drawing shortcut that is more convenient.

TYPICAL OPERATION

In this session you construct boxes by entering their two corners from the keyboard and then you draw some boxes by entering random points on the screen.

1. Start a new drawing.

2. Pick the **Box** command from the Draw menu. Type **4,4 <CR>** as the first corner and **6,6 <CR>** as the second corner.

3. Type **2,2 <CR>** as the first corner and **5,5 <CR>** as the second corner.

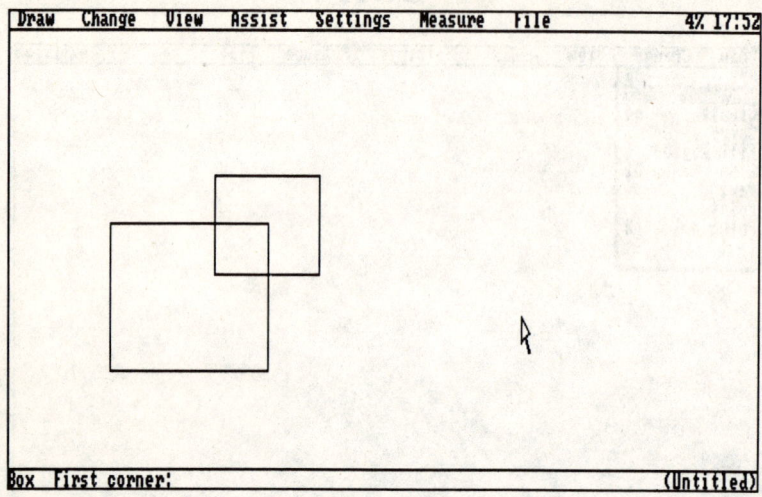

4. Quit AutoSketch, or turn to Module 65, Zoom, to continue the learning sequence.

Module 9
BOX ARRAY

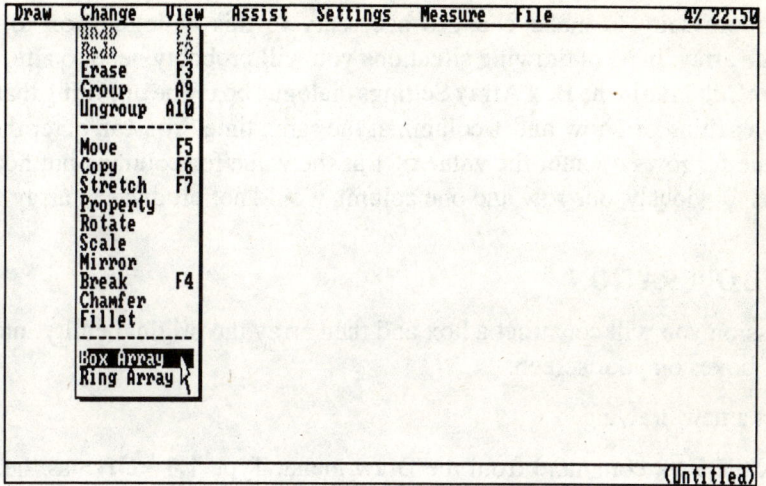

DESCRIPTION

The Box Array command is on the Change menu and on the Settings menu. In the world of Computer Aided Design, the term "array" refers to the process of reproducing an existing entity in an orderly and repeating fashion which produces a multiple copy of the original entity in rows and columns. A column can be remembered as the vertical component of the array and you can remember that the column is vertical if you will associate this concept with the fact that columns in front of a building are vertical. Of course, this leaves the row as the horizontal component of the array. Remember how rows in a garden are horizontal (on flat ground)? The Box Array command in AutoSketch allows you to define a rectangular or box shaped array of entities.

For the Box Array command to work, you must already have an entity in your drawing to array. When Box Array is selected from the Change menu, AutoSketch asks you to Select an object. The object (entity or entities) can be selected by picking with the screen cursor or by using the Crosses/window box. When the Change menu selection has been utilized, AutoSketch allows you to modify the settings of the dialogue box labeled as "Box Array Settings."

APPLICATIONS

Use the Box Array command anytime you need to reproduce an entity in a multiple pattern that results in a box or rectangular repeating pattern of the original entity. The practical application of the Box Array command is best approached by first drawing the entity to be arrayed and then selecting the Box Array command from the Settings menu. This gives you the opportunity to make changes necessary to this dialogue box to produce an appropriate array. In most drawing situations you will probably need to alter the number of Rows or Columns in the Box Array Settings dialogue box. The one thing that you cannot ask for is a setting of 1 row and 1 column at the same time. You can enter the value of 1 as the value for rows or enter the value of 1 as the value for columns but not both at the same time. Obviously, one row and one column would not produce an array of anything.

TYPICAL OPERATION

In this session you will construct a box and then array the original entity into a multiple pattern of boxes on your screen.

1. Start a new drawing.

2. Pick the **Box** command from the Draw menu. Type **1,1 <CR>** as the first corner and **1.75,1.5 <CR>** as the second corner.

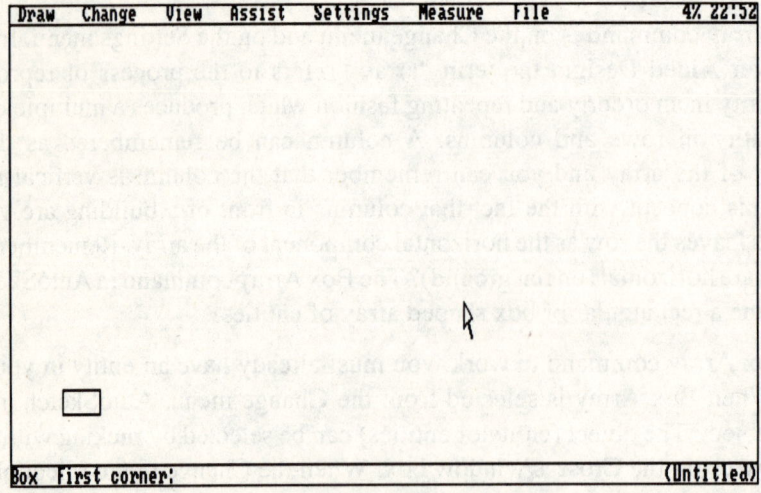

3. Pick the **Box Array** command from the Settings menu.

4. Pick the box to the right of Rows. Type **3 <CR>**. Pick the box to the right of Columns. Type **4 <CR>**.

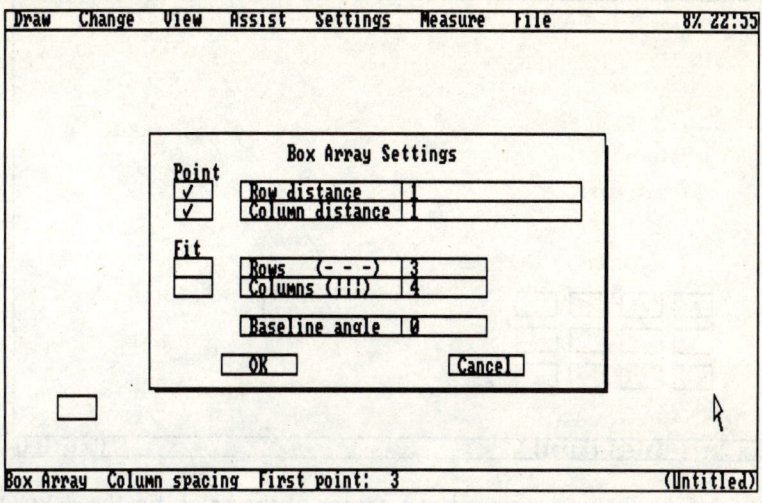

5. Pick the **OK** box.

6. Pick the **Box Array** command from the Change menu.

7. Pick the box on the screen with the screen pointer.

8. Type **1,1 <CR>**. Type **2,1 <CR>**.

9. Type **1,1 <CR>**. Type **1,1.75 <CR>**.

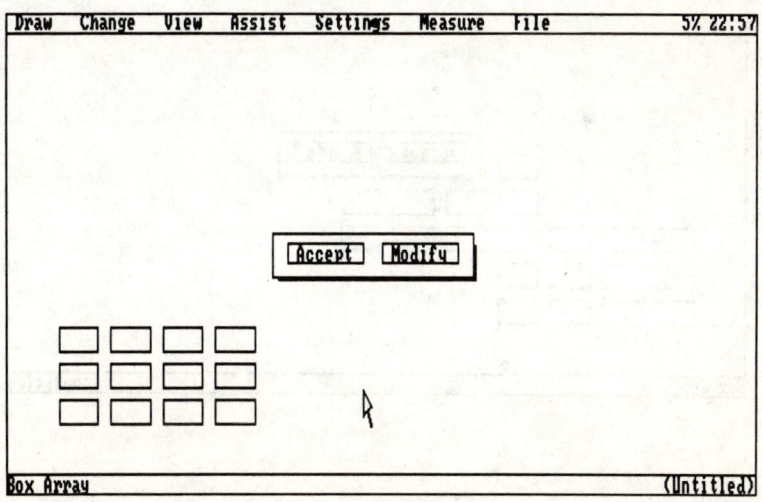

10. Pick **Accept**.

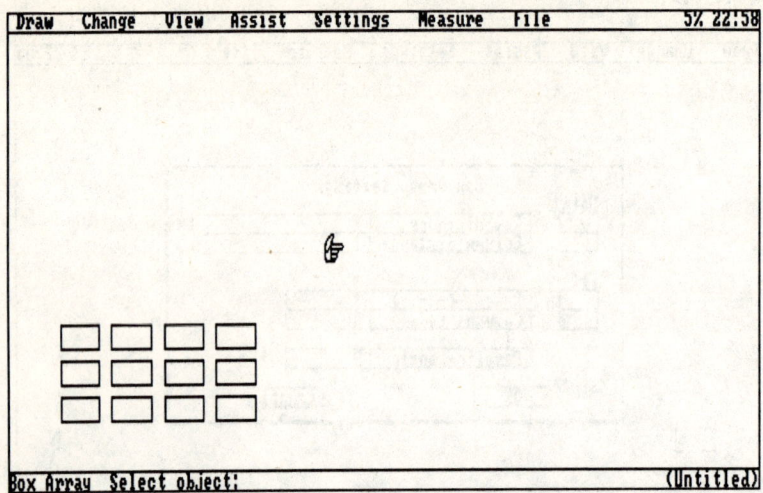

11. Pick the box in the upper right hand corner of the array for the next object to be arrayed.

12. Enter the column spacing. Type **4,2.5 <CR>**. Type **5,2.5 <CR>**.

13. Enter the row spacing. Type **4,2.5 <CR>**. Type **4,3.25 <CR>**.

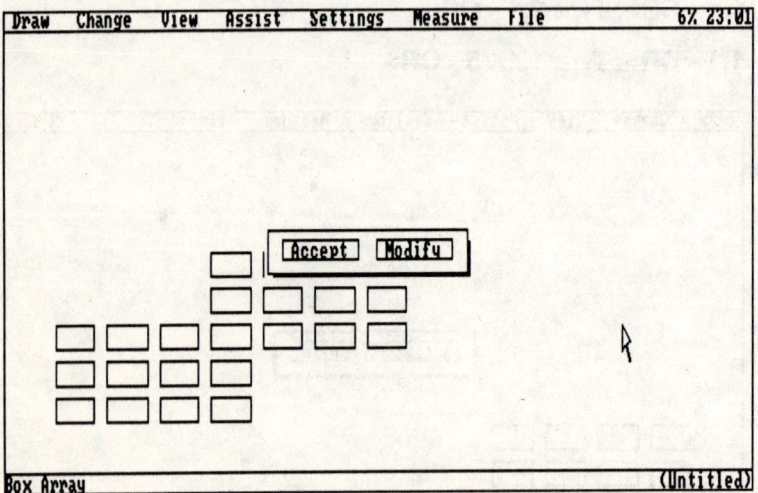

14. Pick **Accept**.

15. Experiment with the Box Array command by changing other settings to see how they work. Satisfy yourself that you understand the Box Array command.

16. Turn to Module 53, Ring Array, to continue the learning sequence.

Module 10
BREAK

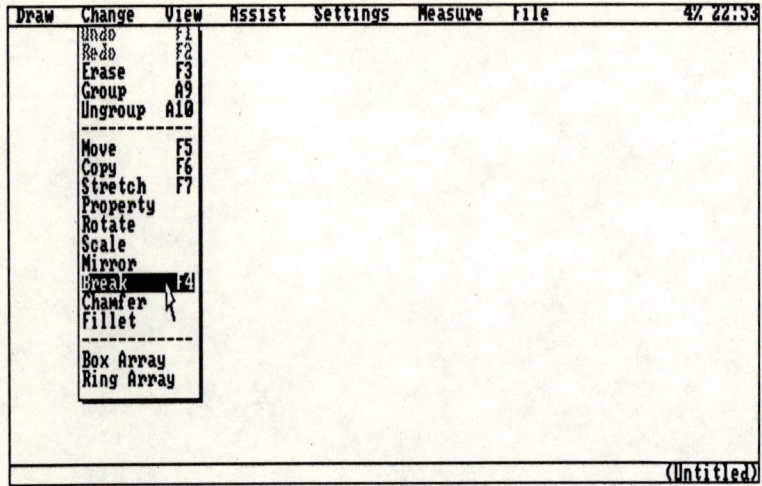

| Draw | Change | View | Assist | Settings | Measure | File | 4% 22:53 |

Undo   F1
Redo   F2
Erase   F3
Group   A9
Ungroup   A10

Move   F5
Copy   F6
Stretch   F7
Property
Rotate
Scale
Mirror
Break   F4
Chamfer
Fillet

Box Array
Ring Array

(Untitled)

DESCRIPTION

The Break command, located on the Change menu, erases a portion of an existing entity, such as a line. This is different from the Erase command which erases an entire entity. The Break command works on lines, arcs, boxes, circles, polygons, and curve frames. When you want to use the Break command, pick Break from the Change menu or press the F4 key. After you have picked the object to be broken, the object becomes dotted. Pick two break points on the entity with the screen pointer and the portion between the two points will be removed. If you are breaking a circle, the break is performed in a counterclockwise direction from the first point you select to the second.

APPLICATIONS

The Break command is often used to place a gap in a drawn object or to erase a portion of an item. Sometimes the drawing activity requires that a line, circle, or arc be partially erased. An example of a practical use for the Break command would be: after drawing a wall in a floor plan with the Line command, the Break command is used to erase portions of the wall to insert doors and windows.

TYPICAL OPERATION

In this operation you draw a circle, lines, and an arc. The entities that you draw are broken to produce a different looking drawing.

1. Start a new drawing.

2. Pick the **Line** command from the Draw menu. Type **6,4.5 <CR>** and **9,4.5 <CR>** as the second point.

3. Type **6,4.5 <CR>** as the first point and **6,7.5 <CR>** as the second point.

4. Type **6,4.5 <CR>** as the first point and **3,4.5 <CR>** as the second point.

5. Type **6,4.5 <CR>** as the first point and **6,1.5 <CR>** as the second point.

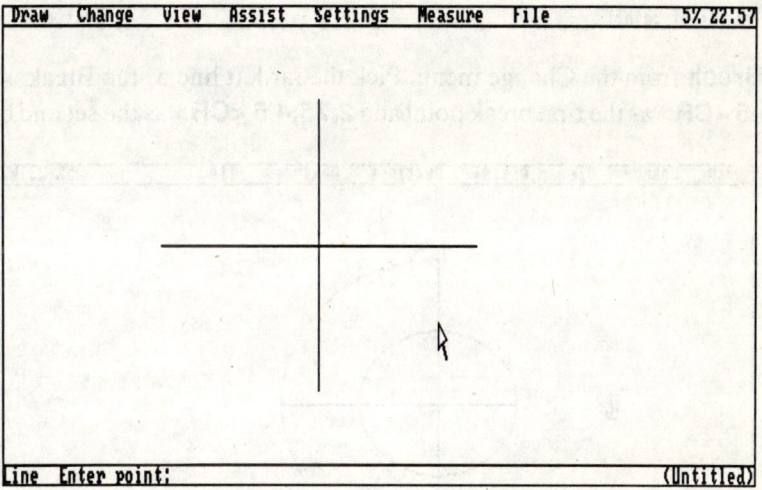

6. Pick **Circle** from the Draw menu. Type **6,4.5 <CR>** as the center point and **6,3 <CR>** as a point on the circle.

7. Pick **Arc** from the Draw menu. Type **6,1.5 <CR>** as the arc start point, **9,4.5 <CR>** as the point on the arc, and **6,7.5 <CR>** as the arc end point.

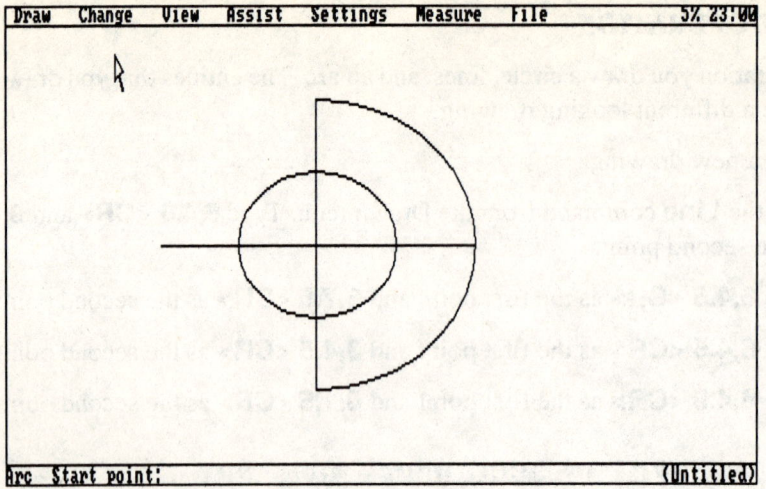

8. Pick **Break** from the Change menu. Pick the far left line as the Break object. Type **4.5,4.5 <CR>** as the first break point and **2.75,4.5 <CR>** as the second break point.

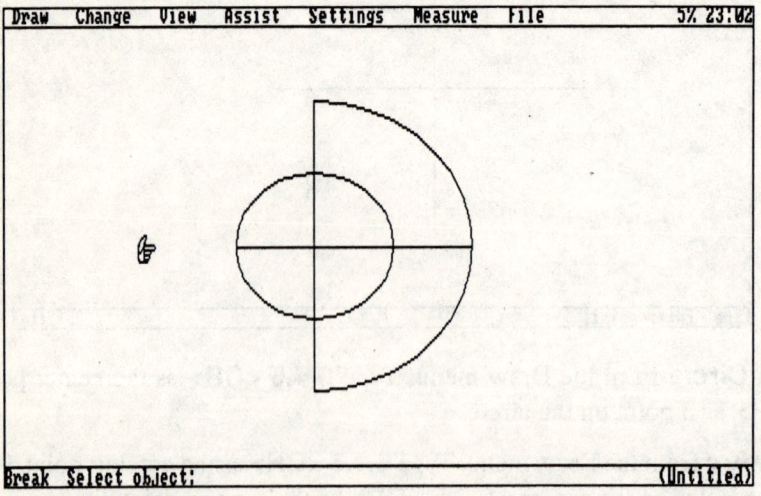

9. Pick **Break** from the Change menu. Pick anywhere on the circle. Type **6,3 <CR>** as the first break point and **6,6 <CR>** as the second break point.

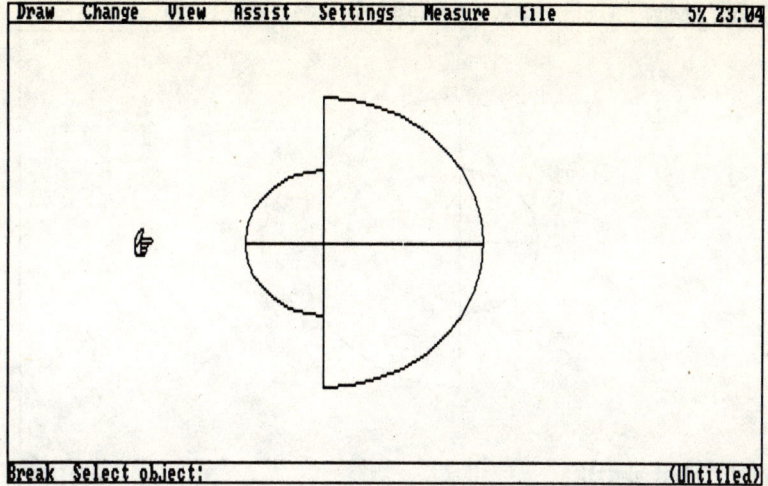

10. Pick **Break** from the Change menu. Pick anywhere on the line at the right side of the drawing. Type **7.5,4.5 <CR>** as the first break point and **9.5,4.5 <CR>** as the second break point.

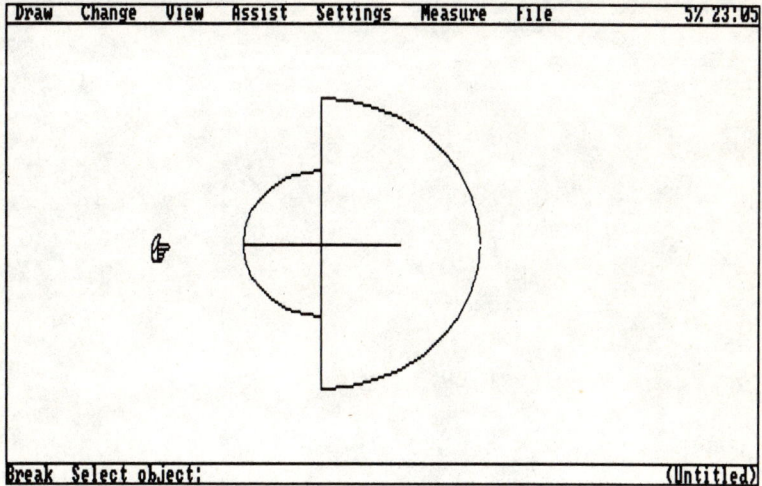

11. Break the arc to leave a gap in it. Where you put the two points on the arc will determine the size of the break. Look at the following illustration to help you determine where to pick the two break points.

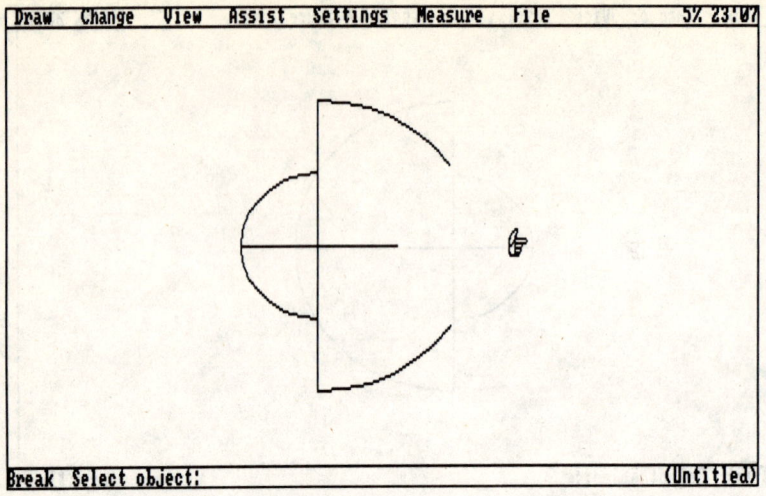

12. Quit AutoSketch, or turn to Module 6, Attach, to continue the learning sequence.

Module 11
CHAMFER

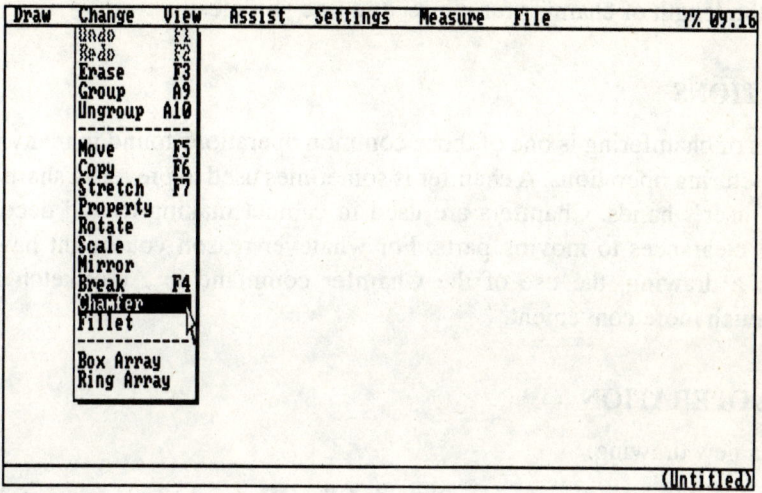

DESCRIPTION

Chopping off a portion of a corner of a board is one description of a chamfer. You can also think of it as a straight fillet. If you don't know how to pronounce the word, begin your pronunciation of the word the same way you begin to pronounce the word champ and instead of ending the word with the "P" sound, substitute the "FER" sound. The Chamfer command in AutoSketch is found in both the Change menu and the Settings menu. When the chamfer distance is set to zero, AutoSketch will join the two lines at exactly the same point. Anytime you need to change the settings of the first or second distances for Chamfer, pick the Chamfer command in the Settings menu.

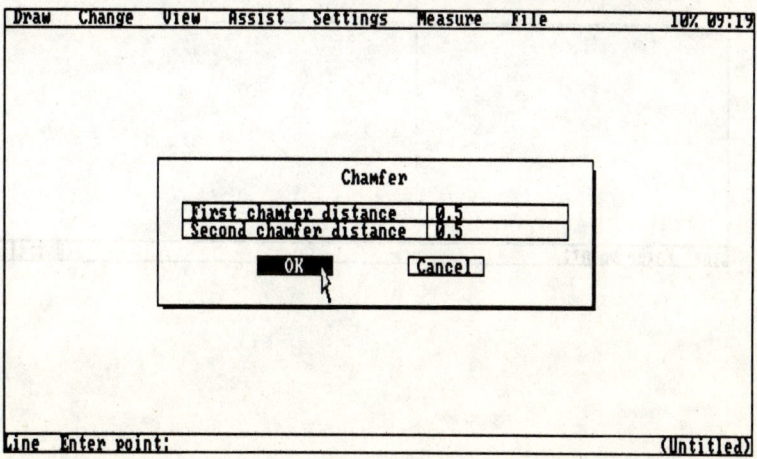

The default setting for Chamfer is 0.5 inches. When you change the setting for First chamfer distance in the Chamfer dialogue box it automatically changes the setting of the Second chamfer distance to echo the first. You must manually change the setting for the second distance if you want it to differ from the first. The software uses the First chamfer distance to chamfer the first line you select and uses the Second chamfer distance to determine the length of chamfer for the second line you pick.

APPLICATIONS

The process of chamfering is one of those common operations found in many machining and manufacturing operations. A chamfer is sometimes used to prevent a sharp edge from cutting the user's hands. Chamfers are used in cabinet making to add decoration and operational clearances to moving parts. For whatever reason you might have to use a chamfer in a drawing, the use of the Chamfer command in AutoSketch makes the operation much more convenient.

TYPICAL OPERATION

1. Start a new drawing.

2. Pick **Line** from the Draw menu. Type **1,4.5 <CR>** as the beginning of the line and type **10,4.5 <CR>** as the end of a horizontal line.

3. Type **6,1 <CR>** to begin the vertical line and type **6,8 <CR>** to end the line.

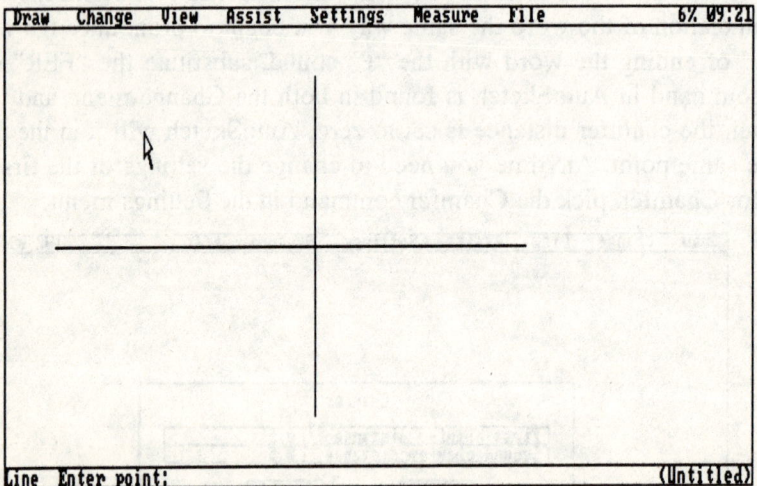

4. Pick **Text** from the Draw menu. Type **6.25, 5.5 <CR>** and to enter the text type **1 <CR>**. Type **4.75,4.75 <CR>** and type **2 <CR>**. Type **6.25, 3.5 <CR>** and type **3 <CR>**. Type **7.25,4.75 <CR>** and type **4 <CR>**.

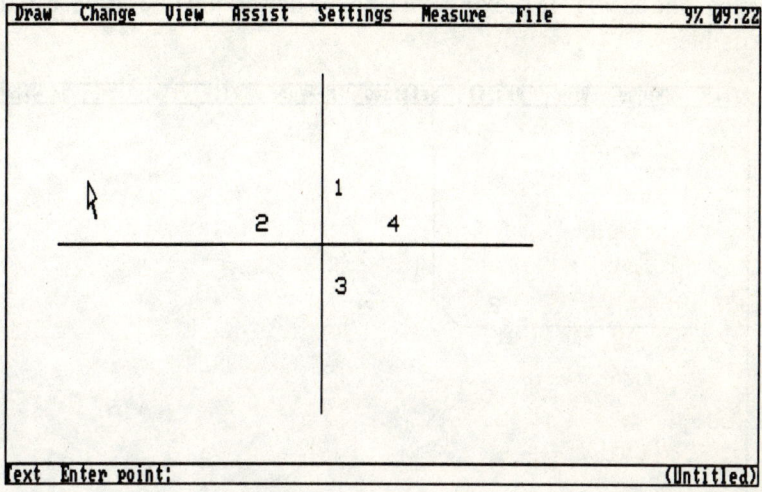

5. Pick **Chamfer** in the Settings menu. If the First and Second chamfer distances are not set to 0.5 as shown in the following illustration, pick on the First chamfer distance and change it to 0.5.

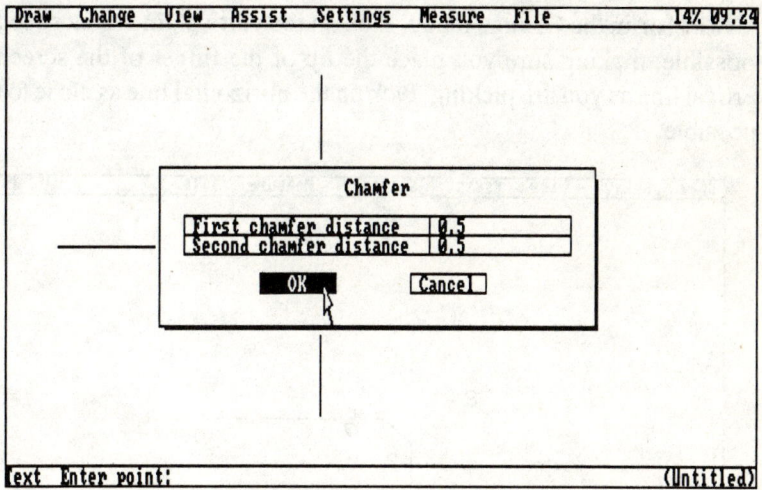

6. Pick **OK**.

7. Pick **Chamfer** in the Change menu. Pick on the vertical line as close to the numeral 1 as possible, making sure you place the tip of the finger of the screen pointer on the vertical line as you are picking. Pick on the horizontal line as close to the numeral 2 as possible.

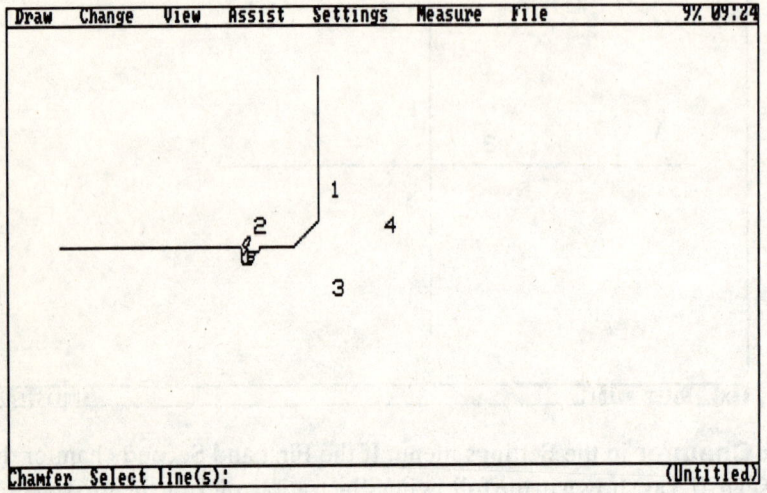

8. Pick **Undo** from the Change menu.

9. Pick **Chamfer** in the Change menu. Pick on the vertical line as close to the numeral 3 as possible, making sure you place the tip of the finger of the screen pointer on the vertical line as you are picking. Pick on the horizontal line as close to the numeral 4 as possible.

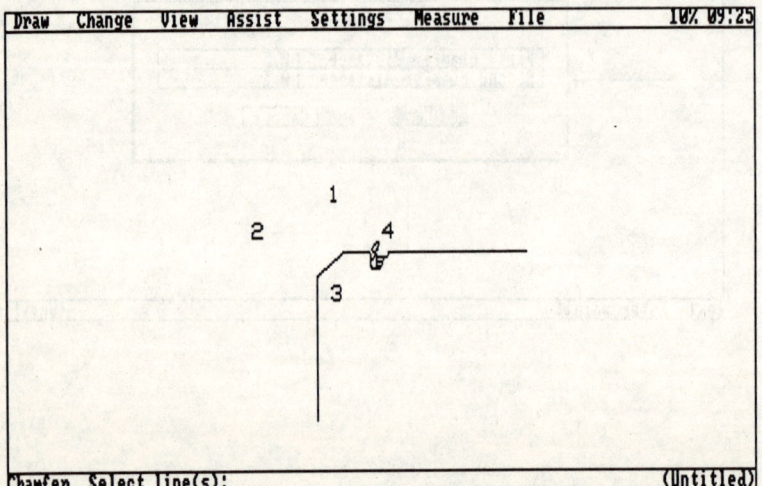

10. Experiment more with the Chamfer command. Try drawing a box with the Box command and see what happens when you use the Chamfer command to modify it. Try other values in the chamfer settings and see how they affect the operation of the command.

11. Turn to Module 59, Stretch, to continue the learning sequence.

Module 12
CIRCLE

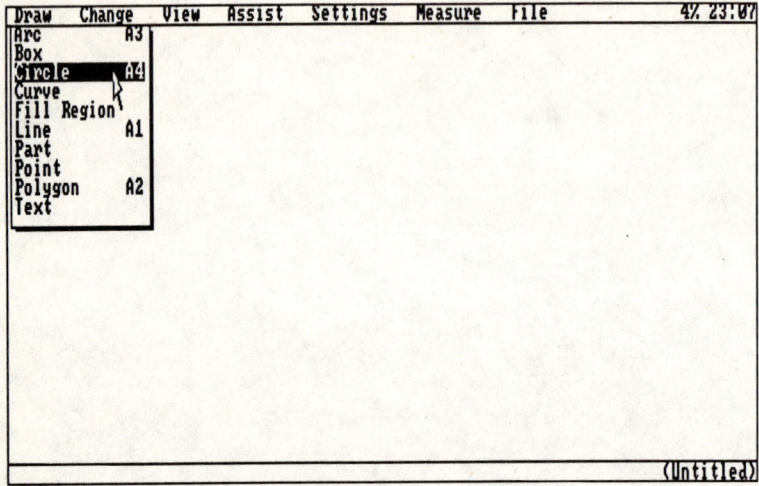

DESCRIPTION

The Circle command, located on the Draw menu, is for producing circles in AutoSketch. Pick the command from the menu, or press Alt-F4 to activate the Circle command. AutoSketch prompts at the bottom of the screen "Circle Center point:" and you are expected to enter the location of the center of the circle. The next prompt is "Circle Point on circle:" and you are then expected to enter a point on the circumference of the circle. The location of the first or second points can be accomplished by moving the screen pointer and picking or by entering the X,Y screen location value from the keyboard. After drawing the circle, AutoSketch repeats the command for you again. You can draw a series of circles without having to pick the command again until you are ready to move on to another command. A circle is a single drawing entity in the same way that a line is a single drawing entity. The Stretch command has no effect on a circle.

APPLICATIONS

Circle is a frequently used command. It is used in the creation of mechanical, electrical, and architectural drawings. The ability to select only the center and a point on the circumference is a limiting factor in the use of this command. You may need to do some clever planning, and possibly draw some auxillary construction lines to draw the required circles with only the center point/point on circumference method.

TYPICAL OPERATION

In this session you draw four circles and two lines. The Attach command is used to locate some of the points.

1. Begin a new drawing.

2. Pick **Circle** from the Draw menu. Type **6,4.5 <CR>** as the center point and **6,3 <CR>** as a point on the circle.

3. Draw another circle of the same size by typing **6,3 <CR>** as the center point, and **6,4.5 <CR>** as a point on the circle.

Now draw two lines to use for construction of more circles. Use the center of the second circle to locate the beginning of the first line and use polar coordinates to locate the lines. The first line will be 2.25 inches long and at an angle of 225 degrees from its origin. The second line will begin at the end of the first line and will be 3 inches long at an angle of 135 degrees.

4. Pick **Line** from the Draw menu. Type **6,3 <CR>** as the first point and **P(2.25,225) <CR>** as the second point.

5. Continue the line by typing **/LPOINT <CR>** as the first point and **P(3,135) <CR>** as the second point.

Add text to the three end points of the lines. These points will be used to construct more circles.

6. Pick **Text** from the Draw menu. Type **6,2.5 <CR>** as the entry point, then type **1 <CR>** as the text.

7. Type **4,1 <CR>** as the entry point, then type **2 <CR>** as the text.

8. Type **2,3.7 <CR>** as the entry point, then type **3 <CR>** as the text.

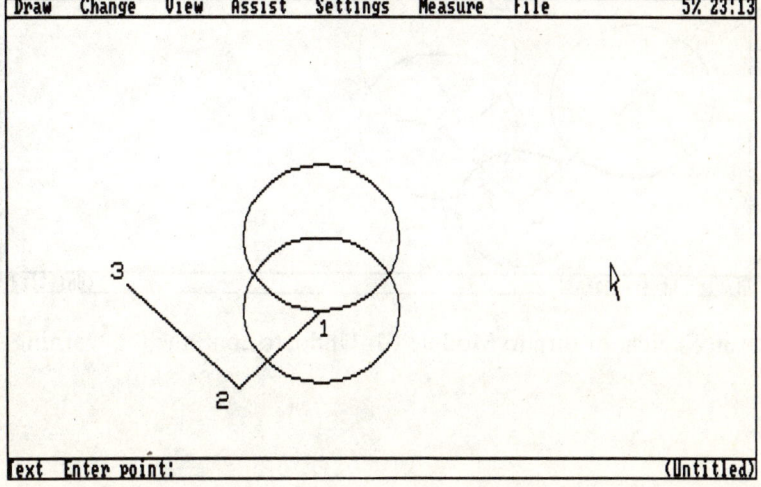

9. Pick **Attach** from the Assist menu.

10. Pick **Circle** from the Draw menu.

11. Pick on the vertex at point 2 to specify the point as the circle center point. Pick close to the midpoint of the line between 1 and 2 as a point on the circle.

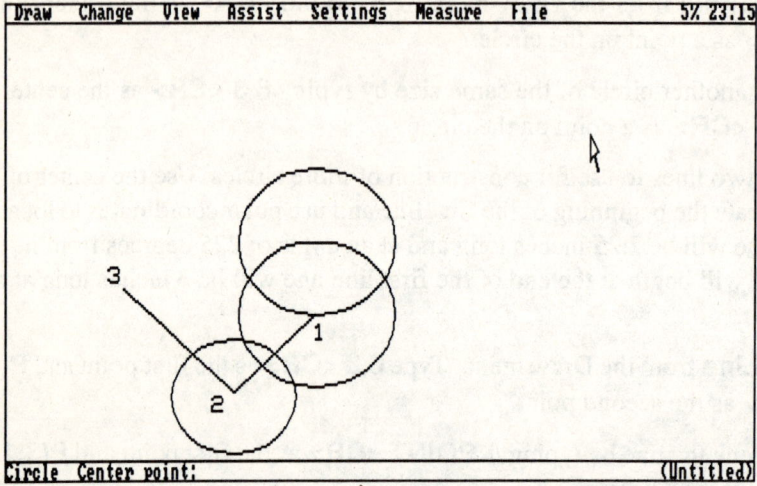

12. Pick on the line at point 3, specifying it as the circle center point. Pick close to the midpoint of the line between 3 and 2 as a point on the circle.

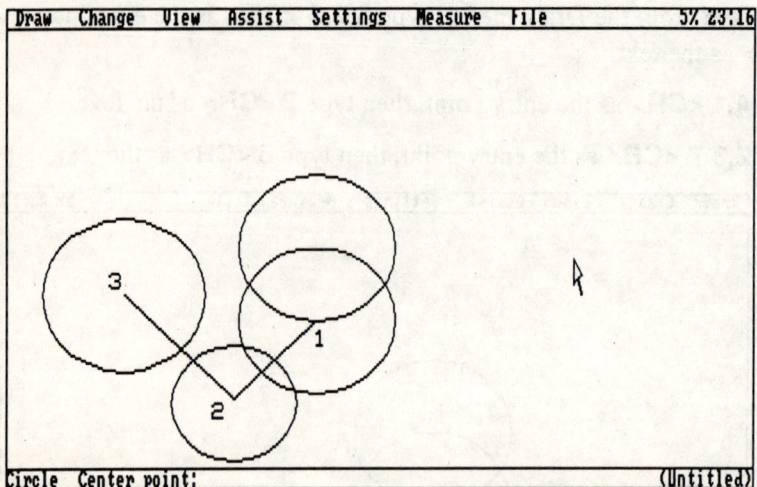

13. Quit AutoSketch, or turn to Module 61, Undo, to continue the learning sequence.

Module 13
COLOR

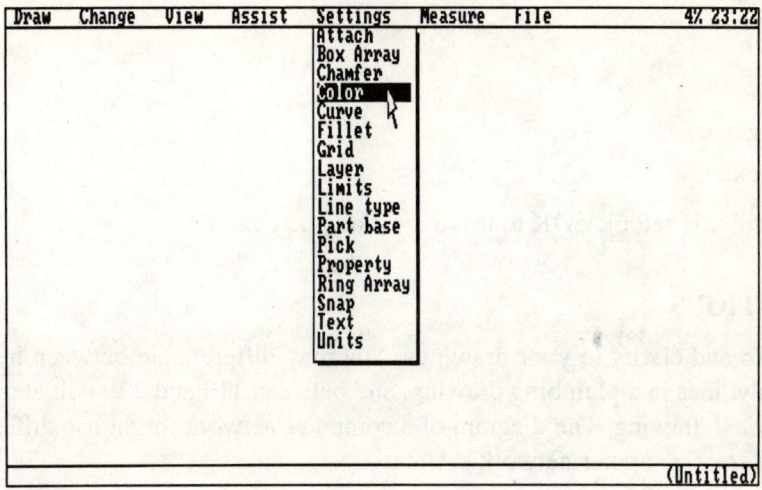

DESCRIPTION

The Color command, located on the Settings menu, allows you to change the color of new objects that you draw. When you select the command, the following dialogue box appears:

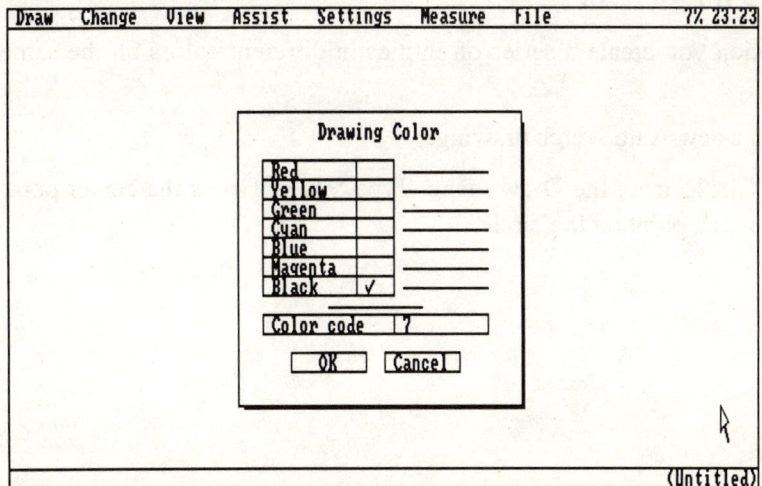

You set the desired color either by picking the check box next to the color name, or by typing the color number in the Color code box. The color numbers are:

1 Red

2 Yellow

3 Green

4 Cyan

5 Blue

6 Magenta

7 Black

When the color is set, pick OK to leave the dialogue box.

APPLICATIONS

Use color to add clarity to your drawings. You may differentiate between hot and cold water supply lines in a plumbing drawing, and between 110 and 220 volt electrical lines in an electrical drawing. The diagram of a computer network might use different colors to label different computer network systems.

Use the Color command on the Settings menu to establish the color for subsequent drawing activities. Use the Property command on the Settings menu to change the color of an existing drawing entity.

TYPICAL OPERATION

In this session you create a series of entities in different colors on the same layer of a drawing.

1. Begin a new AutoSketch drawing.

2. Pick **Circle** from the Draw menu. Type **5,5 <CR>** as the center point. Type **6,6 <CR>** as a point on the circle.

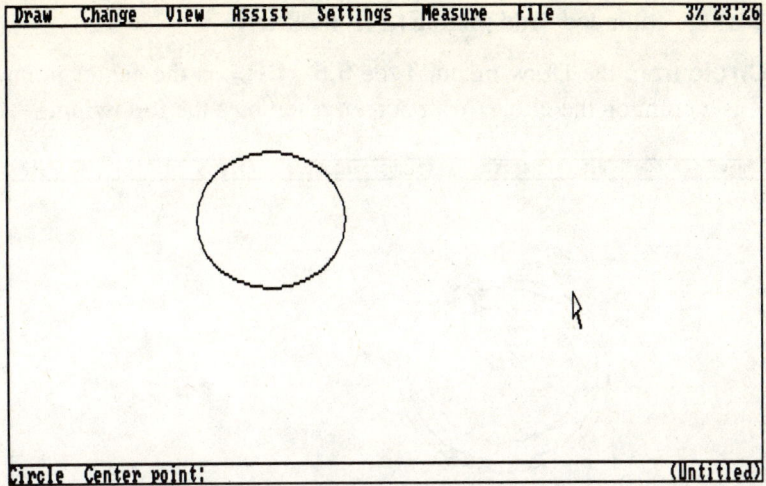

3. Pick **Color** from the Settings menu.

4. Pick the check box next to Red.

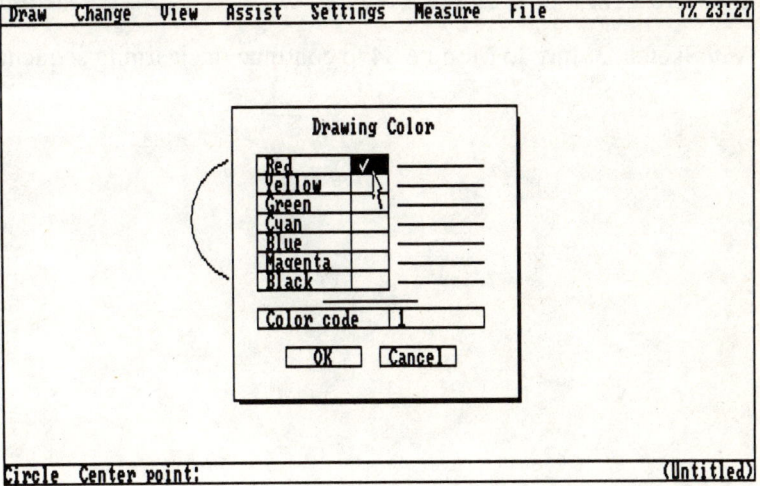

5. Pick **OK**.

6. Pick **Circle** from the Draw menu. Type **5,5 <CR>** as the center point. Type **6,6.5 <CR>** as a point on the circle.

7. Pick **Color** from the Settings menu.

8. Type **3** as the color code and press **Enter**. Pick **OK**.

9. Pick **Circle** from the Draw menu. Type **5,5 <CR>** as the center point. Type **7,5 <CR>** as a point on the circle. Your screen resembles the following.

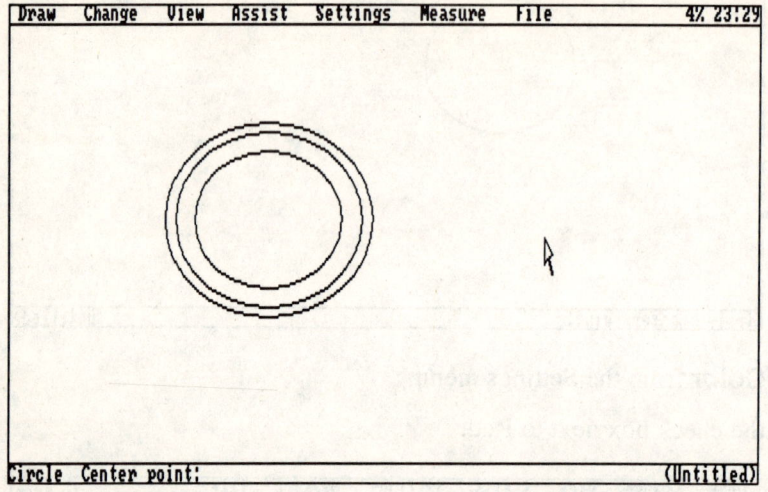

10. Quit AutoSketch, or turn to Module 34 to continue the learning sequence.

Module 14
COORDS

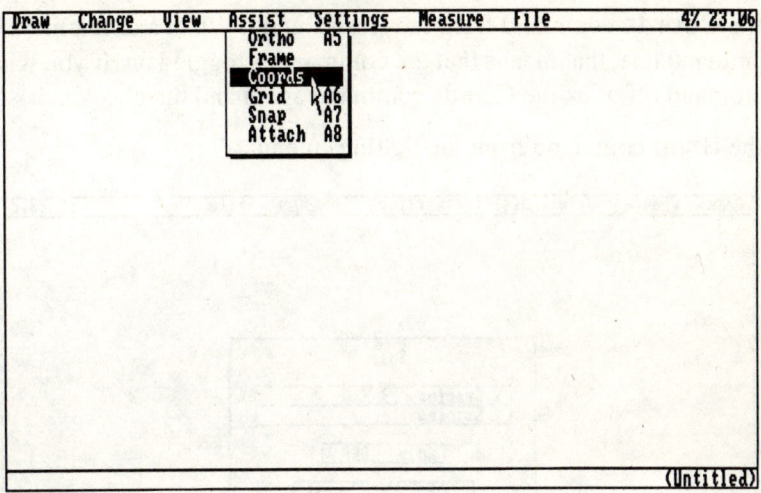

DESCRIPTION

When you pick Coords from the Assist menu, you are able to keep track of where your screen pointer is in reference to its X and Y location on the drawing (indicated in the form of X,Y). This is made possible by two sets of numbers that are separated by a comma located on the prompt line at the bottom of the AutoSketch screen. These two sets of numbers continuously change as the pointer is moved about the screen and are called the Running Coordinates display. Coords can be toggled on and off by continuing to pick the Coords command in the Assist menu.

APPLICATIONS

The most practical application of the Coords command in everyday use for the production of an actual drawing is usually in conjunction with the Snap command. By setting the Snap to a useful value and turning on the running coordinates you can snap to locations on the drawing with accuracy equal to that of entering all values from the keyboard. I also find that the running coordinates displayed at the bottom of the screen aid me in keeping track of where I am on a drawing especially when the view has been zoomed to some magnification that I find difficult to picture in my mind. This new Coords command in AutoSketch is one tool that I find myself automatically turning on before I do any work on a drawing.

TYPICAL OPERATION

This operation consists of using the Snap and Coords command to produce simple geometric figures.

1. Start a new drawing.

2. Pick the **Coords** command from the Assist menu. When a check mark appears on the command line, that means that the command is toggled on. If you wish to toggle the command off, pick the Coords command again and the check mark disappears.

3. Pick the **Snap** command from the Settings menu.

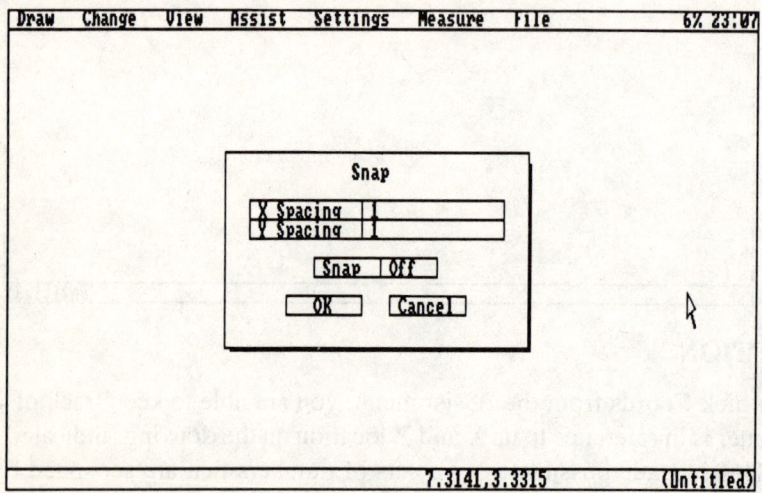

NOTE
Notice that the X and Y spacing of the Snap spacing is set to a default of 1 unit. For this exercise we will leave snap set to 1 unit. If for some reason your snap settings are at some other value than 1, then change them at this time.

4. Pick the **Off** box to turn on Snap. Pick the **OK** box. Move your screen pointer around the screen. Notice that the exact location of the cursor is marked by a small crosshair and that all values displayed in the Running Coordinates line remain in units of whole numbers. This makes it simple to locate your cursor on the screen without fractional values entering into the X and Y location.

5. Select the **Line** command from the Draw menu. Move the screen cursor until the Running Coordinates indicate 1.0000,1.0000 and pick that point for the beginning of the line. The values 1.0000 and 1.0 mean the same thing.

6. Move the cursor to 1.0000,8.0000 and pick that point. You now have a vertical line on your screen that is 8 units long.

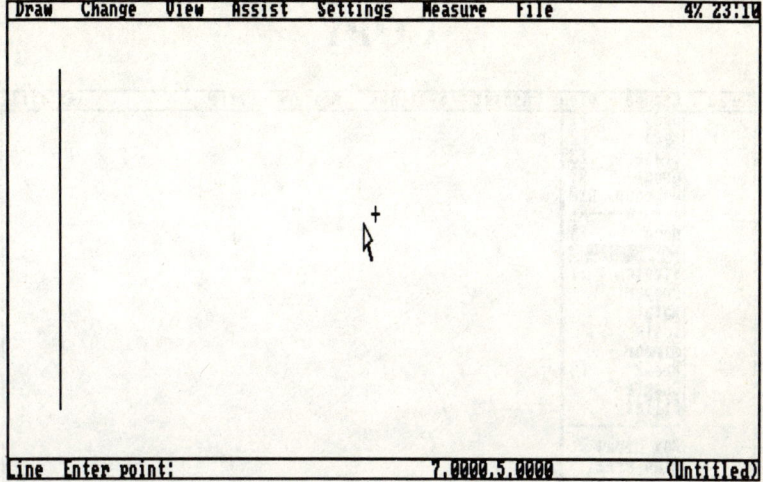

7. Since it is now obvious to you how to use the Coords command, experiment with this tool by drawing some more lines and thinking about where you want the line to be as you pick each point. Can you draw a rectangle within a rectangle and then draw a circle in the middle of both? Try it and see what happens.

8. Turn to Module 31, Line, to continue the learning sequence.

Module 15
COPY

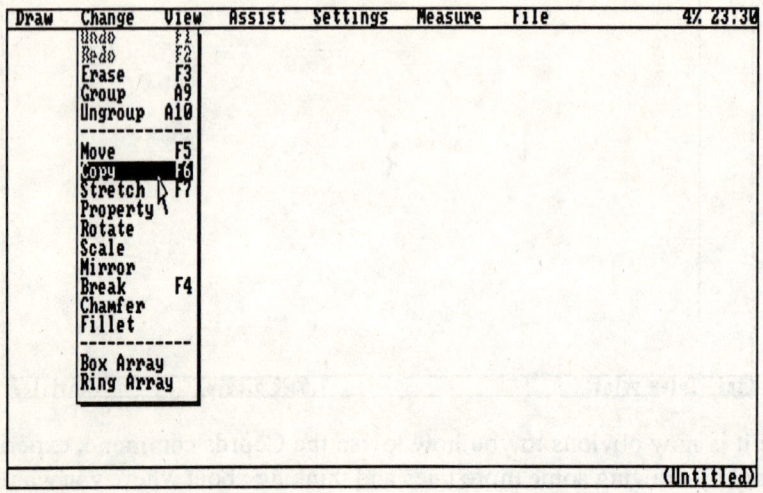

DESCRIPTION

The Copy command is used to copy one or more objects in a drawing. Select the Copy command from the Change menu or press the F6 key. There are three basic steps in using the Copy command. First, you must select the object or objects to be copied. This can be done with the screen pointer to select a single object, or with the Crosses/window box to select several objects at one time. Second, you pick a base point. This base point should be thought of as the beginning of a vector. A vector has direction and magnitude (distance). Third, you pick an insertion point. The insertion point can be thought of as the end of the vector. The object to be copied is reproduced in a position determined by the direction and magnitude of the vector created by the base and insertion points. When the base point is selected, the object(s) to be copied is dragged on the screen with the screen pointer as it is moved.

APPLICATIONS

Copy is a convenient command for the reproduction of any entity or group of entities. The Copy and Move commands are very similar. The major difference between the two commands is that the Move command moves one or more selected objects from one place to another, while the Copy command duplicates one or more selected objects.

TYPICAL OPERATION

This operation draws a picture of a bike, using the Copy command to reproduce several components.

1. Start a new drawing.

Draw the circle and copy it. The center of the first circle is located at 3,4. The radius of the circle is 1.25. The second circle is copied at 5 inches to the right of the first circle.

2. Pick **Circle** from the Draw menu. Type **3,4 <CR>** as the center point and **1.75,4 <CR>** as a point on the circle.

3. Pick **Copy** from the Change menu. Pick the circle. Type **3,4 <CR>** as the reference point, then type **8,4 <CR>** to specify the position of the copy.

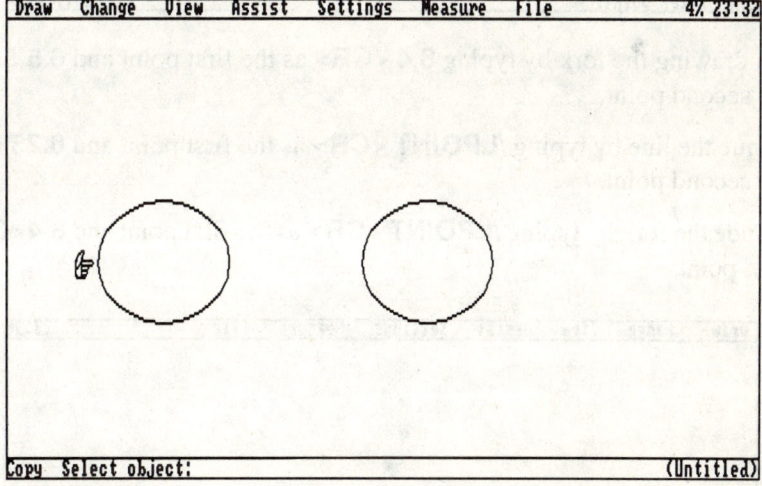

4. Pick **Line** from the Draw menu. Type **3,4 <CR>** as the first point and **5.75,4 <CR>** as the second point.

5. Type **/LPOINT <CR>** as the first point and **7.25,5.5 <CR>** as the second point.

6. Type **/LPOINT <CR>** as the first point and **3,4<CR>** as the second point.

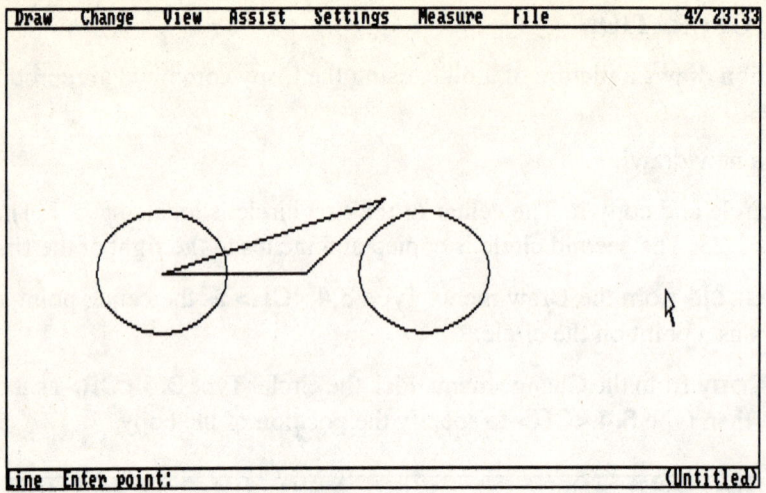

7. Begin drawing the fork by typing **8,4 <CR>** as the first point and **6.5,5.75 <CR>** as the second point.

8. Continue the line by typing **/LPOINT <CR>** as the first point and **6.25,5.5 <CR>** as the second point.

9. Conclude the fork by typing **/LPOINT <CR>** as the first point and **8,4<CR>** as the second point.

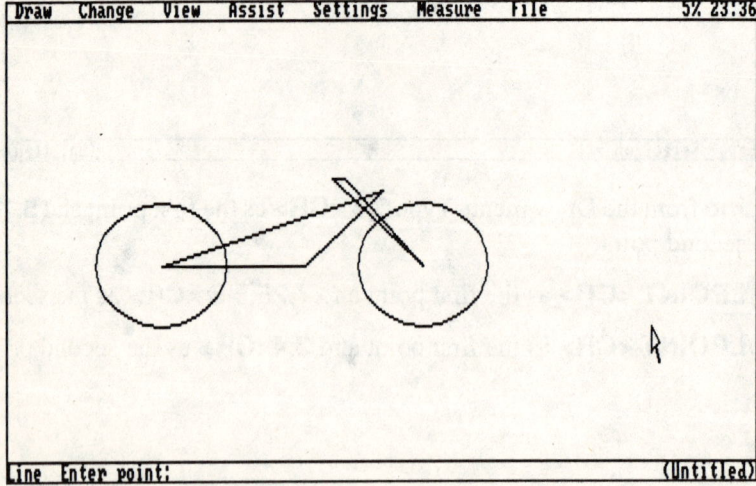

Zoom in on the drawing to construct the handlebars.

10. Pick **Zoom box** from the View menu. Type **4.5,4.75 <CR>** as the first corner and **7,6.25 <CR>** as the second corner.

11. Pick **Arc** from the Draw menu. Type **6.25,5.5 <CR>** as the start point, **5.5,5.75 <CR>** as a point on the arc, and **4.75,5.5 <CR>** as the arc endpoint.

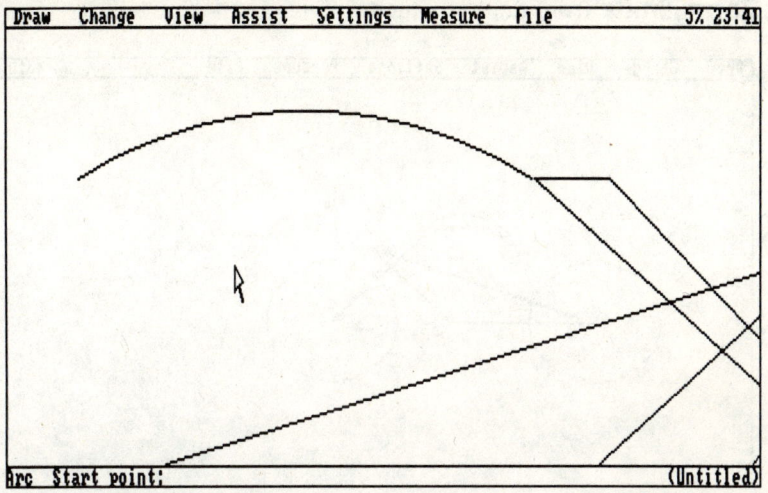

12. Pick **Copy** from the Change menu. Pick the arc. Type **6.25,5.5 <CR>** as the reference point, and **6.5,5.75 <CR>** as the position for the copy.

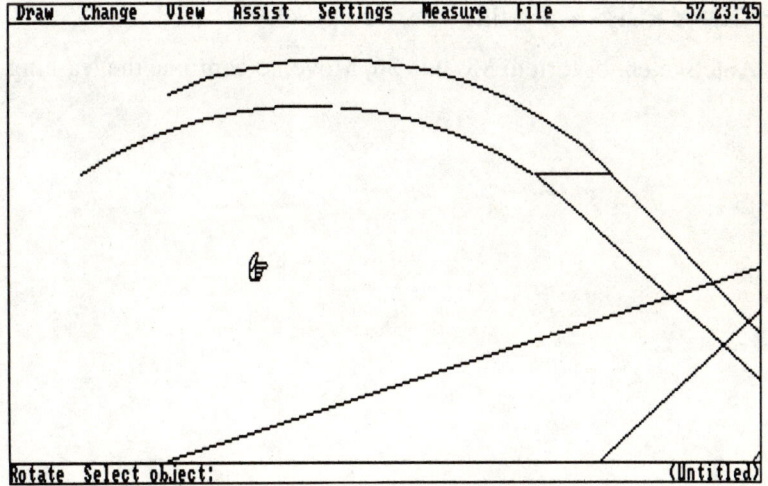

13. Pick the **Attach** command from the Assist menu.

14. Pick **Line** from the Draw menu. Pick the left end of the upper arc, then type **4.7,5.65 <CR>** as the second point.

15. Continue the figure by typing **/LPOINT <CR>** as the first point, then pick the left end of the lower line as the second point.

16. Pick **Zoom limits** from the View menu.

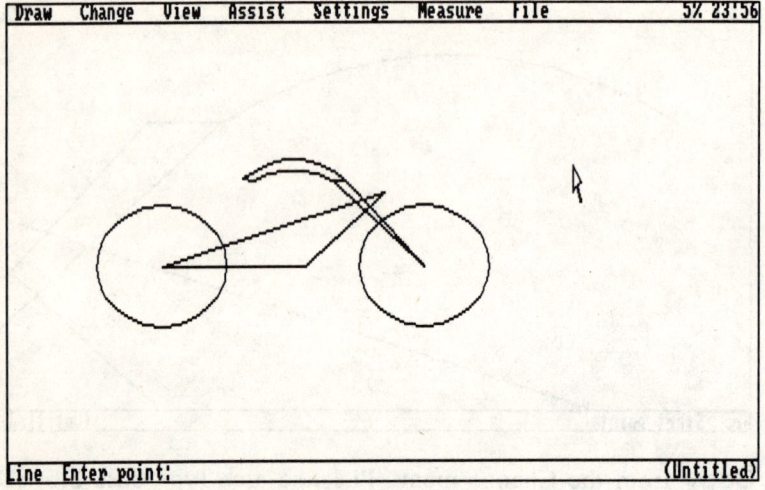

17. Pick **Save as** from the File menu.

18. Type **COPY <CR>** as the filename, then pick **OK**.

19. Quit AutoSketch, or turn to Module 36, Move, to continue the learning sequence.

Module 16
CURVE

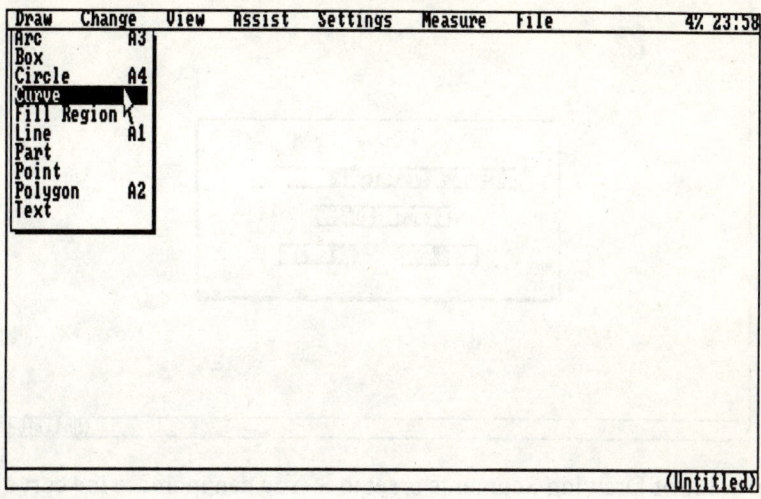

DESCRIPTION

The Curve command is used to draw a B-Spline curve. When you pick the Curve command from the Draw menu, you are asked for a starting point and then a series of control points that define a Frame. The frame looks like a series of connected straight lines.

After you have finished the frame and want to stop picking points, either pick the last point twice in succession or return to the first point and pick it again. By picking the first point twice, you produce a closed curve. AutoSketch then fits a curve to the frame of control points.

The smooth curve passes through the first and last points unless the curve is closed. The curve will be pulled toward the points on the frame. By adding more points to the frame you can cause the curve to more closely fit the frame. The more concentrated the points are in a particular part of the frame, the more pull the points exert. The maximum number of control points for a curve is 100.

A spline curve is one that if you stretch a curve by moving one of its control points, the effects are limited to that point and nearby points.

You can control the precision of the curve's creation by choosing the Curve command from the Settings menu. After making this selection, you are given the opportunity to reset the value of Drawing Segments.

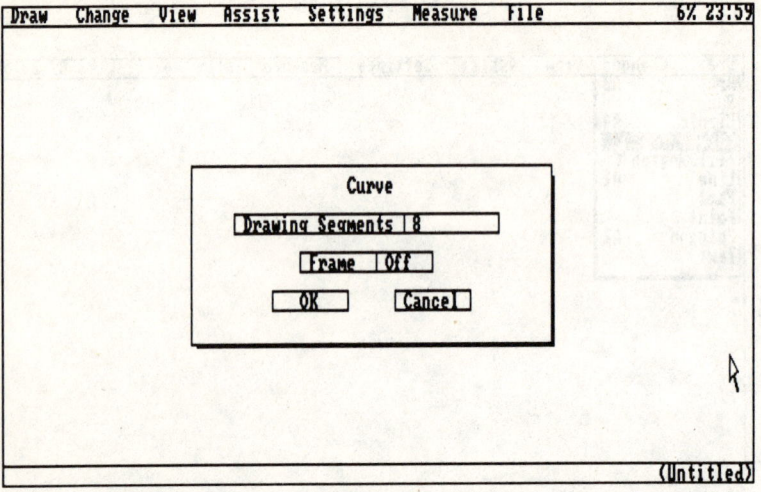

The default value of Drawing Segments is set to 8. You can increase the curve's precision by increasing the value of this setting. The price you pay for more precision is an increase in the time it takes AutoSketch to draw the curve. In this same dialogue box, you can also toggle Frame On or Off. When Frame is On, you can see the curve and the frame. When Frame is Off, you can only see the curve. The Frame toggle can also be switched by picking the Frame command from the Assist menu.

APPLICATIONS

The Curve command could be used to produce a topographical map by picking the frame points on each of the surveyor's points that are at the same elevation. If these points are used to produce a closed Curve, it produces a satisfactory map curve. The Curve could also be used to draw the outline of an airplane's wing or fuselage. The accuracy of the outline could be made very accurate by using many points along the curve's path.

TYPICAL OPERATION

In this session you draw a figure using the Curve command.

1. Begin a new drawing.

2. Draw a vertical line for construction purposes by picking **Line** from the Draw menu. Type **6,.5 <CR>** as the first point and **6,8.5 <CR>** as the second point.

3. Pick the **Curve** command from the Draw menu. Type the following points:

Curve To point: **6,8.5 <CR>**
Curve To point: **5.75,8.5 <CR>**
Curve To point: **5.5,8.5 <CR>**
Curve To point: **5.5,8.25 <CR>**
Curve To point: **5.5,7.875 <CR>**
Curve To point: **5.5,7.625 <CR>**
Curve To point: **5.75,7.5 <CR>**
Curve To point: **5.75,5.375 <CR>**
Curve To point: **4.625,4.875 <CR>**
Curve To point: **3.75,4.25 <CR>**
Curve To point: **4.375,3.125 <CR>**
Curve To point: **3.375,2.5 <CR>**
Curve To point: **3.375,1.75 <CR>**
Curve To point: **4.75,0.75 <CR>**
Curve To point: **6,.5 <CR>**
Curve To point: **6,.5 <CR>**

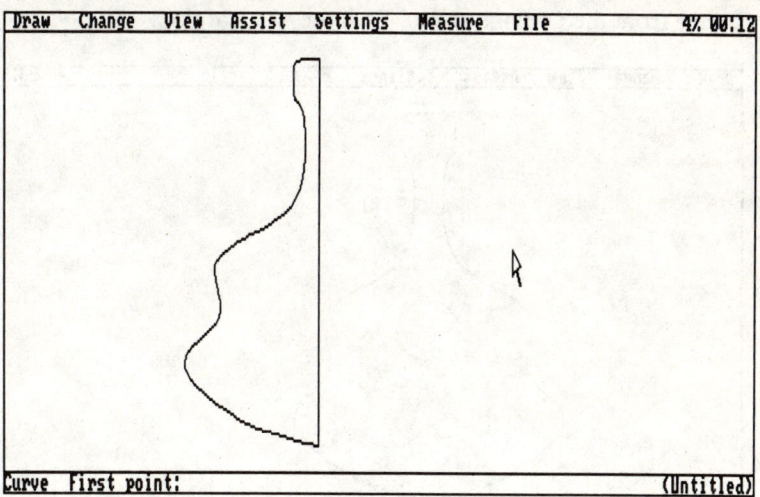

4. Pick the **Frame** command from the Assist menu.

5. Pick the **Mirror** command from the Change menu. Pick on the frame (make sure you do not pick the line or curve). Type **6,.5 <CR>** as the mirror base point and **6,8.5 <CR>** as the second point.

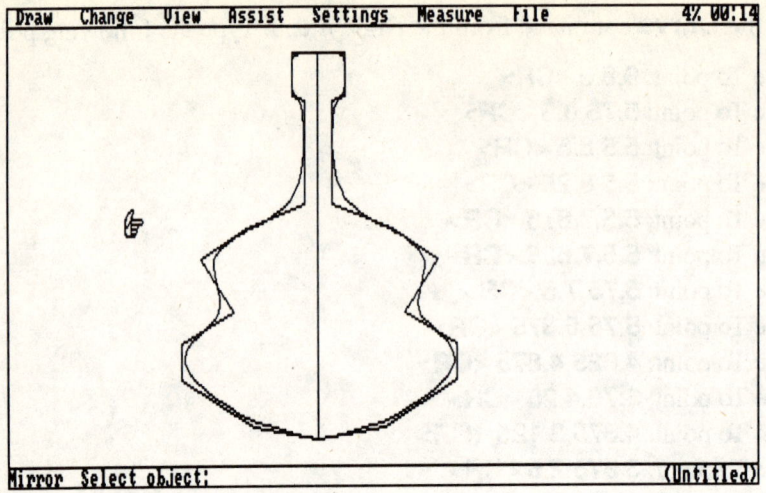

6. Pick **Frame** from the Assist menu.

7. Pick **Circle** from the Draw menu. Type **6,4 <CR>** as the center point and **6.625,4 <CR>** as a point on the circle.

8. Pick **Erase** from the Change menu. Pick the vertical line.

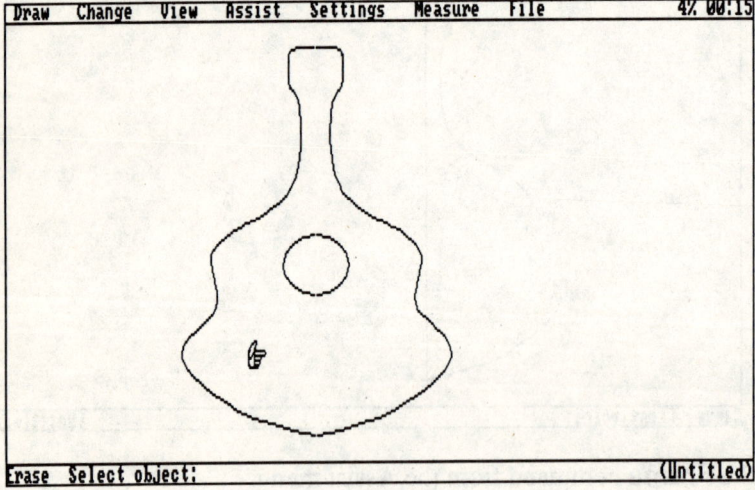

9. Quit AutoSketch, or turn to Module 22, Frame, to continue the learning sequence.

Module 17
DIMENSION

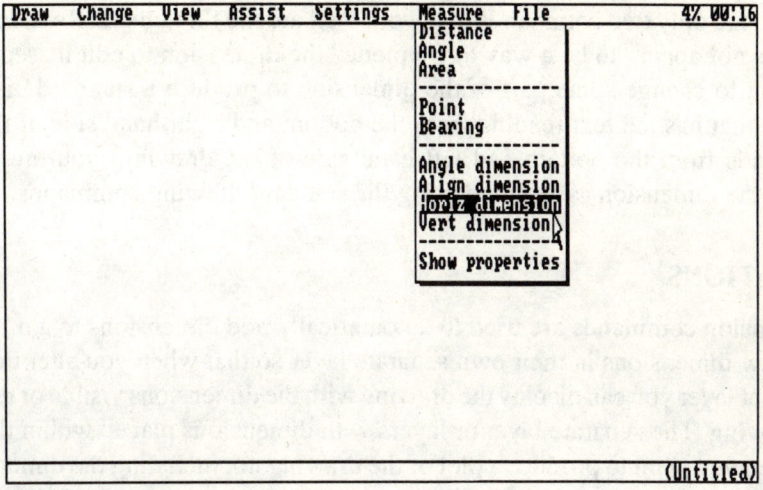

DESCRIPTION

The Dimension command is found in the Measure menu. This command provides semi-automatic dimensioning anytime it is necessary to add a dimension to a drawing. AutoSketch provides three different types of dimensioning, these include: (1) Align dimension, (2) Horiz dimension, and (3) Vert dimension.

The Align dimension produces a linear dimension aligned between two points. To select this item, pick the Measure menu and in the pull-down menu box you can select Align dimension. After picking this command (and all other dimensioning commands) you are required to enter three points. The first point and second point entered define the beginning and ending of the item or distance to be dimensioned and the third point defines the location of the dimension line. After picking the third point, AutoSketch automatically produces a complete dimension. This dimension (and all other dimensions) includes an unbroken dimension line with arrows at each end, two extension lines with appropriate spacing between themselves and the dimensioned object and an overhang past the dimension line. The dimension text is added beyond the dimension line to complete the dimensioning process.

The Horiz dimension command produces a horizontal dimension which is the "X" dimension only and does not recognize any vertical displacement. The Horiz dimension includes the same items that accompany the Align dimension.

The Vert dimension command produces a vertical dimension which is the "Y" dimension only and does not recognize any horizontal displacement. The Vert dimension includes the same items that accompany the Align and Horiz dimension.

The dimensioning commands in AutoSketch work well if all you want to do is allow the program to produce dimensions using its own default settings. If you decide to edit a dimension, the only two commands that work well are the Stretch and Rotate commands. There does not appear to be a way to "explode" the dimension to edit its separate parts. If you want to change some part of the dimension to produce a standard bi-directional dimension that has the text reading from the bottom and right-hand side of the drawing (it now reads from the bottom and left-hand side of the drawing) you must manually reproduce the dimension as required using the standard drawing commands.

APPLICATIONS

The Dimension commands are used to automatically add dimensions to a drawing. You should draw dimensions in their own separate layer so that when you alter the visibility status of that layer you can display the drawing with the dimensions visible or not showing on the drawing. The separate layer or layers with dimensions placed within them is also handy when you want to produce a plot of the drawing not including the dimensions. The dimensions produced automatically in AutoSketch do not comply with internationally established dimensioning standards, but they are sufficient for establishing measurements on a drawing.

TYPICAL OPERATION

In this session you construct some lines and use AutoSketch's semi-automatic dimensioning to show the dimensions. To begin the session, start with a new untitled drawing.

1. Begin a new AutoSketch drawing.

2. Pick **Line** from the Draw menu. Type **2,6 <CR>** as the first point and **7,3 <CR>** as the second point.

3. Pick **Align dimension** from the Measure menu. Type **2,6 <CR>** as the first point and **7,3 <CR>** as the second point. Type **3.25,3.5 <CR>** as the dimension line location.

4. Pick **Vert dimension** from the Measure menu. Type **2,6 <CR>** as the first point and **7,3 <CR>** as the second point. Type **9,5 <CR>** as the dimension line location.

5. Pick **Horiz dimension** from the Measure menu. Type **2,6 <CR>** as the first point and **7,3 <CR>** as the second point. Type **5,7.5 <CR>** as the dimension line location.

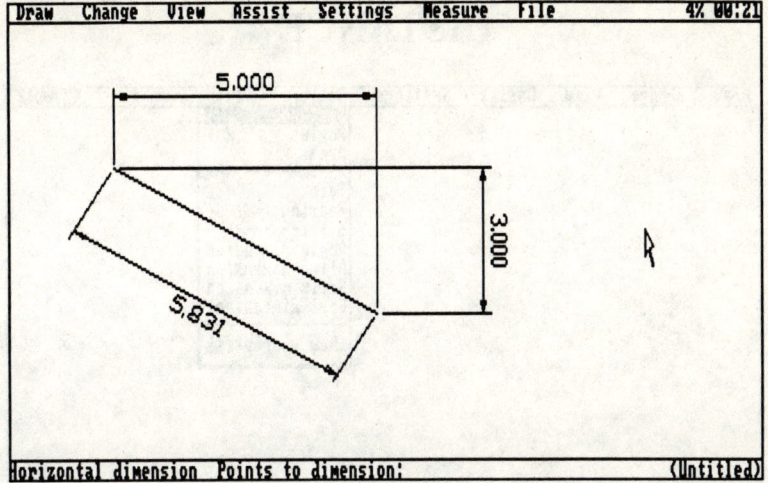

6. Quit AutoSketch, or turn to Module 63, Units, to continue the learning sequence.

Module 18
DISTANCE

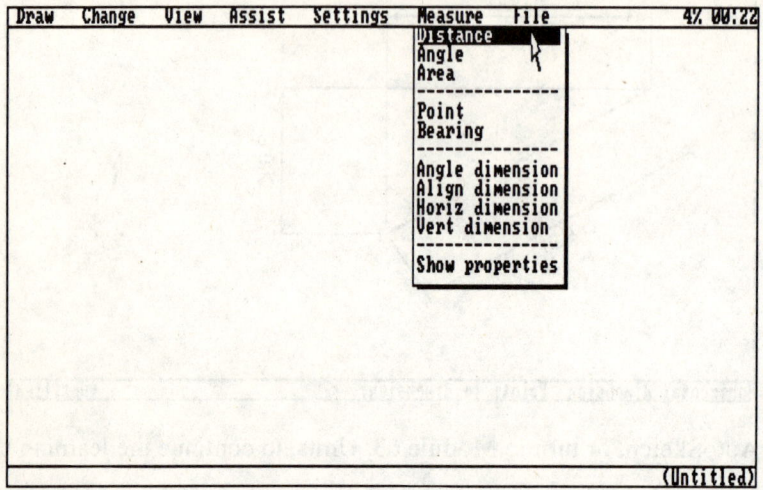

DESCRIPTION

The Distance command calculates the distance between any two points that you pick on the AutoSketch screen. The Distance command is found in the Measure menu at the top of the drawing screen. The distance measurement calculated by the Distance command is displayed in a dialogue box that pops up on the screen after responding to the prompts of the command. You must pick in the check box marked "OK" to proceed with your drawing activities.

APPLICATIONS

Anytime you need to find the distance between any two points on your AutoSketch drawing, the Distance command is the command of choice. There is no further need for you to reach for your calculator and trig tables to find odd distances on a drawing, the Distance command solves all those problems for you.

TYPICAL OPERATION

In this session you draw two lines and find the distance between the ends of the lines using the Distance command.

1. Begin a new AutoSketch drawing.

2. Pick the **Line** command from the Draw menu. Type **2,6 <CR>** as the first point and **7,3 <CR>** as the second point.

3. Type **4,6 <CR>** as the first point and **4,2 <CR>** as the second point.

4. Add letters of identification close to the ends of the lines. Pick **Text** from the Draw menu. Type **1.75,6.25 <CR>** as the entry point and **A <CR>** as the text. Type **7.25,2.75 <CR>** as the entry point and **B <CR>** as the text. Type **4,6.25 <CR>** as the entry point and **C <CR>** as the text. Type **4,1.5 <CR>** as the entry point and **D <CR>** as the text.

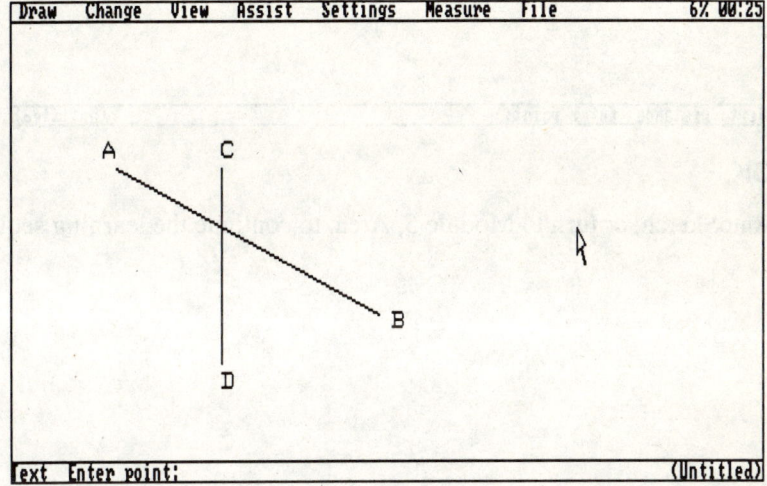

Use the Distance command to find the distance between the ends of two lines. The Attach command will be activated so that all you need do to pick the end of a line is to get the tip of the black arrowhead screen pointer close to the end of a line and the exact end of the line will be attached by the distance command.

5. Pick **Attach** from the Assist menu.

6. Pick **Distance** from the Measure menu. Pick the line end C, then pick line end B.

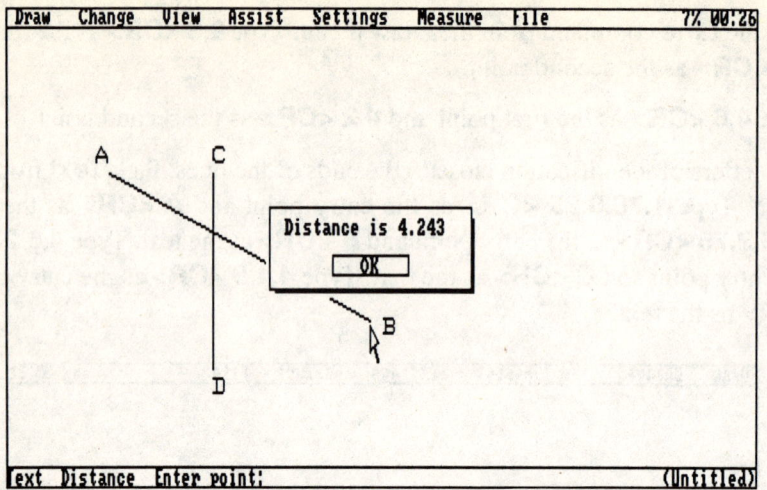

7. Pick **OK**.

8. Quit AutoSketch, or turn to Module 5, Area, to continue the learning sequence.

Module 19
ERASE

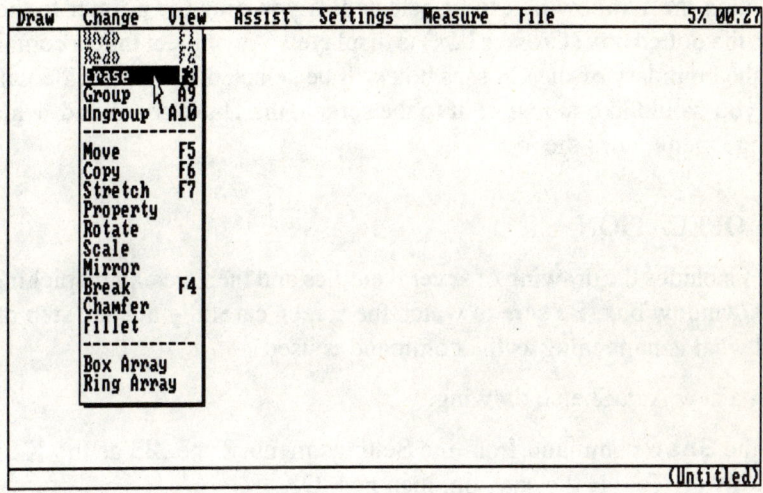

DESCRIPTION

Use the Erase command on the Change menu, or press F3, to remove entities from the drawing. The ERASE command removes complete drawing entities. You can erase a line, but you cannot erase part of a line. To erase part of a line, use the BREAK command instead.

Erase options are described in the following list.

Pick	You may pick the object on the screen.
The Crosses/Window Box	Surround the object in a Crosses/window selection box.
Erase Text	Point to its baseline or use the Crosses/window box to select it.
Erase Curve	Toggle Frame display on and then select the frame.

APPLICATIONS

The Erase command is used anytime you want to remove entire entities. The Crosses/window selection box is used to remove several drawing elements that are close to each other. If you pick a point while using the Erase command and it does not select an object, AutoSketch automatically creates the beginning of a Crosses/window box. Move the pointer diagonally away from this first point to drag the Crosses/window box to select objects to erase. The Crosses/window box works differently, depending on which way you drag to select the second corner of the box. If you drag the pointer to the right of the first corner, the dotted box (Window box) is displayed. Objects must be completely enclosed within the Window box to be selected. If you drag the pointer to the left of the first corner, the dotted box (Crosses box) is displayed. Any object that is contained within or crosses the boundary of the Crosses box will be selected. If you accidentally erase an object and you would like to restore it to the screen, the Undo command, which is found in the Change menu, does the job.

TYPICAL OPERATION

This session includes the drawing of several entities and then erasing by picking and using the Crosses/window box. Be sure to watch the screen carefully at each step of erasure to understand what is happening as the command is used.

1. Begin a new AutoSketch drawing.

2. Pick the **Snap** command from the Settings menu. Type **.25** as the X Spacing and press **Enter**. Toggle the snap on, then pick **OK**.

3. Pick **Grid** from the Assist menu.

Draw three circles by entering the value of the location of their centers from the keyboard and then entering the value of a location on their circumference that is .5 below center.

4. Pick **Circle** from the Draw menu. Type **3,2 <CR>** as the center point and **3,1.5 <CR>** as a point on the circle.

5. Type **3.75,3.25 <CR>** as the center point and **3.75,2.75 <CR>** as the point on the circle.

6. Type **4.5,2 <CR>** as the center point and **4.5,1.5 <CR>** as the point on the circle.

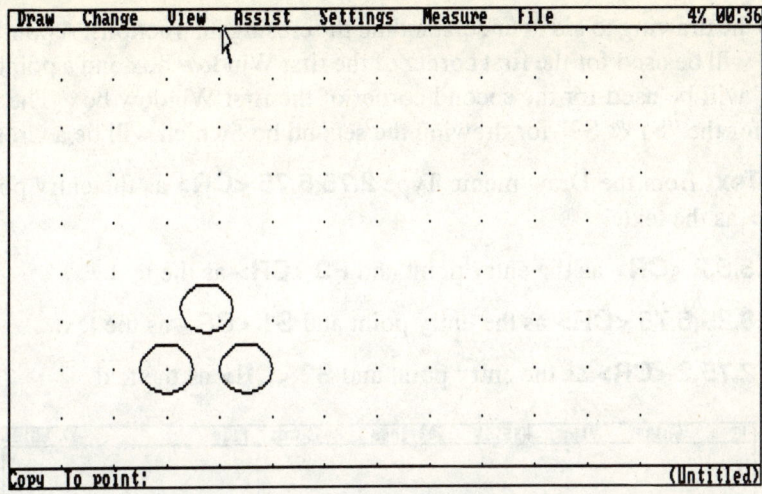

Copy the circles twice with the Copy command. First select the three circles by surrounding them with a Window box and then choose the beginning and ending points of a vector that describes the direction and distance for the new copy to be placed from the original object.

7. Pick **Copy** from the Change menu. Type **2.25,4 <CR>** as the first window point and **5.5,1 <CR>** as the second window point.

8. Type **3.75,2.25 <CR>** as the copy reference point and **7.5,4 <CR>** as the position of the copy.

9. Type **2.25,4 <CR>** as the first window selection point and **5.5,1 <CR>** as the second window selection point.

10. Type **3.75,2.25 <CR>** as the reference point and **3,6 <CR>** as the position for the copy.

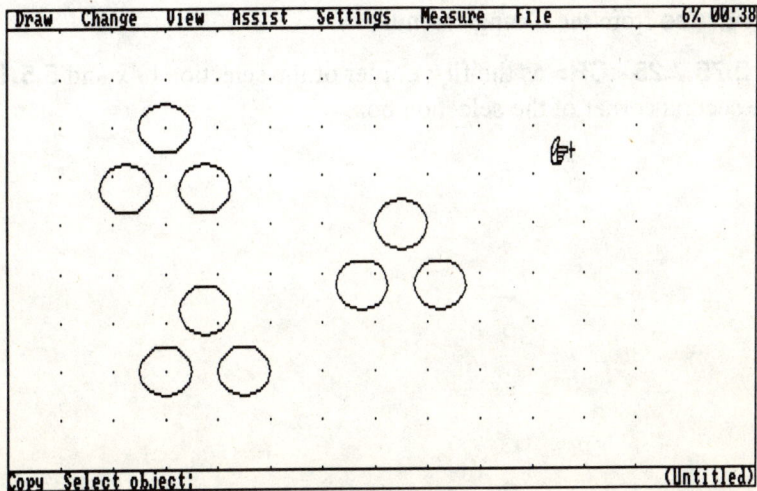

Add text to the drawing to aid in understanding the erasing instructions. A point very close to the "P1" will be used for the first corner of the first Window box and a point very close to the "P2" will be used for the second corner of the first Window box. The same logic holds true for the "S1 & S2" for drawing the second box which will be a Crosses box.

11. Pick **Text** from the Draw menu. Type **2.75,6.75 <CR>** as the entry point and **P1 <CR>** as the text.

12. Type **5.5,2 <CR>** as the entry point and **P2 <CR>** as the text.

13. Type **8.25,6.75 <CR>** as the entry point and **S1 <CR>** as the text.

14. Type **2.75,2 <CR>** as the entry point and **S2 <CR>** as the text.

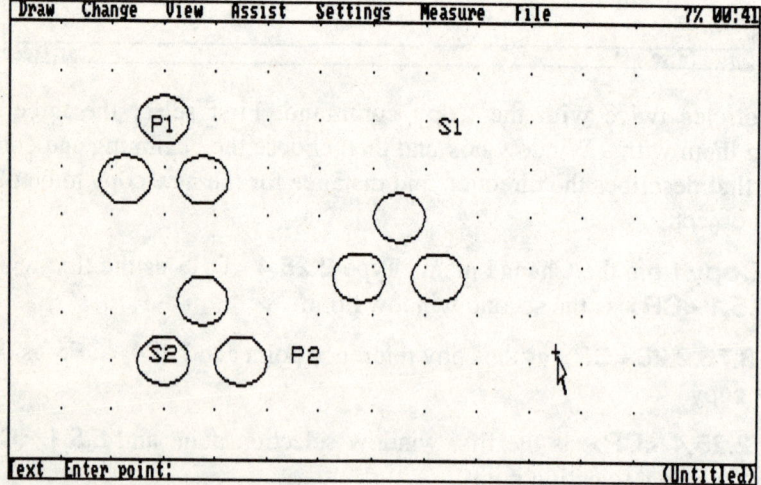

Erase some of the circles using a Window box. The Window box only causes the erasure of items enclosed by the box.

15. Select **Erase** from the Change menu.

16. Type **2.75,7.25 <CR>** as the first corner of the selection box and **5.5,1.75 <CR>** as the second corner of the selection box.

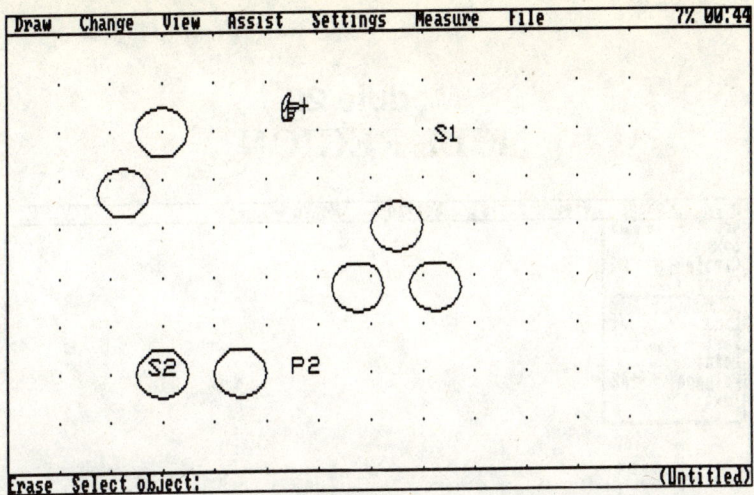

Notice that only two circles and the "P1" were erased because they were the only items completely included in the Window box.

Erase some of the circles using a Crosses box. Any items that are even partially included in the Crosses box will be erased.

17. Pick **Erase** from the Change menu. Type **8,7 <CR>** as the first corner and **2,4 <CR>** as the second corner.

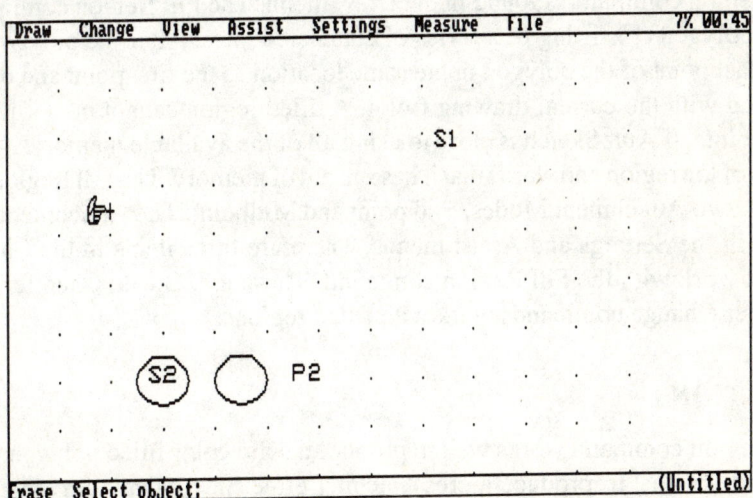

18. Quit AutoSketch, or turn to Module 10, Break, to continue the learning sequence.

Module 20
FILL REGION

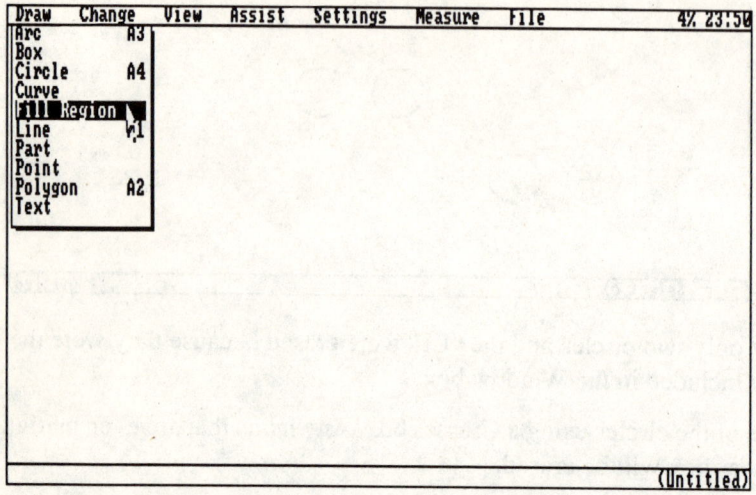

DESCRIPTION

The Fill Region command is found in the Draw menu. The Fill Region command is used to draw a polygon consisting of a series of connected lines. After the polygon is closed, select the last point of the polygon in the same location as the first point and the enclosed area is filled with the current drawing Color. A filled region cannot be defined by more than 100 points. If AutoSketch is close to using all of the available memory, it draws only the outline of the region and warns that it has run out of memory. The Fill Region command works with two Attachment Modes, End point and Midpoint. The Attachment Modes are controlled in the Settings and Assist menus. There are three items in the Change menu that do not work with the Fill Region command. These are, Break, Chamfer, and Fillet. All the other Change commands work with filled regions.

APPLICATIONS

The Fill Region command works well to produce a solid color filled polygon. It could be used (with restraint) to produce a crosshatching effect in cutaway drawings (sectional drawings). It is important to use Fill Region sparingly. Filled regions are very demanding on your computer's RAM capacity (memory) and disk storage. The other negative component that must be considered is the tremendous wear and tear that this type of drawing object (entity) places on your plotter pen or printer ribbon. Filled regions can dramatically increase your paper drawing output expense.

TYPICAL OPERATION

In this operation you use the Fill Region command to draw a stylized representation of an object that is very familiar to those of us living here in the Midwestern part of these United States.

1. Start a new drawing.

2. Pick **Attach** from the Assist menu. This makes it easier to close the polygon when using the Fill Region command.

3. Draw the first circle. Pick **Circle** from the Draw menu. Type **5,6 <CR>** to locate the center. Type **5.25,6 <CR>** to produce a circle with a radius of .25 inches.

4. Draw the base of the windmill. Pick **Line** from the Draw menu. Type **5,6 <CR>**, **6,.25 <CR>**. Type **/LPOINT <CR>** and **4,.25 <CR>**. Type **/LPOINT <CR>** and **5,6 <CR>**. Type **4,.25 <CR>** and **5.5,3 <CR>**. Since Attach has been turned On, the line you just entered is at the exact midpoint of the line to the right. Type **6,.25 <CR>** and **4.5,3 <CR>**.

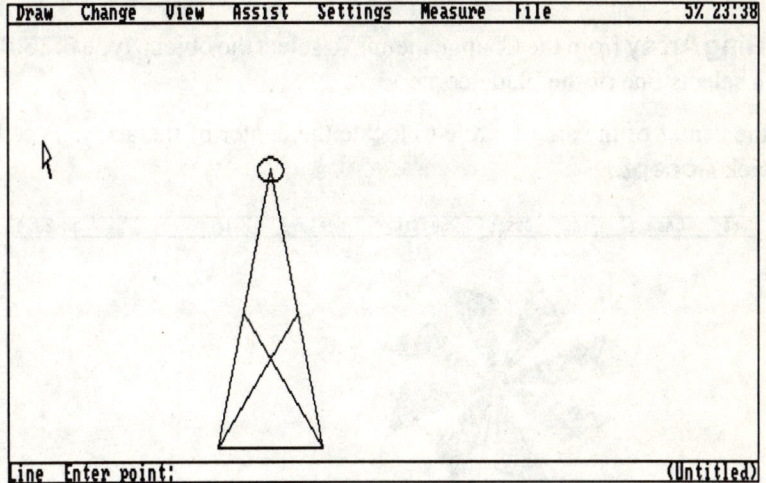

5. Draw the blade. Pick **Fill Region** from the Draw menu. Type **5,6 <CR>**, **5.75,3.75 <CR>**, **6.25,4.75 <CR>**, and **5,6 <CR>**.

6. Make 7 copies of the blade. Pick **Ring Array** from the Settings menu. Change the Number of items to **8** and press **Return**.

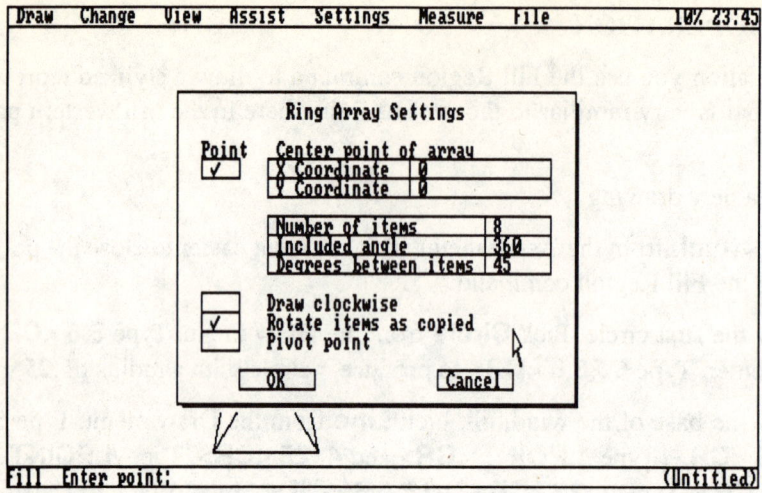

7. Check the Ring Array Settings dialogue box on your screen and make sure that all your settings are the same as the one shown above. After you are satisfied with your results, Pick **OK**.

8. Pick **Ring Array** from the Change menu. To select the object, type **6.25,4.75 <CR>** which selects one of the blade corners.

9. Use the center of the small circle to locate the center of the array. Type **5,6 <CR>** and pick **Accept**.

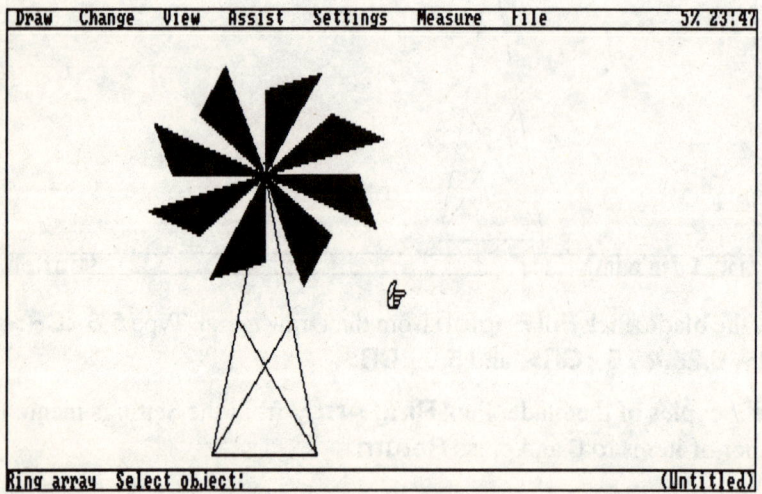

10. Draw the outer circle. Pick **Circle** from the Draw menu. Type **5,6 <CR>** and **7,6 <CR>**.

11. Turn to Module 60, Text, to continue the learning sequence.

Module 21
FILLET

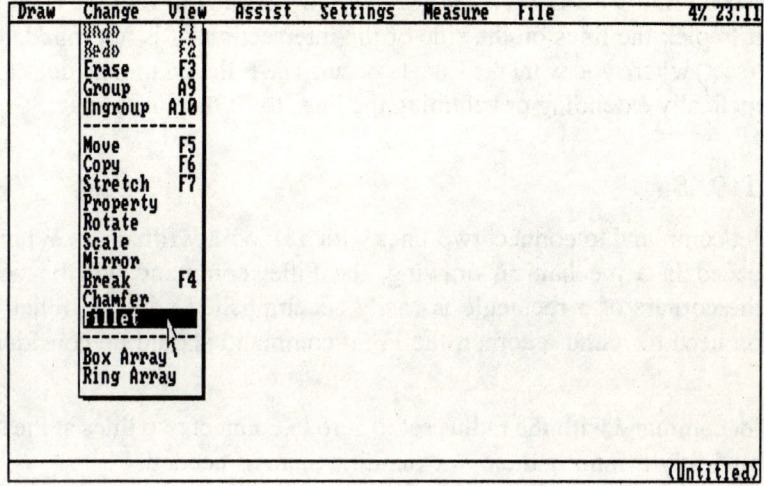

DESCRIPTION

The Fillet command is found in the Change menu and the Settings menu. When you select
Fillet from the Settings menu, the following dialogue box appears.

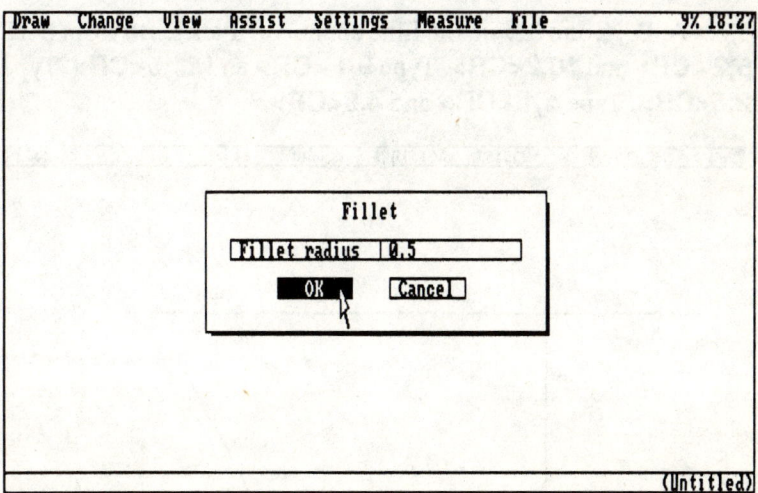

The default setting for Fillet radius is 0.5. When you are satisfied with your fillet radius and are ready to fillet some lines, pick Fillet from the Change menu. It is necessary for you to have already drawn the lines to be filleted before you choose Fillet from the Change menu. After you have picked the Fillet command AutoSketch prompts you to Select a line. Pick a line close to the location of where you want the fillet to occur. You are prompted to select a second line. Pick the second line close to where you want the fillet to occur. It is important to pick the lines on the side of the intersection (it is not mandatory for the lines to intersect) where you want the fillet to occur. The Fillet command does a marvelous job of automatically extending or trimming the lines to fit the curve exactly.

APPLICATIONS

Use the Fillet command to connect two lines with a smoothly fitted arc. When a fillet or round is needed in a mechanical drawing, the Fillet command will be your choice. Rounding the corners of a rectangle is easily accomplished with the Fillet command. Anytime you need to round a corner, the Fillet command should be considered for the job.

Use the Fillet command with the radius set to zero to connect two lines at the same exact point, automatically trimming them or extending them as needed.

TYPICAL OPERATION

In this activity, you draw four lines and then use the Fillet command to round corners and trim lines at their intersection.

1. Draw lines A, B, X, and Y with the Line command. Pick **Line** from the Draw menu. Type **5,2 <CR>** and **10,2<CR>**. Type **9,1 <CR>** and **11,5<CR>**. Type **1,6 <CR>** and **12,6<CR>**. Type **4,1 <CR>** and **4,8<CR>**.

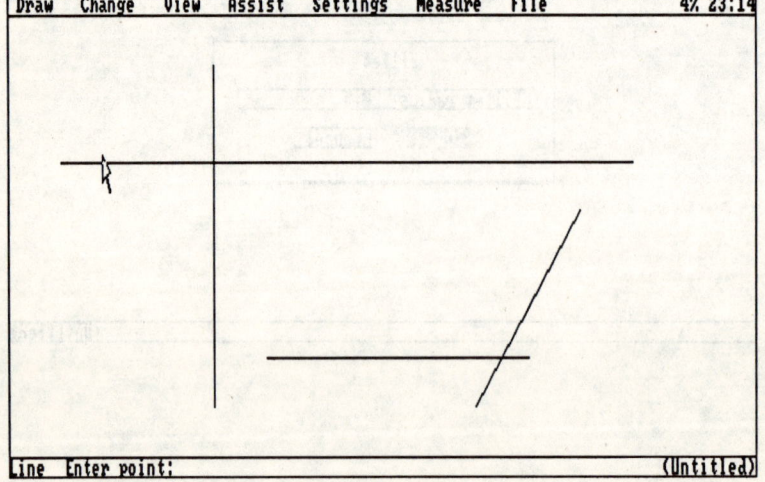

2. Enter all letters identifying lines with the Text command. Pick **Text** from the Draw menu. Type **.5,5.875 <CR>** and **X <CR>**. Type **3.875,8.125 <CR>** and **Y <CR>**. Type **6,1.625 <CR>** and **A <CR>**. Type **10.5,3.375 <CR>** and **B <CR>**.

3. Enter numerals defining points to use while using the Fillet command. Type **5,5.5 <CR>** and **1 <CR>**.

4. Type **4.25,4.625 <CR>** and **2 <CR>**.

5. Type **3.625,6.625 <CR>** and **3 <CR>**.

6. Type **3,5.5 <CR>** and **4 <CR>**.

7. Type **5,2.25 <CR>** and **5 <CR>**.

8. Type **3.625,2.5 <CR>** and **6 <CR>**.

9. Type **8.75,2.25 <CR>** and **7 <CR>**.

10. Type **9.5,2.75 <CR>** and **8 <CR>**.

11. Type **10.5,4.75 <CR>** and **9 <CR>**.

12. Type **10.25,6.25 <CR>** and **10 <CR>**.

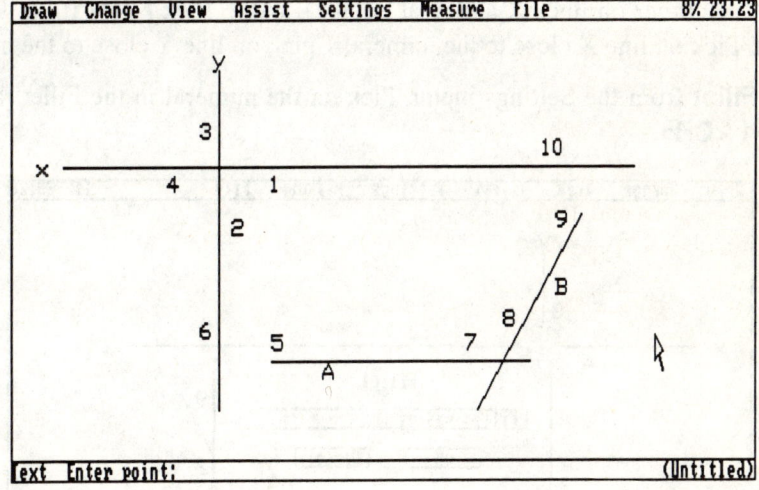

13. Pick **Fillet** from the Settings menu.

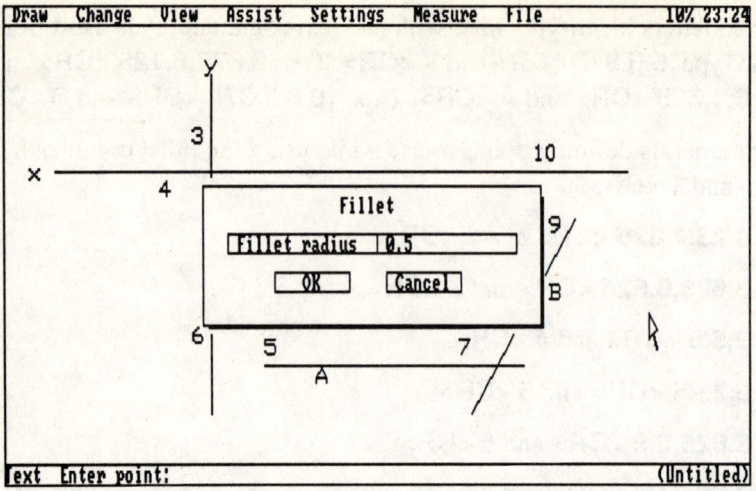

14. If your Fillet radius is not set to 0.5, change it and then pick **OK**.

15. Break lines X and Y close to their intersection. Pick **Break** from the Change menu. Type **4.5,6 <CR>** and **4.5,6 <CR>** and **3.625,6 <CR>**. Pick anywhere on line Y to select it. Type **4,5.5 <CR>** and **4,6.5 <CR>**

16. Fillet the corner on lines X and Y at points 1 and 2. Pick **Fillet** from the Change menu. Pick on line X close to the numeral 1 pick on line Y close to the numeral 2.

17. Pick **Fillet** from the Settings menu. Pick on the numeral in the Fillet radius box. Type **1 <CR>**.

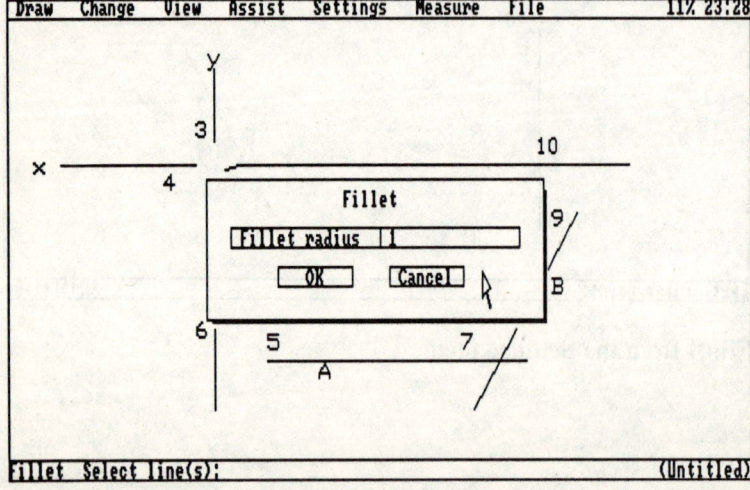

18. After checking to make sure that your fillet radius is now set to 1 inch, pick the **OK** box.

19. Fillet the corner on lines X and Y at points 3 and 4. Pick on line X close to the numeral 4, then pick on line Y close to the numeral 3.

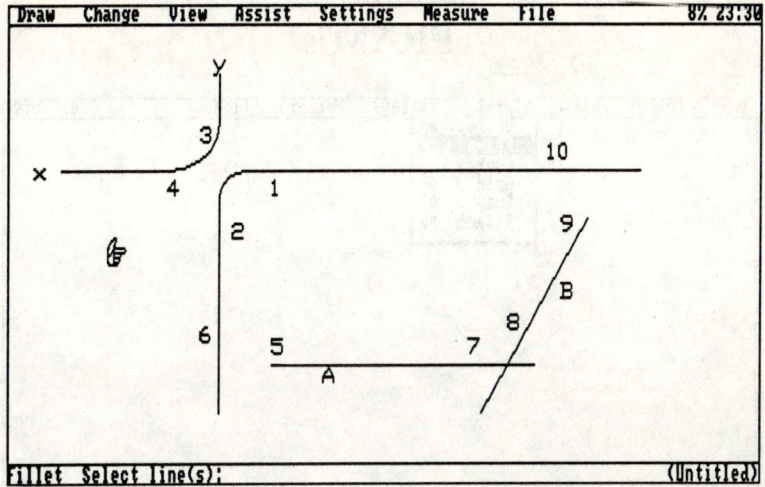

20. Now change the fillet radius to zero to hook up some lines at their intersection point. Pick **Fillet** from the Settings menu. Pick on the 1 in the Fillet radius box. Type **0 <CR>** and pick **OK**.

21. Pick on line A close to the numeral 5. Pick on line Y close to the numeral 6.

22. Pick on line A close to the numeral 7. Pick on line B close to the numeral 8.

23. Pick on line B close to the numeral 9. Pick on line X close to the numeral 10.

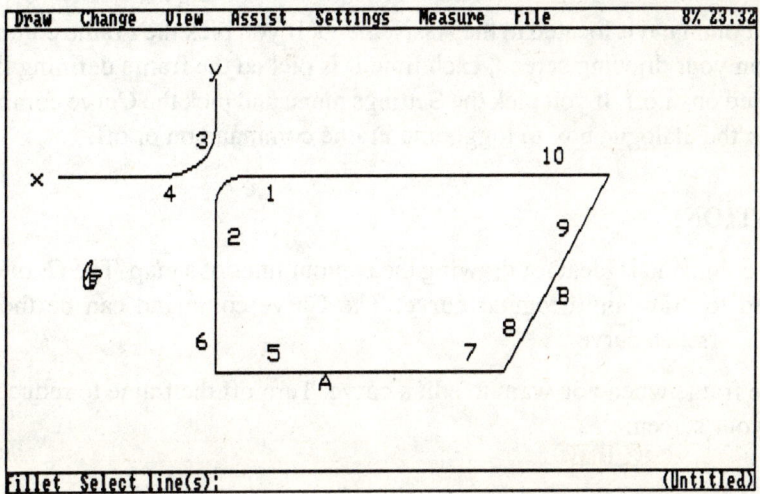

24. Turn to Module 11, Chamfer, to continue the learning sequence.

Module 22
FRAME

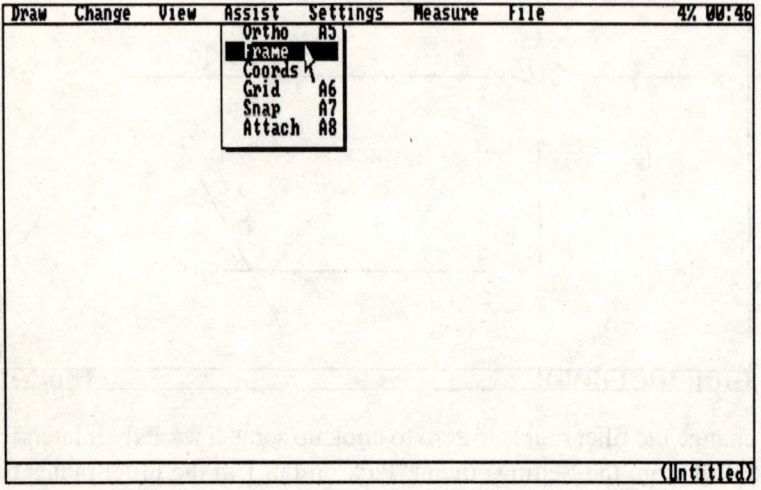

DESCRIPTION

The Frame command, located on the Assist menu, controls the visibility of the frame defining any curve produced with the Curve command. The Frame command makes the editing of a curve by erasing, stretching, moving and other modifications easier because the frame of the curve is what must be picked for editing.

The Frame command is located in the Assist menu. If you pick the Frame command when a curve is on your drawing screen, each time it is picked the frame defining the curve is either toggled on or off. If you pick the Settings menu and pick the Curve command, there is a place in the dialogue box to toggle the Frame command on or off.

APPLICATIONS

The Curve command is ideal for drawing the contour lines of a map. The Curve command can be used to draw any irregular curve. The Curve command can be thought of as AutoSketch's french curve.

Turn on the frame when you want to edit a curve. Turn off the frame to reduce the visual clutter on your screen.

TYPICAL OPERATION

In this session you draw a curve with the Curve command and then toggle the frame on and off with the Frame command. Start with a new untitled drawing.

1. Begin a new AutoSketch drawing.

2. Pick the **Curve** from the Draw menu. Type the following points to define the curve:

Curve First point: **1,2 <CR>**
Curve To point: **3,3 <CR>**
Curve To point: **5,7 <CR>**
Curve To point: **6,7 <CR>**
Curve To point: **8,3 <CR>**
Curve To point: **10,2 <CR>**
Curve To point: **10,2 <CR>**

3. Pick **Frame** from the Assist menu.

4. Pick **Stretch** from the Change menu. Type **8,3 <CR>** as the first corner and **8,3 <CR>** as the second corner. Type **8,3 <CR>** as the stretch base and **9,5 <CR>** as the stretch-to point.

5. Pick **Frame** from the Assist menu, deactivating the Frame setting.

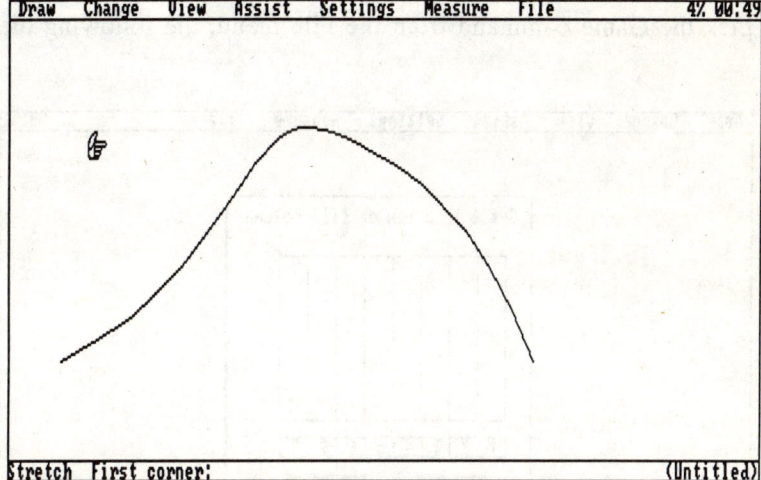

6. Quit AutoSketch, or turn to Module 47, Polygon, to continue the learning sequence.

Module 23
GAME

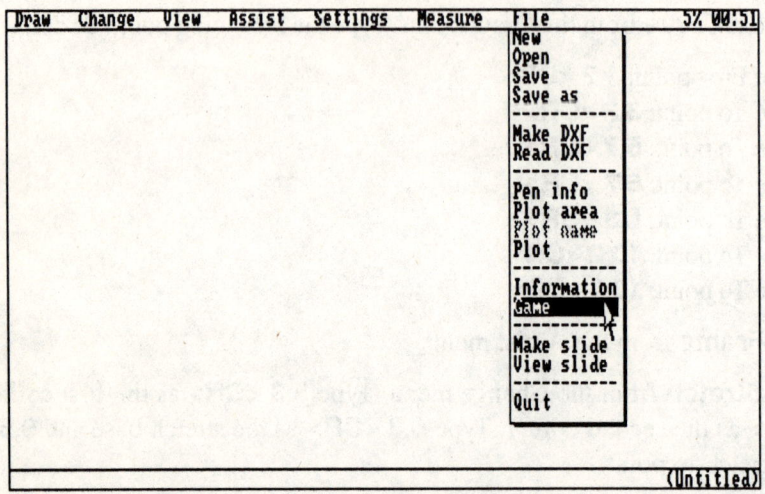

DESCRIPTION

When you pick the Game command from the File menu, the following dialogue box appears.

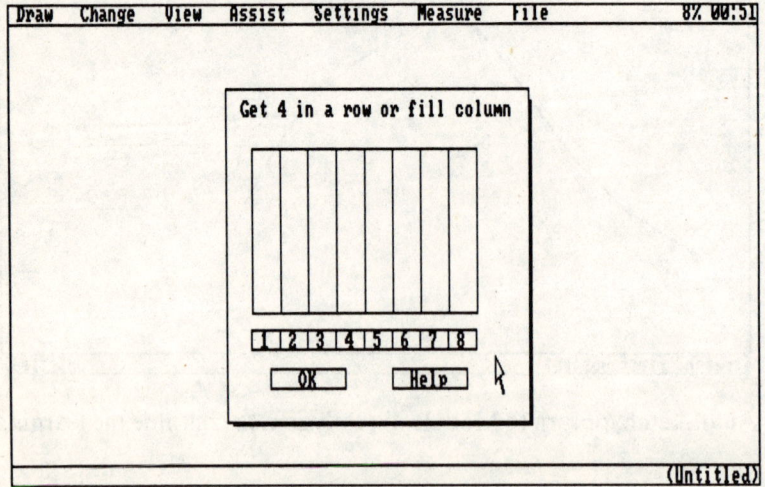

The object of the game is to place 4 X's in a row, either horizontally, vertically, or diagonally. You also win if you are the one to place the last character in a column. (A column holds eight characters.) You may review the rules at any time by picking Help.

APPLICATIONS

Use the Game command to relieve stress induced by staring at the drawing editor for long time periods. You may pick OK at any time to suspend the game, returning to it by again picking Game from the File menu.

TYPICAL OPERATION

In this session you play the AutoSketch game.

1. Pick **Game** from the File menu.

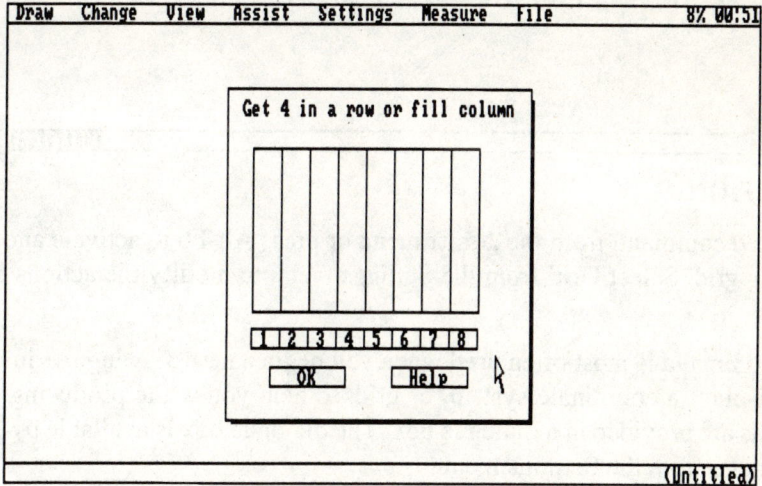

2. Alternate with the computer in placing characters on the screen by picking the numbers beneath the desired columns.

3. Continue playing until you win.

This concludes the learning sequence.

Module 24
GRID

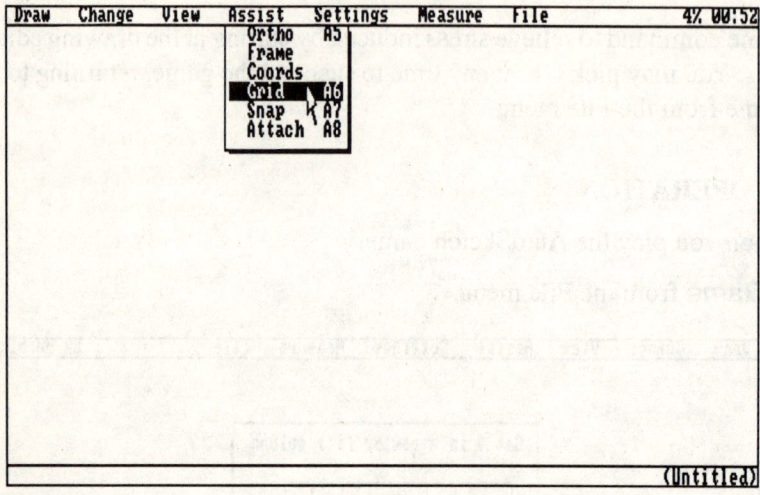

DESCRIPTION

Pick the Grid command from the Assist menu or press Alt-F6 to activate and deactivate the drawing grid. Select Grid from the Settings menu to modify the actions of the Grid command.

The Grid command is most often used when you begin a new drawing. As implied by its name, it displays a coordinate system, or grid, to help you while producing a drawing. Grid options are provided in a dialogue box. The dialogue box is available by picking the Grid command from the Settings menu.

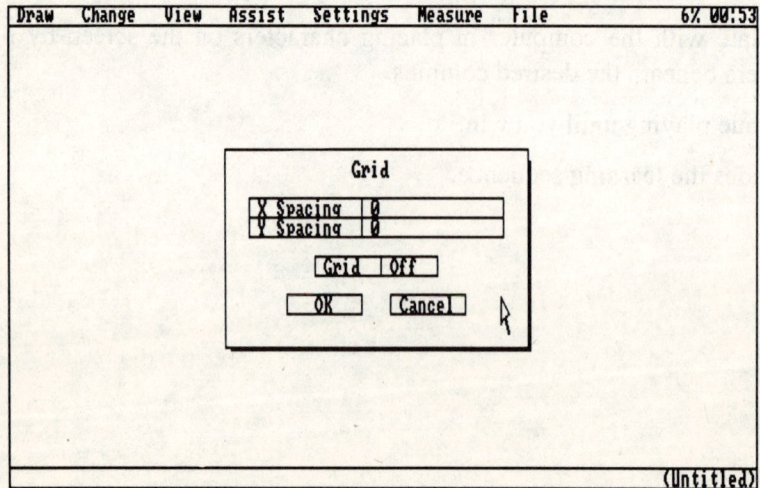

The options are described in the following list.

On   Activates the grid

Off   Deactivates the grid

X Spacing   Typing a value of 0 allows the grid spacing to automatically follow the Snap spacing. The Snap is a function of AutoSketch that is toggled on and off to allow the screen cursor to snap (or jump) to established grid coordinates. For example, a Snap setting of .25 causes the screen cursor to jump by .25-inch increments. Typing a non-zero number specifies the coordinate spacing for the grid. It is possible, although not especially useful, to specify grid and snap coordinates which are completely unrelated using this method. The X spacing sets the horizontal distance between grid dots. When you use the dialogue box and type in an X spacing value, the Y spacing value is also set; so always set the value of X first and then, if different, set the Y value.

Y Spacing   The Y spacing sets the vertical spacing between the grid dots.

APPLICATIONS

The Grid command displays a visual grid, or matrix of dots, on the screen. It has no effect on the drawing and does not force alignment of any type. It is purely a visual reference. Usually, you want the visible grid to follow the snap resolution. However, if the snap resolution is small, it is often more useful to have the visible grid appear at some multiple of snap resolution. In most cases, it is best to leave Grid set to zero and then the grid follows the setting set for Snap.

Because there are only a fixed number of pixels on your graphics screen, you can reach a point where the grid is so dense that it would obscure the screen. At this point, which varies with your graphics hardware, AutoSketch displays the following dialogue box.

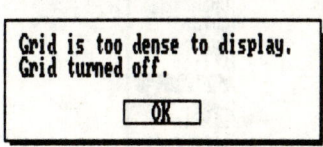

You have the option of either working without the grid displayed, or changing the grid setting to a larger value. This is an excellent situation for making the grid an integer multiple of the snap.

Typically, you draw with the Grid set to zero (0). This forces the displayed grid to follow whatever parameters you set for Snap.

TYPICAL OPERATION

In this activity you activate the drawing grid.

1. Begin a new untitled drawing.

2. The default setting for Snap is already set to 1. Turn on the Grid so it follows the snap setting by picking **Grid** from the Assist menu.

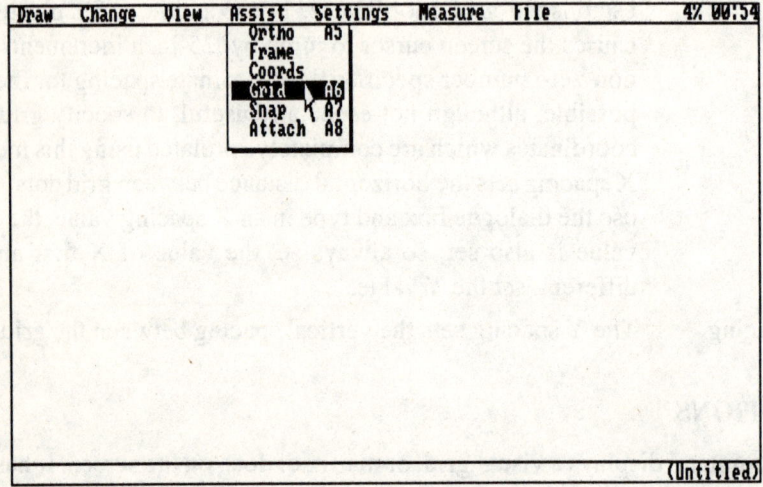

There are times when you do not want the Grid to follow the Snap. Sometimes the setting of the Snap makes the Grid too dense to show on the screen. If this should happen you can change the Grid to a larger spacing or to any other spacing you desire. Reset the Grid to 2 inch spacing and leave the Snap as it is.

3. Pick **Grid** from the Settings menu.

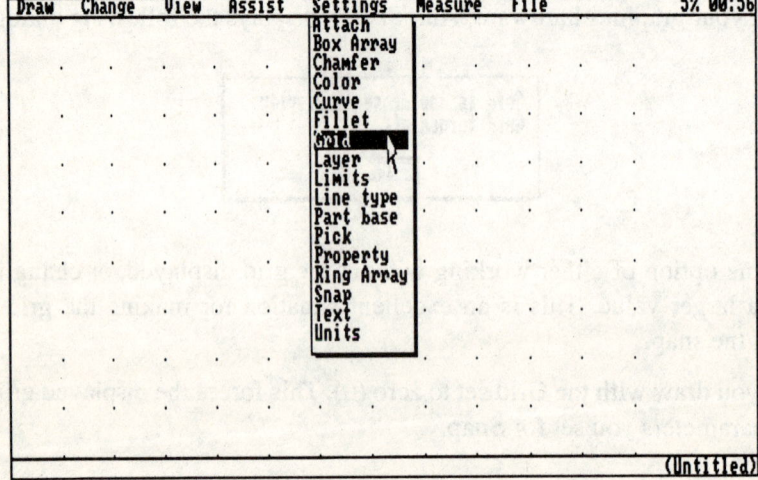

4. Move the screen pointer so it highlights the box to the right of the "X Spacing" and type **2 <CR>**. Pick **OK**.

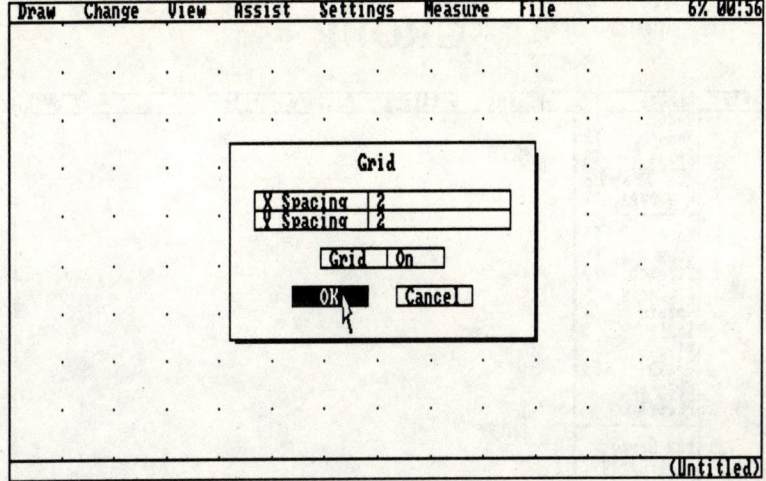

5. Pick **Quit** from the File menu and discard the drawing, or continue your work session by picking **New** from the File menu.

6. Turn to Module 14, Coords, to continue the learning sequence.

Module 25
GROUP

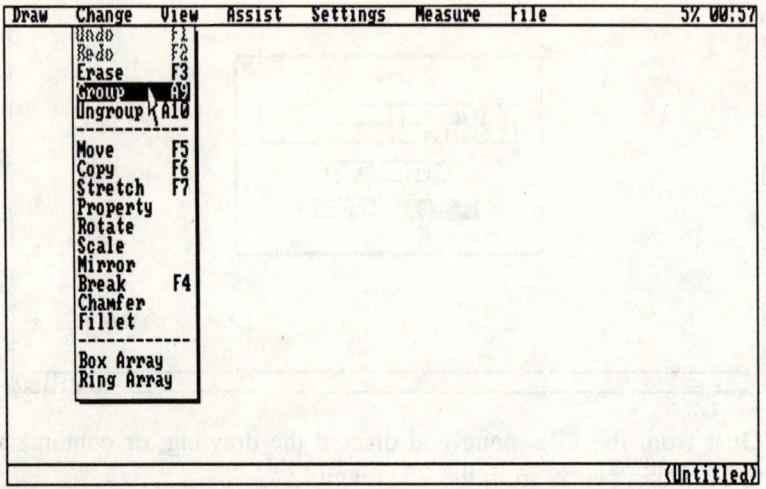

DESCRIPTION

The Group command, located on the Change menu or activated by pressing Alt-F9, is used to collect a group of objects so that they can be manipulated as a single unit. You can group and ungroup objects whenever you like.

If you want to use the Group command to identify objects (entities) as a group, you can select the Group command from the Change menu or press the Alt and F9 keys simultaneously. After selecting the Group command there are several different things you can do with it.

- You can turn individual entities into a group.
- You can combine entities and other groups.
- You can combine groups with other groups.
- You can create a group within a group up to a nesting depth of eight.
- You can produce groups with up to 100 objects and an object can be either an entity or a group.

The editing commands work differently on groups than they do on entities. When the Property of a group is changed (Color, Layer, Line type), all the objects in the group are changed. The Break command does not work on a group. The Stretch command only acts as a Move command on a group and does not stretch the group.

If you must use the editing commands, the Ungroup command must be used first to break the group back into its individual parts.

APPLICATIONS

Many times, when drawing plans, it becomes necessary to copy groups of entities many times to create the finished drawing. This is accomplished much more easily if the objects are grouped together using the Group command. As an example, if you were drawing an office layout showing furniture and you wanted to copy a drawing of a chair 10 times in the office, the chair drawing could be turned into a group and then copied as if it were a single entity as many times as desired.

The Group command is very similar to AutoCAD's Block command.

TYPICAL OPERATION

In this session you draw the popular "Happy Face," combine its parts together as a group, and then use the Copy command to reproduce it as many times as you want.

1. Begin with a new drawing.

2. To draw the circles for the face, pick **Circle** from the Draw menu. Type **6,4 <CR>** as the center point and **8,4 <CR>** as a point on the circle.

3. Type **5.5,4.25 <CR>** as the center point and **6,4.25 <CR>** as a point on the circle.

4. Type **5.75,4.25 <CR>** as the center point and **6,4.25 <CR>** as a point on the circle.

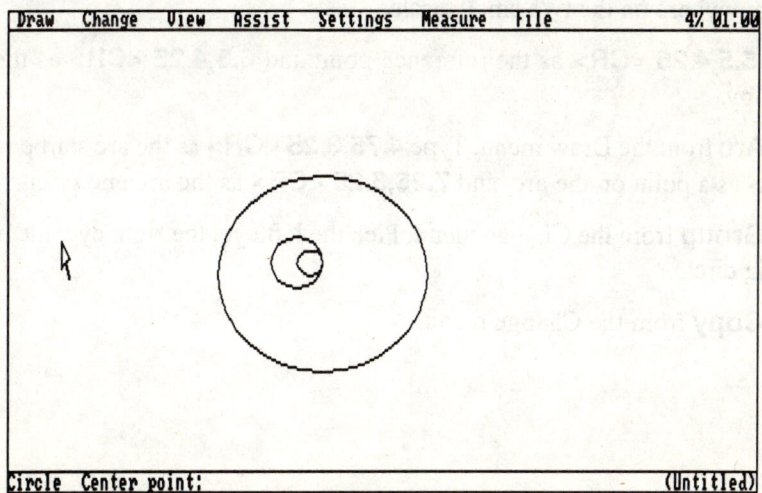

5. Pick **Group** from the Change menu.

6. Pick the middle-sized circle.

7. Pick the smallest circle. Notice that both circles you picked are now drawn with dotted lines.

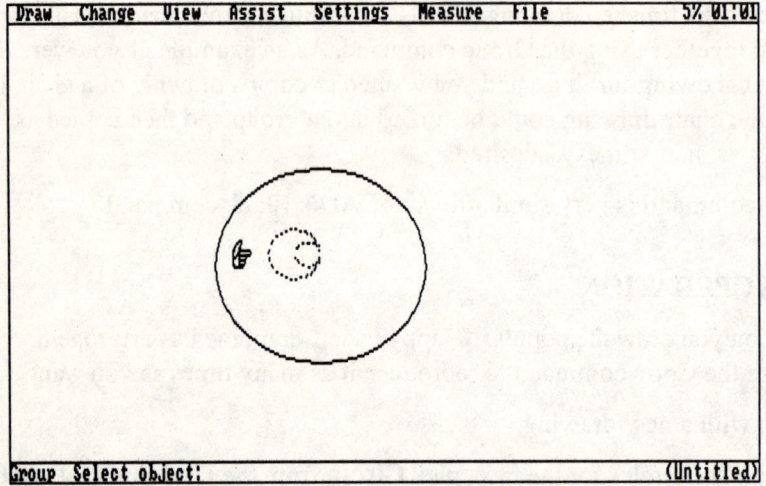

8. Pick the **Group** command from the Change menu. The two small circles are now one group.

9. Pick the **Copy** command from the Change menu.

10. Pick anywhere on the two small circles.

11. Type **5.5,4.25 <CR>** as the reference point and **6.5,4.25 <CR>** as the point for the copy.

12. Pick **Arc** from the Draw menu. Type **4.75,3.25 <CR>** as the arc start point, **6,2.75 <CR>** as a point on the arc, and **7.25,3.25 <CR>** as the arc end point.

13. Pick **Group** from the Change menu. Pick the left eye, the right eye, the mouth, and the big circle.

14. Pick **Copy** from the Change menu.

15. Pick any part of the face. Type **6,4 <CR>** as the reference point and **9,6.75 <CR>** for the copy point.

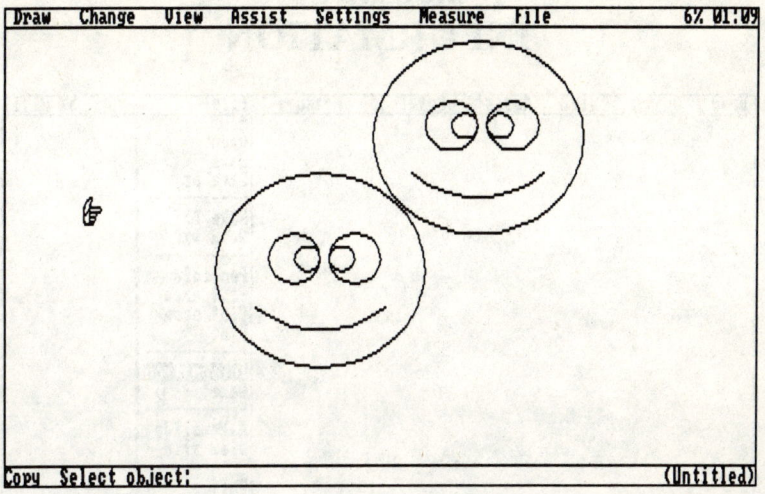

16. Pick **Save as** from the File menu. Type **group** as the filename, press **Enter**, and pick **OK** in the dialogue box.

17. Quit AutoSketch, or turn to Module 41, Part and Part Base, to continue the learning sequence.

Module 26
INFORMATION

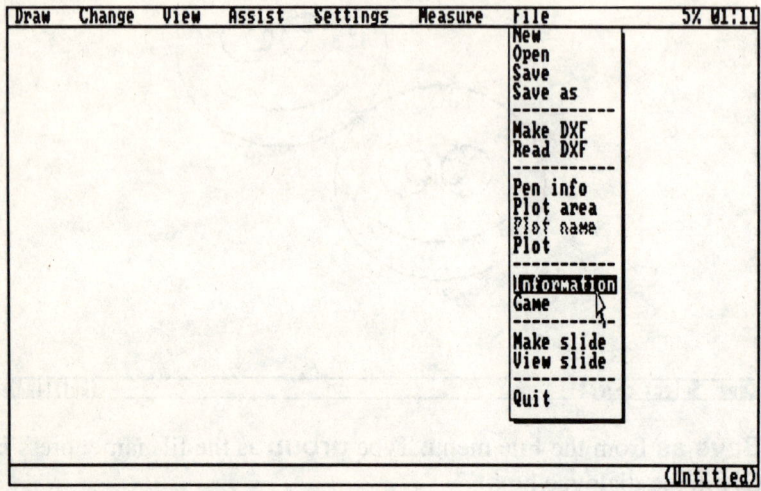

DESCRIPTION

The Information command is located in the File menu. This command provides a dialogue box with program information on your screen including the following:

- The name of the program you are using (AutoSketch)
- The program authors
- Copyright information
- The Release number and date
- Your hardware configuration
- A clever Latin quotation
- An "OK" box to pick to move on to another command

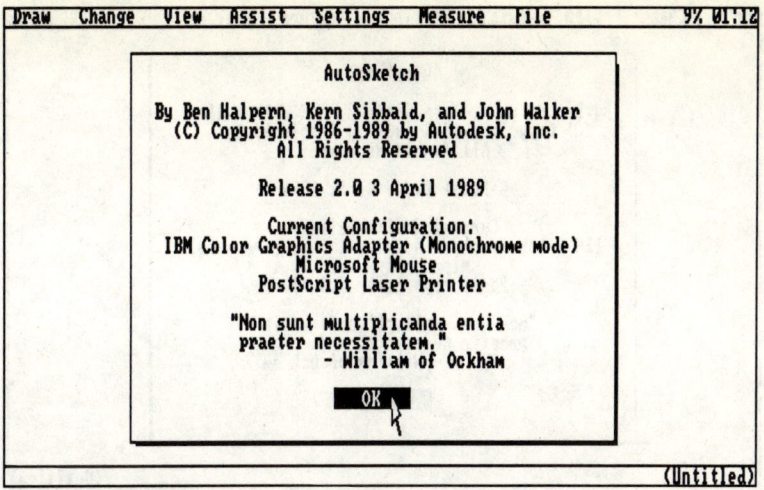

```
 Draw  Change  View  Assist  Settings  Measure  File          9% 01:12
┌────────────────────────────────────────────────────────────────────┐
│              ┌──────────────────────────────────────┐               │
│              │              AutoSketch                │               │
│              │                                        │               │
│              │  By Ben Halpern, Kern Sibbald, and John Walker         │
│              │   (C) Copyright 1986-1989 by Autodesk, Inc.            │
│              │           All Rights Reserved          │               │
│              │                                        │               │
│              │        Release 2.0 3 April 1989        │               │
│              │                                        │               │
│              │          Current Configuration:        │               │
│              │  IBM Color Graphics Adapter (Monochrome mode)          │
│              │            Microsoft Mouse             │               │
│              │         PostScript Laser Printer       │               │
│              │                                        │               │
│              │     "Non sunt multiplicanda entia      │               │
│              │      praeter necessitatem."            │               │
│              │         - William of Ockham            │               │
│              │                                        │               │
│              │              ▐ OK ▌                    │               │
│              └──────────────────────────────────────┘               │
│                                                          (Untitled)  │
└────────────────────────────────────────────────────────────────────┘
```

APPLICATIONS

The Information box is probably most useful for finding out what version of AutoSketch you are working with. The first digit of the software version refers to a major revision. The first digit to the right of the decimal point refers to a minor revision. The second digit to the right of the decimal point is typically a bug-fix release, and is of interest only to individuals who have experienced a problem with the product. A typical minor release change would be the correction of an obscure printer driver anomaly. Normally, there is no need to update software to follow the minor release changes unless you are experiencing the particular problem that the release corrects. If your printer isn't printing, your mouse isn't moving, or your screen is not showing its full potential, check the information dialog box to verify that your software configuration matches your installed hardware.

TYPICAL OPERATION

In this session you call up the Information command's dialogue box and move on to another command.

1. Begin a new AutoSketch drawing.

2. Pick **Information** from the File menu.

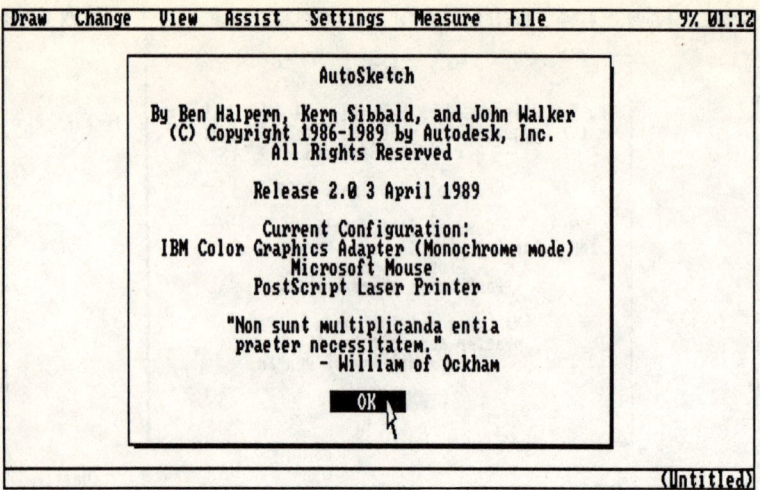

3. Pick **OK**.

4. Pick **Quit** from the File menu and discard the drawing, or continue your work session by picking **New** from the File menu.

5. Turn to Module 30, Limits, to continue the learning sequence.

Module 27
LAST PLOT BOX

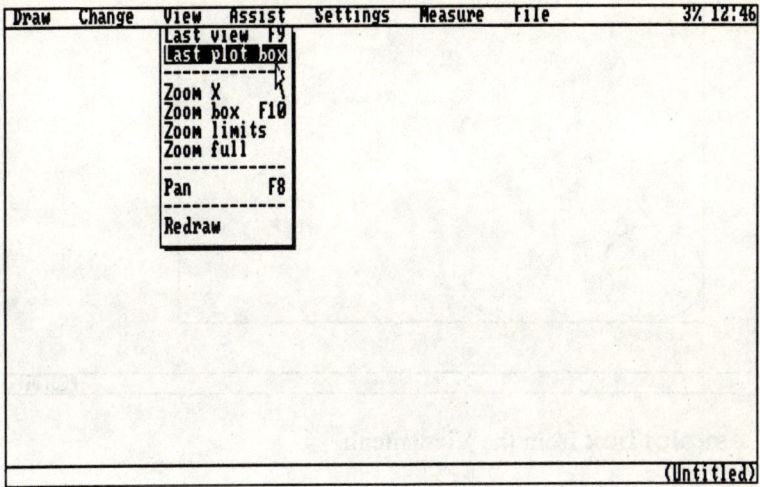

DESCRIPTION

The Last plot box command, located on the View menu, changes the current view to correspond with the most recently used plot box. It changes only the screen view, it does not modify the drawing itself, or its plotting configuration.

APPLICATIONS

The Last plot box command is used to view the screen corresponding to the most recently used plot box. The command provides a simple way to make your screen correspond to the current plot area selection. It is especially useful for extremely large or extremely small plot boxes. It is indispensible when things go wrong and you can't find the plot box on the screen, possibly because you specified the plot area a hundred times larger or smaller than you intended.

TYPICAL OPERATION

This activity uses the PLOTDEMO drawing that you created in the Plot and Plot Name module, then modified the plot area with the Plot Area command. In this session you use the Last plot box command to force the screen view to correspond to the most recently used plot box.

1. If PLOTDEMO is not the current drawing, open it from the File menu. Your screen appears as follows.

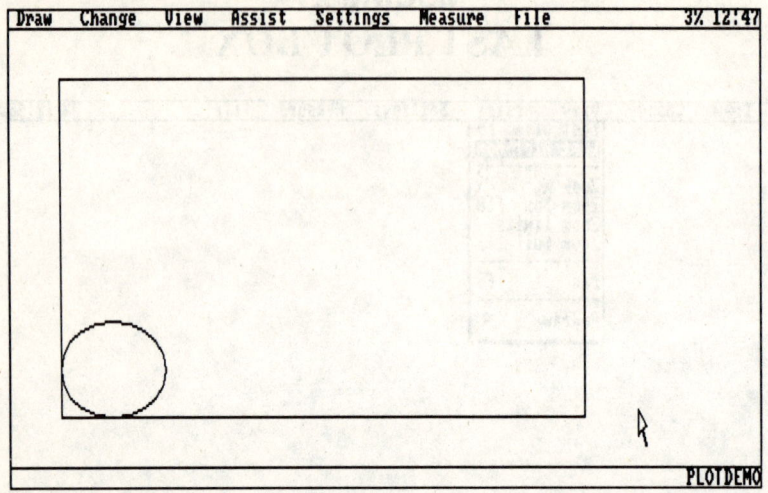

2. Pick **Last plot box** from the View menu.

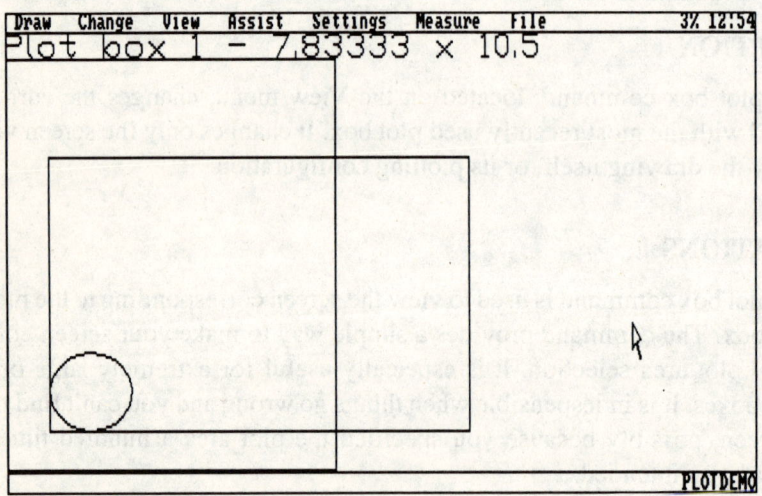

3. Save the drawing and turn to Module 42, Pen Info, to continue the learning sequence.

Module 28
LAST VIEW

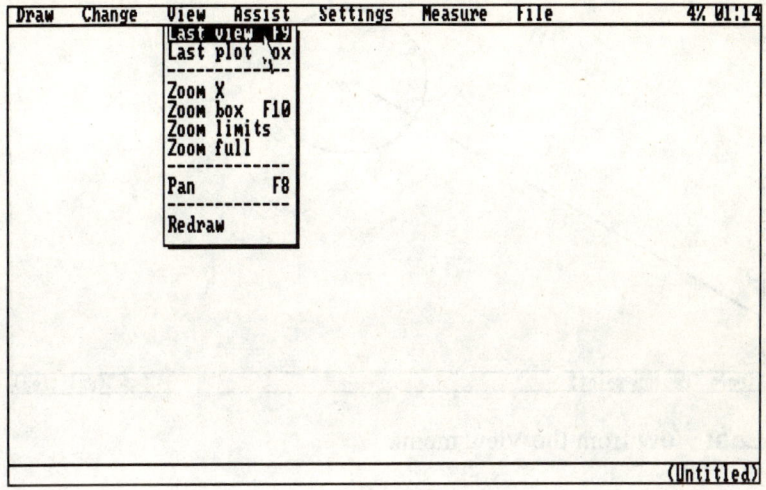

DESCRIPTION

The Last view command, located on the View menu or activated by pressing F9, does exactly what its name implies. It toggles between the view shown on the screen and the last view displayed prior to the last Zoom or Pan selected in the drawing.

APPLICATIONS

The Last view command is used to view the screen that was previously displayed. If you need to zoom in on an area for more precise work and then you want to go back to the previous view, the Last view command does this for you.

TYPICAL OPERATION

In this session you draw a line and a circle. You use the Zoom box command to change the view and then the Last view command to go back to the previous screen.

1. Begin a new AutoSketch drawing.

2. Pick **Line** from the Draw menu. Type **1,1 <CR>** as the first point and **9,6 <CR>** as the second point.

3. Pick **Circle** from the Draw menu. Type **9,6 <CR>** as the center point and **9.25,6 <CR>** as the point on the circle.

4. Pick **Zoom box** from the View menu. Type **8,5 <CR>** as the first corner and type **9.75,6.5 <CR>** as the second corner.

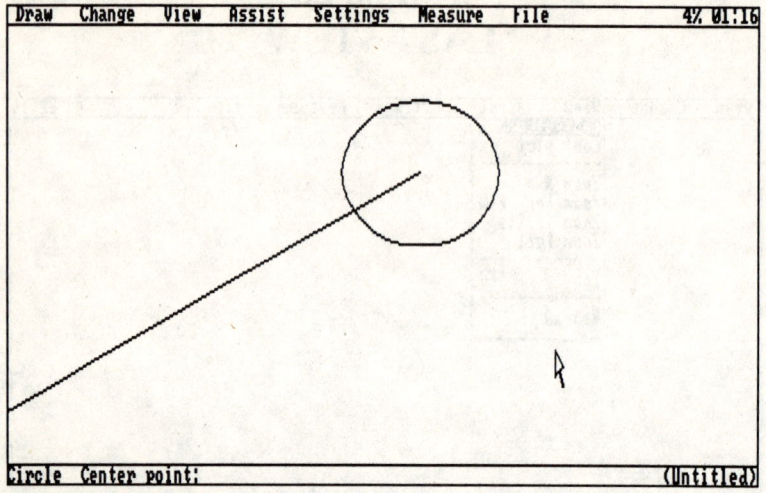

5. Pick **Last view** from the View menu.

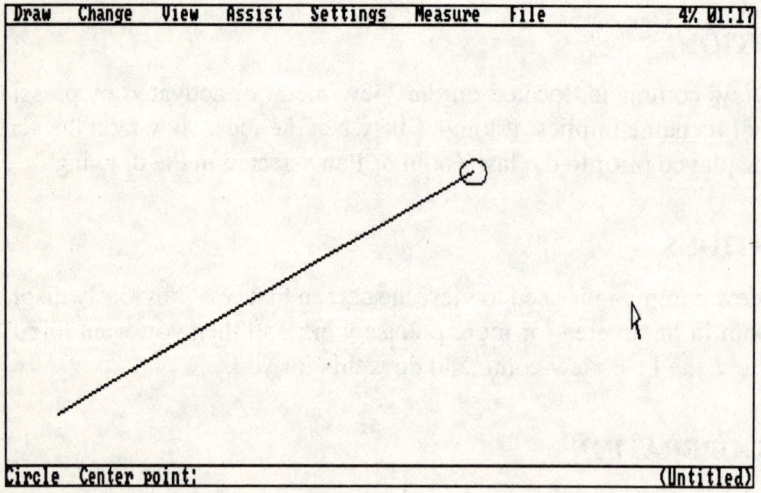

6. Quit AutoSketch, or turn to Module 55, Save and Save As, to continue the learning sequence.

Module 29
LAYER

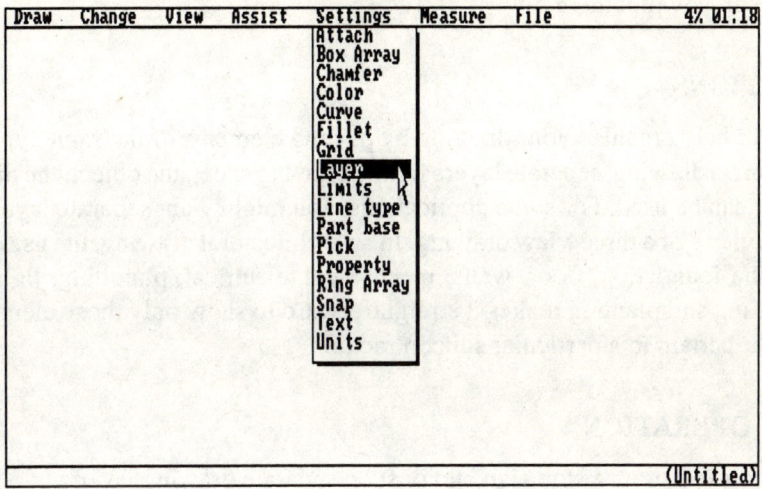

DESCRIPTION

The Layer command is used to draw objects having multiple planes. When you select the Layer command from the Settings menu, AutoSketch displays the following dialogue box.

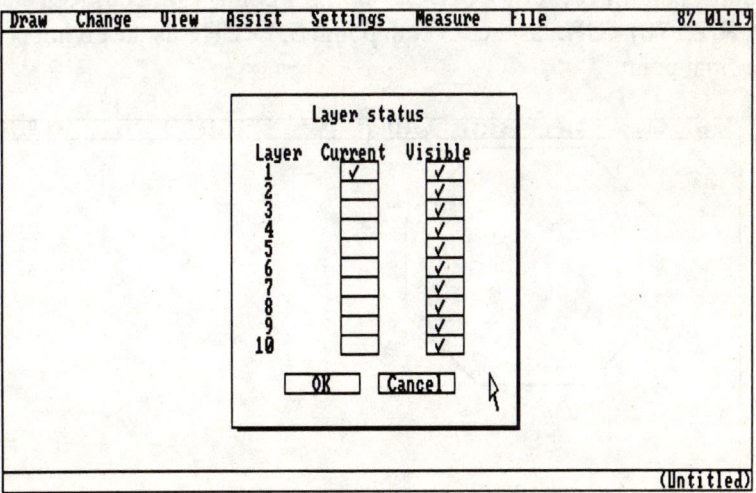

The first column of check boxes contains one check, indicating the current drawing layer. The second column of check boxes contains a check for each visible layer. (By default, all 10 AutoSketch layers are visible.) Making a layer invisible helps to control the clutter on the screen. For example, you might turn off the mechanical layer of an architectural drawing while working on the plumbing layer. You cannot select objects on invisible layers, nor can you plot them.

APPLICATIONS

Use layers to help organize your drawing by placing elements of the same type together. In a mechanical drawing, separate layers for the drawing sheet, the object, the dimensions, and the text can be used. For some applications, you might want separate layers for each of the three views of a three-view drawing. In an architectural drawing, the use of separate layers for the foundation, floor, walls, mechanical, electrical, plumbing, lighting, roof, interior design, and planting makes it straightforward to show only those elements of the drawing that pertain to a particular subcontractor.

TYPICAL OPERATION

In this session you draw a stop sign and post on separate drawing layers.

1. Begin a new AutoSketch drawing.

2. Pick **Polygon** from the Draw menu. Type **5,4 <CR>** as the first point, **P(2,45) <CR>** as the second point, **P(2,90) <CR>** as the third point, **P(2,135) <CR>** as the fourth point, **P(2,180) <CR>** as the fifth point, **P(2,225) <CR>** as the sixth point, **P(2,270) <CR>** as the seventh point, **3,4 <CR>** as the eighth point, and **5,4** as the final point.

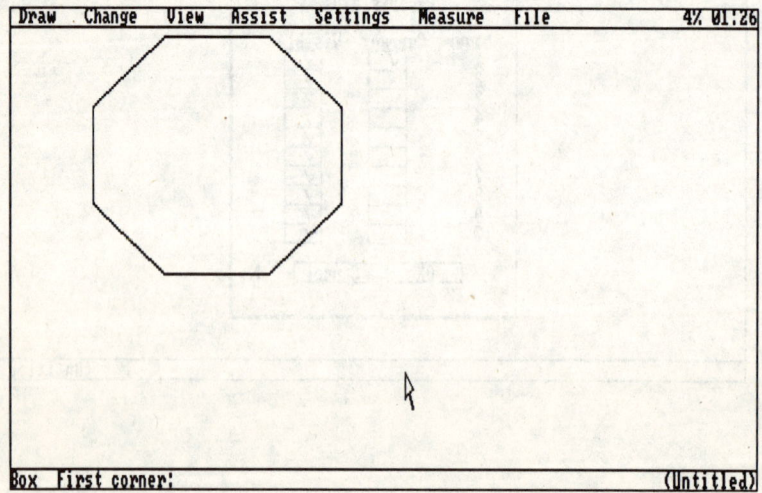

3. Pick **Layer** from the Settings menu.

4. Pick **2** as the current layer.

5. Pick **OK** in the dialogue box.

6. Pick **Box** from the Draw menu. Type **3.9,0 <CR>** as the first corner point and **4.1,4** **<CR>** as the second corner point.

7. Pick **Line type** from the Settings menu. Pick **Hidden** in the dialogue box, type **1** **<CR>** as the scale factor, then pick **OK**.

8. Pick **Box** from the Draw menu. Type **3.9,4 <CR>** as the first corner point and **4.1,7** **<CR>** as the second corner point.

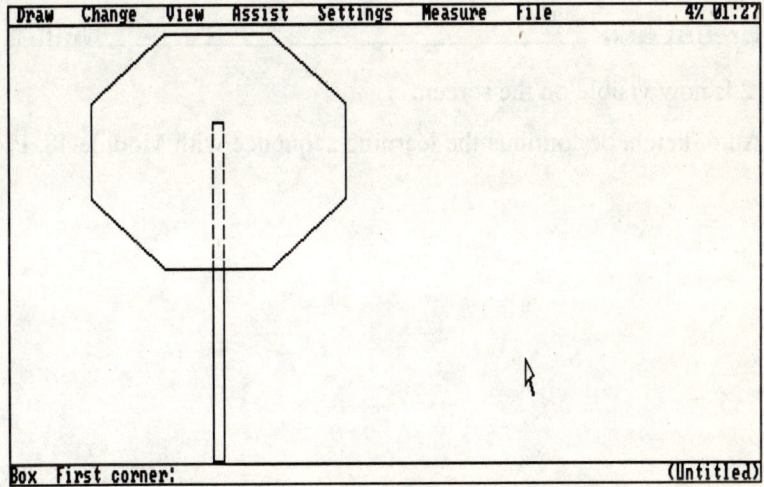

9. Pick **Layer** from the Settings menu. Pick the Visible check box for layer one.

10. Pick **OK** in the dialogue box.

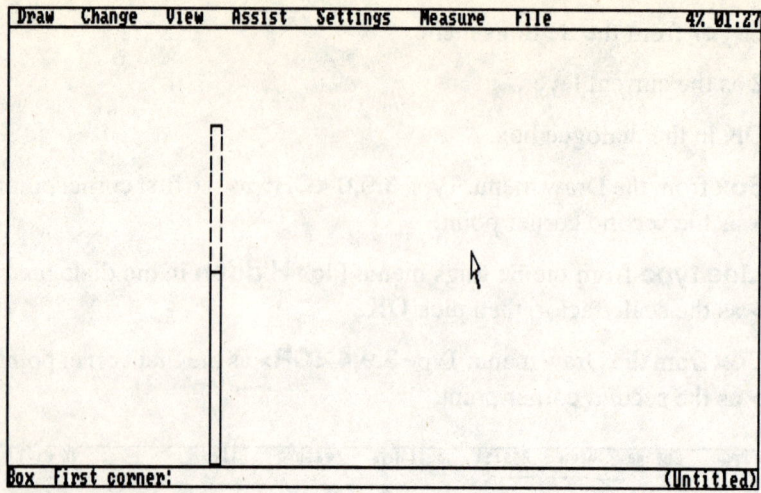

Only layer 2 is now visible on the screen.

11. Quit AutoSketch, or continue the learning sequence with Module 48, Property.

Module 30
LIMITS

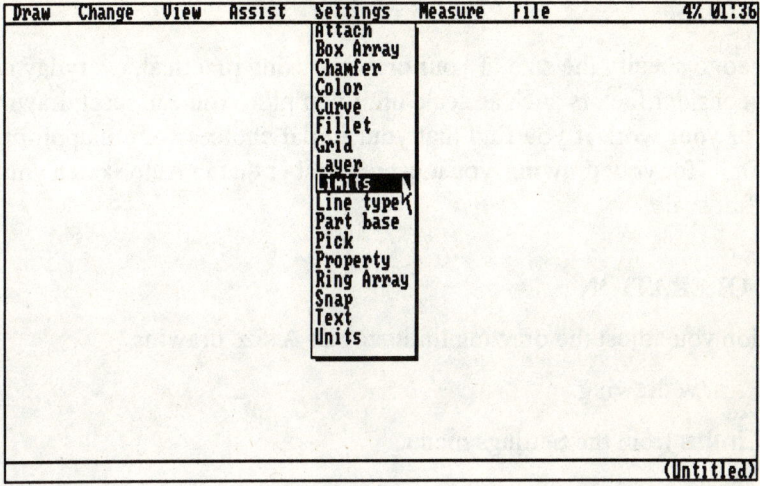

DESCRIPTION

The Limits command is used to establish the size of your drawing. You may think of the Limits command as choosing the size of your drawing sheet in manual drafting. The drawing sheet in AutoSketch must be large enough to accommodate what you are drawing at full scale. The concept of always drawing in full scale is sometimes difficult for the AutoSketch novice. When you select Limits from the Settings menu, the following dialogue box appears.

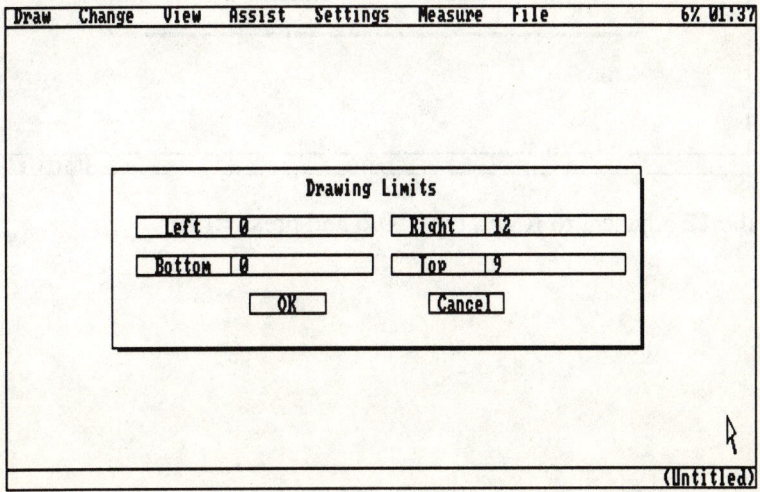

To reset the drawing limits you specify values for the Left, Right, Bottom, and Top of the drawing in drawing units. Type the new values in the boxes provided, or accept the default values. Pick OK to make the changes effective, or pick Cancel to leave the limits unchanged.

APPLICATIONS

Limits is used to specify the size of your drawing using practical, everyday dimensions. You do not consider factors such as scale until you plot. You can reset drawing limits in the middle of your work if you find that your initial choices were inappropriate. When choosing Limits for your drawing, you must remember that in AutoSketch you are always drawing at full scale.

TYPICAL OPERATION

In this session you adjust the drawing limits for an A size drawing.

1. Begin a new drawing.

2. Pick **Limits** from the Settings menu.

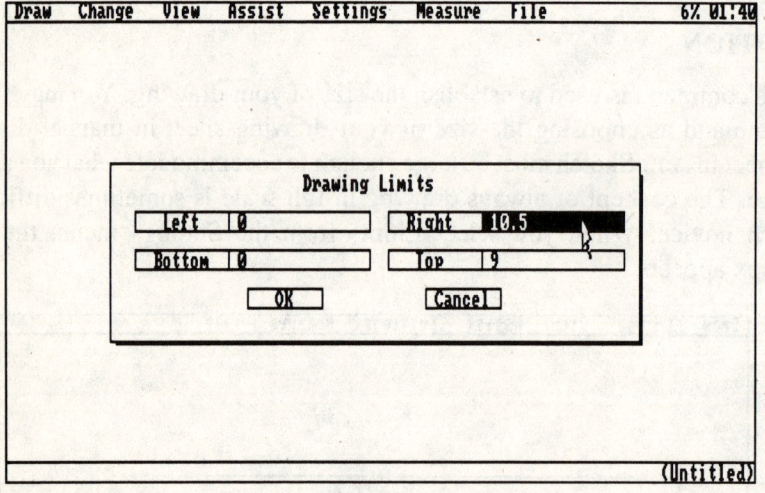

3. Pick the **12** adjacent to Right, type **10.5** and press **Enter**.

4. Pick the **9** adjacent to Top, type **8** and press **Enter**.

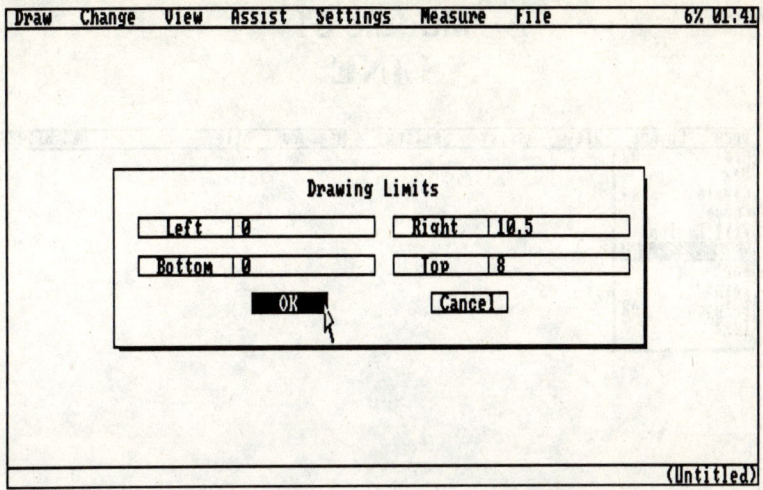

5. Pick **OK**.

6. Pick **Quit** from the File menu and discard the drawing, or continue your work session by picking **New** from the File menu.

7. Turn to Module 58, Snap, to continue the learning sequence.

Module 31
LINE

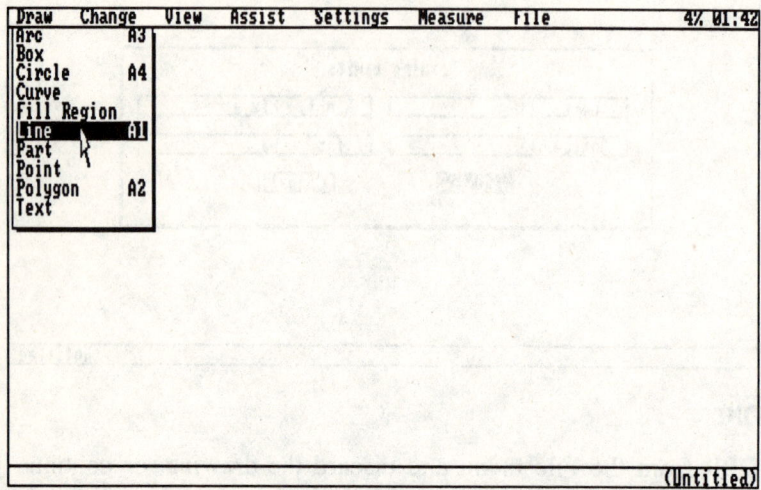

DESCRIPTION

The Line command, located on the Draw menu or activated by pressing Alt-F1, is used to draw individual straight line entities. Drawing a line in AutoSketch requires the definition of two points, the starting point and the endpoint. Even if several lines are drawn connected end to end, AutoSketch still treats each line as a single entity.

Drawing a line in AutoSketch can be accomplished in several ways. The starting point for a line can be defined by moving the screen pointer to the desired location and picking that point, or the exact X,Y coordinates can be entered from the keyboard. After the starting point of the line has been selected, the endpoint of the line can also be selected by moving the screen pointer and picking, or the coordinates can be typed in from the keyboard. When the start point has been selected, there is a rubber-band line stretching from the start point to where the screen pointer is positioned.

After drawing a line, AutoSketch automatically brings the Line command prompt back to the bottom of the screen and assumes that you are drawing another line. To change to an activity other than drawing lines you must pick something else in a menu or press the proper buttons to start another command.

APPLICATIONS

A line is one of the basic drawing elements. A line extends between two endpoints. AutoSketch treats a line as a single entity, not as a series of points. The line command is used in all types of drawing. Walls in a house plan are usually drawn using lines. Straight parts in machines are drawn using lines. Most parts of drawings that are straight are drawn using the Line command.

TYPICAL OPERATION

In this example, you draw a figure using a series of lines.

1. Begin with a new drawing.

2. Pick the **Line** command from the Draw menu. Type **1,1 <CR>** as the first point and **1,6 <CR>** as the second point.

3. Type **1,6 <CR>** as the first point and **7,6 <CR>** as the second point.

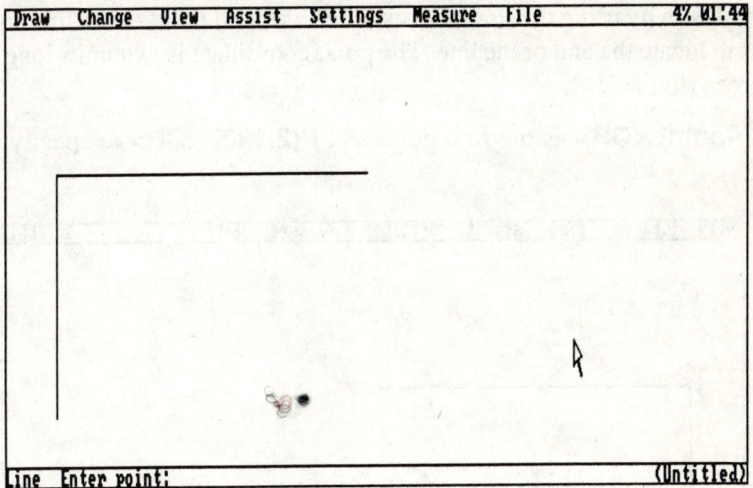

Draw a short vertical line on the right side of the figure by using the /lpoint system variable (the last point picked) as the starting point of the line and then use relative coordinates to pick the end point of the line (relative coordinates are calculated from the last point picked) zero units in the X direction and one unit in the -Y direction (straight down).

4. Type **/lpoint <CR>** as the first point and **R(0,-1) <CR>** to specify the second point.

5. Type **7,5 <CR>** as the first point and **3,1 <CR>** as the second point.

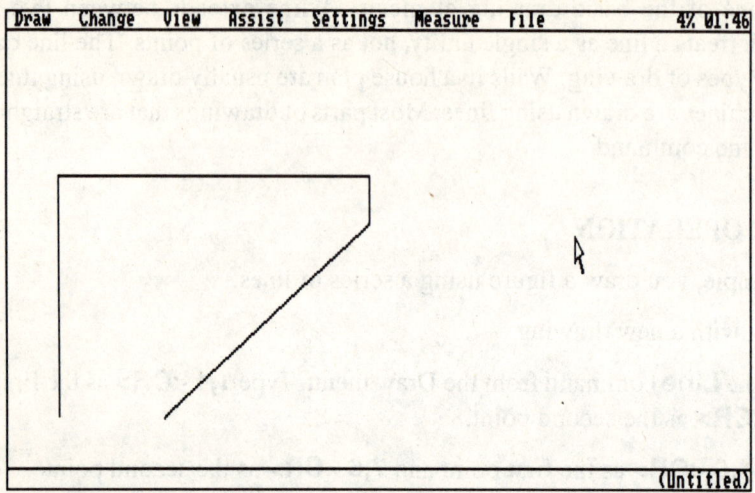

Finish the polygon by using the /lpoint to establish the start point of the line and use polar coordinates to locate the end of the line. The polar coordinate is two units long at an angle of 180 degrees (to the left).

6. Type **/lpoint <CR>** as the first point and **P(2,180) <CR>** to specify the second point.

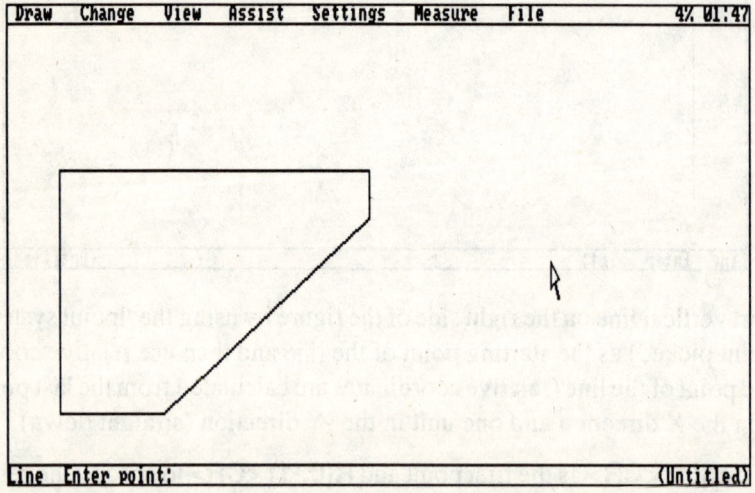

7. Pick **Quit** from the File menu and discard the drawing, or continue your work session by picking **New** from the File menu.

8. Turn to Module 37, New, to continue the learning sequence.

Module 32
LINE TYPE

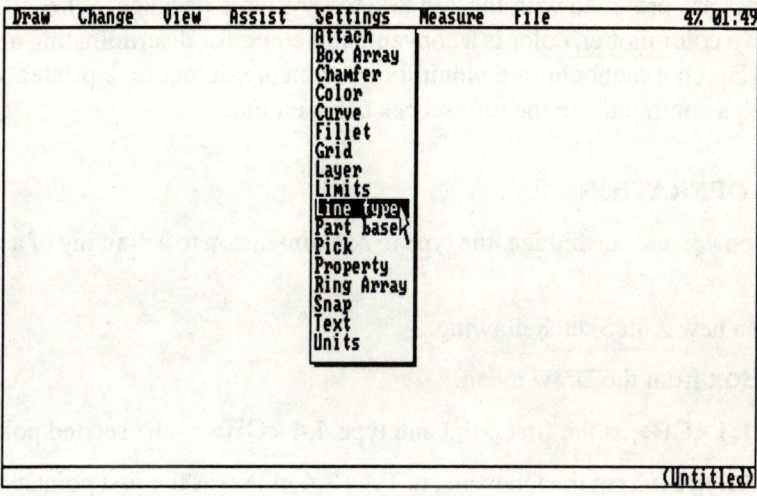

DESCRIPTION

Use the Line type command on the Settings menu to change the line type that AutoSketch uses for drawing new entities. When you pick the command, the following dialogue box appears.

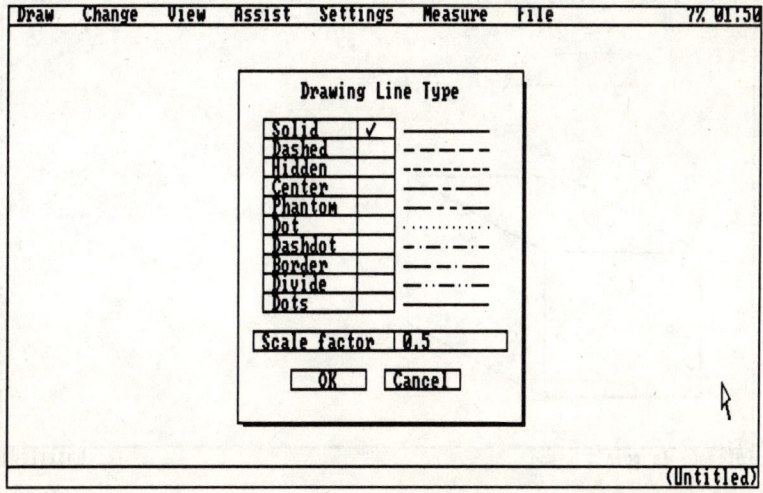

Select a new line type by picking the selection box to the right of the type. The Scale factor is used to specify the relative length of the line segments in segmented lines.

APPLICATIONS

Ten line types are provided with the AutoSketch software package. When using a color monitor and a color plotter, color is a convenient method for discriminating among lines. When working on a monochrome monitor or producing output on a printer, varying the line type helps communicate the differences between lines.

TYPICAL OPERATION

In this session you use the hidden line type to add dimension to a drawing of a rectangular solid.

1. Begin a new AutoSketch drawing.

2. Pick **Box** from the Draw menu.

3. Type **1,1 <CR>** as the first point and type **4,4 <CR>** as the second point.

4. Pick **Polygon** from the Draw menu. Type **1,4 <CR>** as the first point, type **P(3,30)** as the second point, type **P(3,0) <CR>** as the third point, and type **4,4** as the fourth point.

5. Pick **Polygon** from the Draw menu. Type **4,1 <CR>** as the first point, type **P(3,30) <CR>** as the second point, and type **P(3,90) <CR>** as the third point.

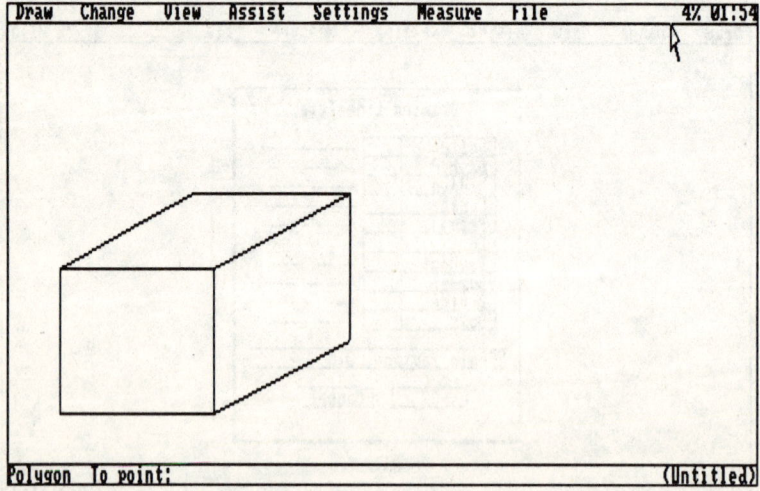

6. Pick **Line type** from the Settings menu.

7. Select **Hidden** as the line type.

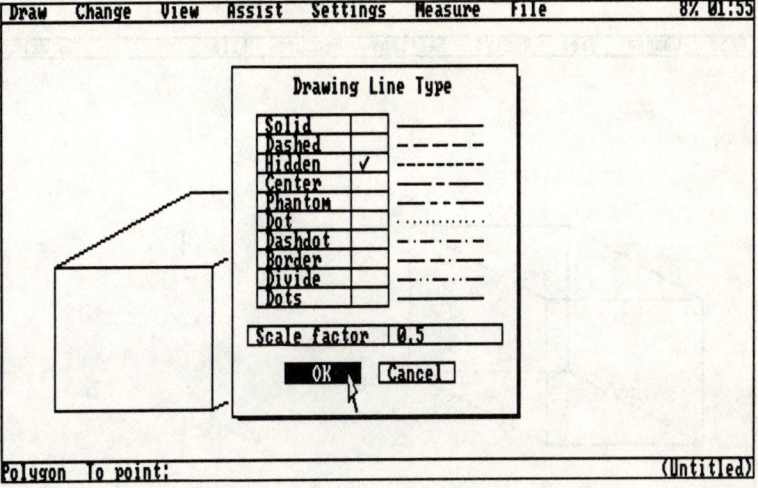

8. Pick **OK**.

9. Pick **Line** from the Draw menu. Type **1,1 <CR>** as the first point and type **P(3,30) <CR>** as the second point. Type **/LPOINT <CR>** as the first point and type **P(3,180) <CR>** as the second point.

10. Pick **Attach** from the Settings menu. Turn off all Attachment modes except End point. Enable Attach.

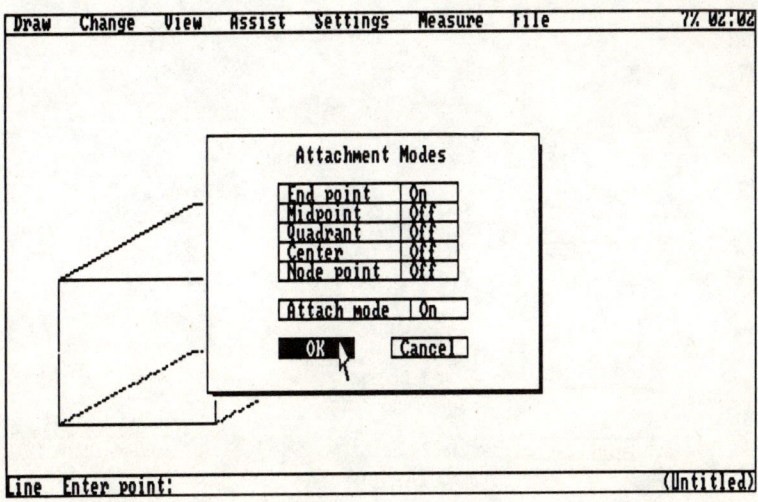

11. Pick **OK**.

12. Pick **Line** from the Draw menu. Select the two rear vertices, drawing the final hidden line.

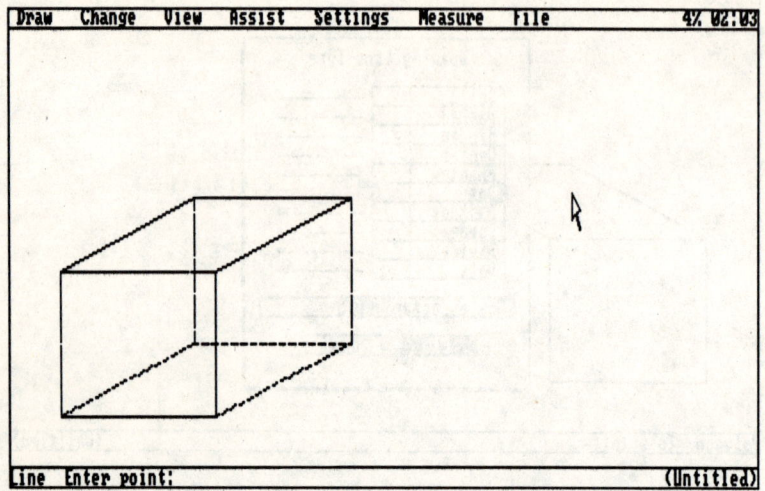

13. Quit AutoSketch, or turn to Module 29, Layer, to continue the learning sequence.

Module 33
MAKE DXF

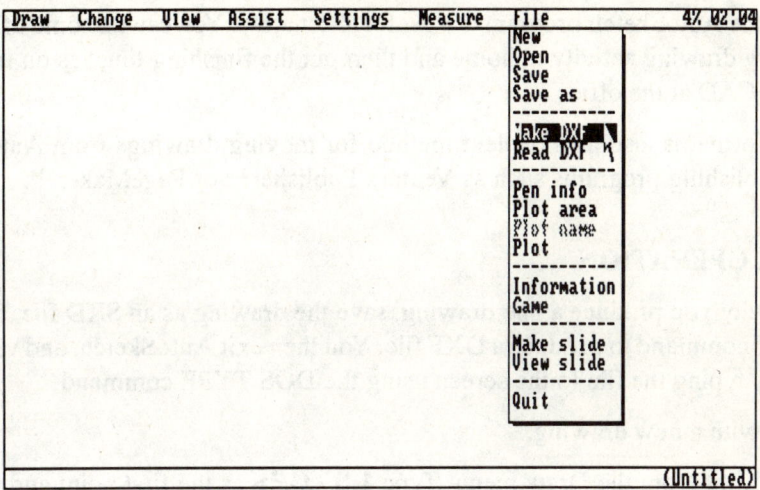

DESCRIPTION

The Make DXF (Drawing eXchange Format) command is found in the File menu and is used to produce a DXF file that can be read by AutoCAD version 2.5 or higher, Generic Cad, and many other CAD programs with DXF import capability. The DXFIN command in AutoCAD reads the DXF file and makes an AutoCAD drawing from the DXF file made in AutoSketch. A DXF file is an ASCII file that completely describes a drawing. This ASCII file can be manipulated and altered for the modification of a drawing without actually looking at the drawing on a graphics screen. After making a DXF file, you can look at it and manipulate the file using the Edlin program that comes with DOS, the File Editor from DOS 4.0, or a wordprocessor such as WordStar™ (using the non-document mode).

AutoCAD is a much more powerful program than AutoSketch, therefore the DXF process works well going from AutoSketch up to AutoCAD, since AutoCAD understands all of AutoSketch's commands. Going from AutoCAD down to AutoSketch using the DXF method does not work well because AutoSketch is not powerful enough to understand all of AutoCAD's commands. Only experimentation can tell you if your work converts well in this direction.

When you make an AutoSketch drawing and save it, the filename always has a filename extension of .SKD. When you do a Make DXF, the filename is saved with the extension .DXF.

APPLICATIONS

The Make DXF command is very useful for converting your AutoSketch drawings made at home to DXF files to be read and used at work on your AutoCAD workstation. When you use AutoCAD at work and want to be able to do some drawing work at home, but you cannot afford the AutoCAD software or the required hardware for your home computer, the AutoSketch program is a useful alternative. You can do some of your more rudimentary drawing activity at home and then put the finishing touches on the drawing using AutoCAD at the office.

The DXF format is also an excellent method for moving drawings from AutoSketch to desktop publishing programs such as Ventura Publisher™ or PageMaker™.

TYPICAL OPERATION

In this activity you produce a line drawing, save the drawing as an SKD file, and use the Make DXF command to produce a DXF file. You then exit AutoSketch, and view the file contents by typing the file to the screen using the DOS TYPE command.

1. Start with a new drawing.

2. Pick **Line** from the Draw menu. Type **1,3 <CR>** as the first point and **9,6 <CR>** as the second point.

3. Pick the **Save** command from the File menu.

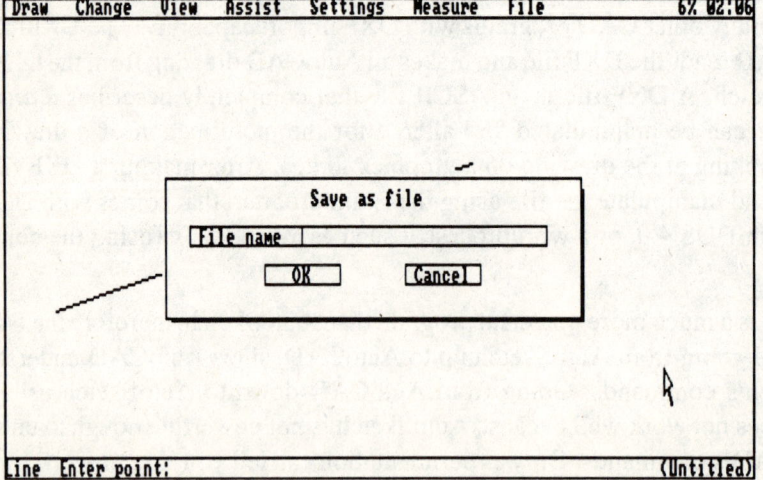

4. Move the screen pointer to highlight the box to the right of "File name" and type **DRAWING <CR>**. Pick **OK**.

5. Pick **Make DXF** from the File menu.

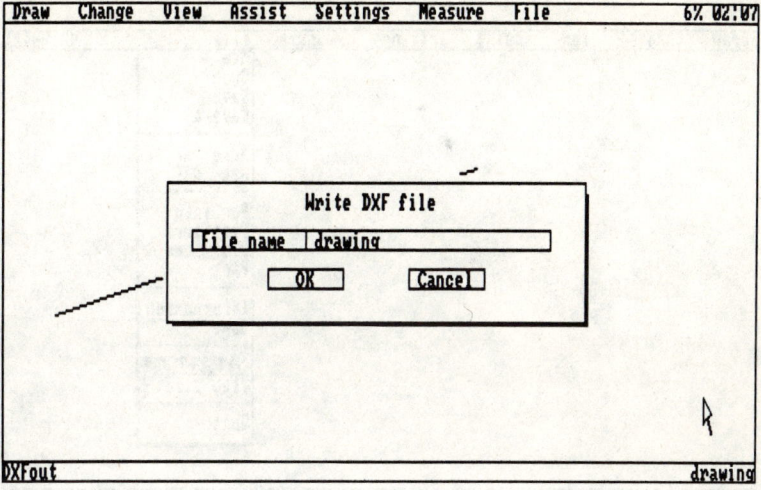

6. Pick **OK**.

7. Quit AutoSketch and return to DOS.

8. Type **TYPE DRAWING.DXF** and press **Enter**

9. Turn to Module 50, Read DXF, to continue the learning sequence.

Module 34
MAKE SLIDE

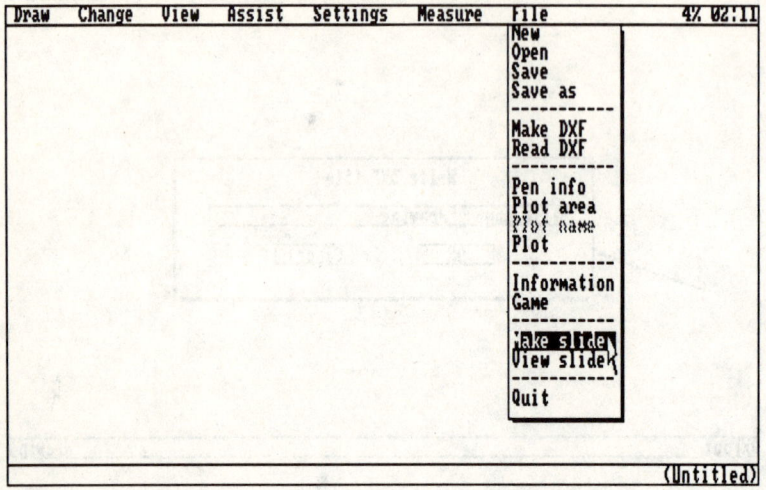

DESCRIPTION

The Make slide command, located on the File menu, is used to create image files that can be recalled by AutoSketch™, AutoCAD™, or moved to a desktop publishing program such as Xerox Ventura Publisher™ or PageMaker™.

The Make slide and View slide commands in AutoSketch are used to make and view slide files. Slide files, which have the extension .SLD (in AutoCAD and AutoSketch), are created with the drawing editor and saved with the Make slide command. They are viewed using the View slide command by specifying the slide filename.

APPLICATIONS

The Make slide command is important to AutoSketch users who integrate slide files (with the extension .SLD) with other programs. For example, Ventura Publisher 1.1 and 2.0 readily accepts AutoSketch .SLD files. The ability to combine the power of multiple programs like AutoSketch, AutoCAD, and Ventura Publisher, gives microcomputer users capabilities that were unavailable only a short time ago. Make slide is additionally useful to users of AutoCAD's Release 9 and 10 for the construction of icons for custom screen menus.

Unlike DXF format, where the additional capabilities of AutoCAD are lost when Autosketch reads an AutoCAD DXF file, all information in a slide file is transferred between the two programs. As a result, AutoSketch is an excellent, low cost program for viewing AutoCAD slide files.

TYPICAL OPERATION

In this session you create a small presentation graphic, then you save it as a slide file. You view the slide in the Typical Operation for Module 64, View Slide.

1. Begin a new AutoSketch drawing.

2. Pick **Text** from the Draw menu. Type **1.75,5.3 <CR>** as the text enter point and type **REGIONAL SALES <CR>** as the text.

3. Type **1.75,4.75 <CR>** as the text enter point and **EASTERN $105,345.00 <CR>** as the text.

4. Type **1.75,4.25 <CR>** as the text enter point and **WESTERN $112,200.00 <CR>** as the text.

5. Pick **Box** from the Draw menu. Type **1.5,3.75 <CR>** as the first point and type **7,6 <CR>** as the second point.

6. Pick **Make slide** from the File menu.

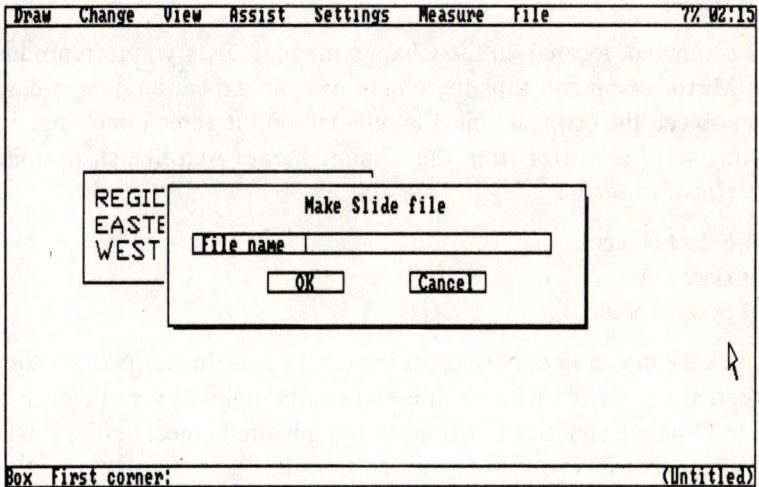

7. Pick the selection box adjacent to the File name, type **SALES**, press **Enter**, and pick **OK** in the dialogue box.

8. Quit AutoSketch, or turn to Module 64, View Slide, where you view the slide, to continue the learning sequence.

Module 35
MIRROR

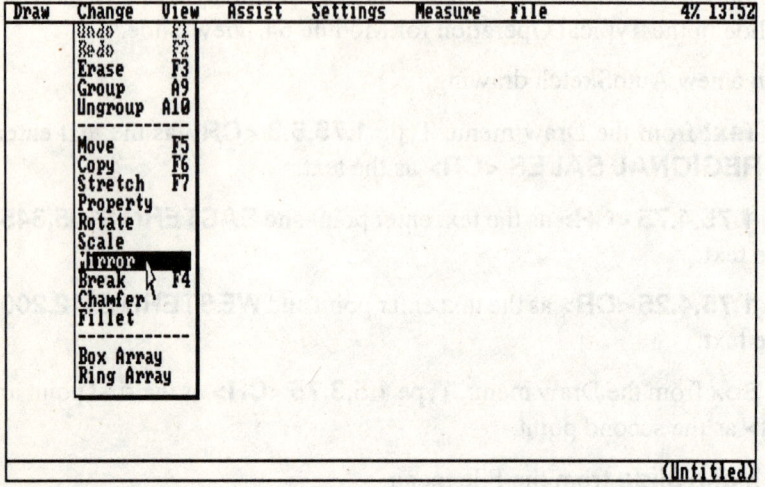

DESCRIPTION

The Mirror command, located on the Change menu, allows you to reproduce a mirror image. The Mirror command flips the object over an axis at any angle desired. When mirroring an object, the original object is retained on the screen unchanged. To use the Mirror command, pick Mirror from the Change menu. AutoSketch responds with the following series of prompts.

> Mirror Select object:
> Mirror Base point:
> Mirror Second point:

When you pick the mirror line, it becomes the mirror axis. In AutoSketch, the mirror line may be placed at any angle. You can drag the second point of the mirror line. Dragging allows you to visualize tentative positions of the mirrored object before final placement. When you mirror text, it is still read from left to right.

APPLICATIONS

The Mirror command has many applications for increasing your drawing productivity. Any time a drawing needs to have objects repeated around a line, the Mirror command is available to reproduce the object. The figure that is mirrored can be any entity or group of entities.

TYPICAL OPERATION

In this session you use the Line, Arc, and Mirror commands to produce the object shown in the following drawing.

1. Begin a new AutoSketch drawing.

2. Pick **Line** from the Draw menu. Type **4,5 <CR>** as the first point and type **6,5 <CR>** as the second point. Type **/LPOINT <CR>** as the first point and type **6,7 <CR>** as the second point.

3. Pick **Arc** from the Draw menu. Type **4,5 <CR>** as the start point, type **4,7 <CR>** as a point on the arc, and type **6,7 <CR>** as the end point.

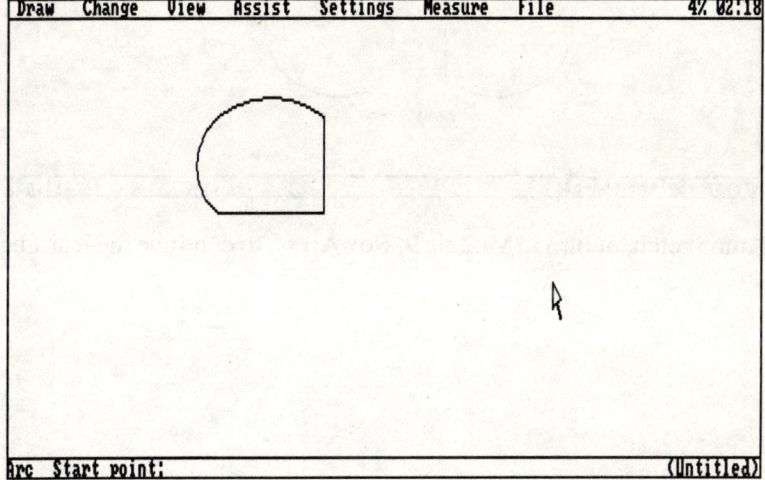

4. Pick **Mirror** from the Change menu. Enclose the figure in a window/crossing box.

5. Type **4,4.5 <CR>** as the base point and type **5,4.5 <CR>** as the second point.

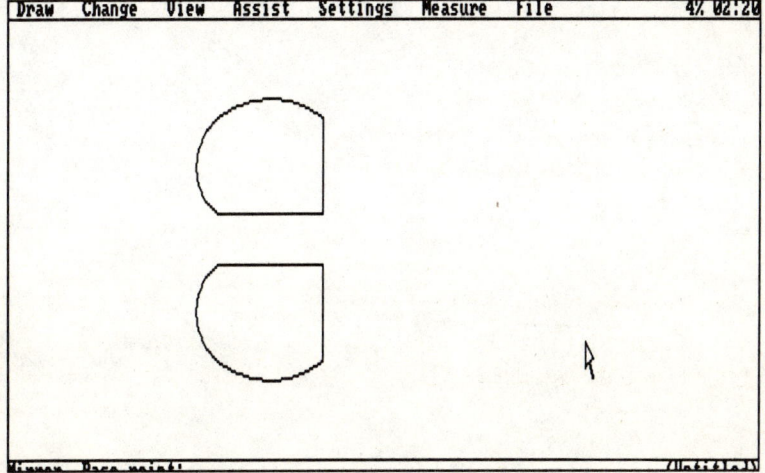

6. Enclose both figures in a window/crossing box.

7. Type **6.5,4 <CR>** as the base point and type **6.5,5 <CR>** as the second point.

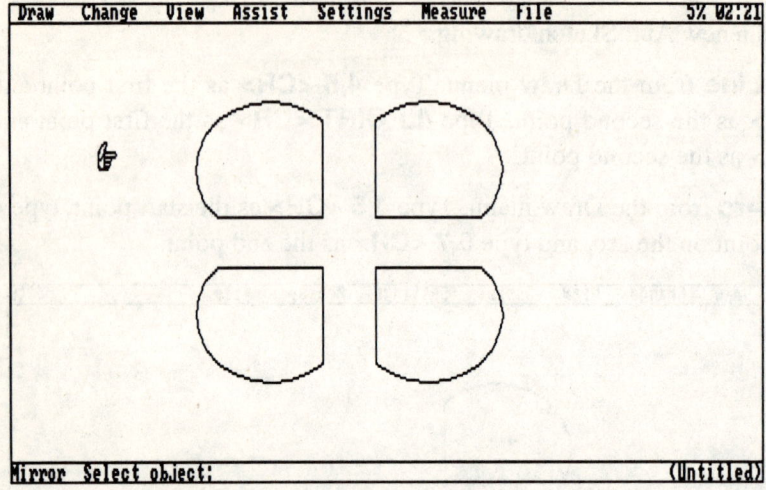

8. Quit AutoSketch, or turn to Module 9, Box Array, to continue the learning sequence.

Module 36
MOVE

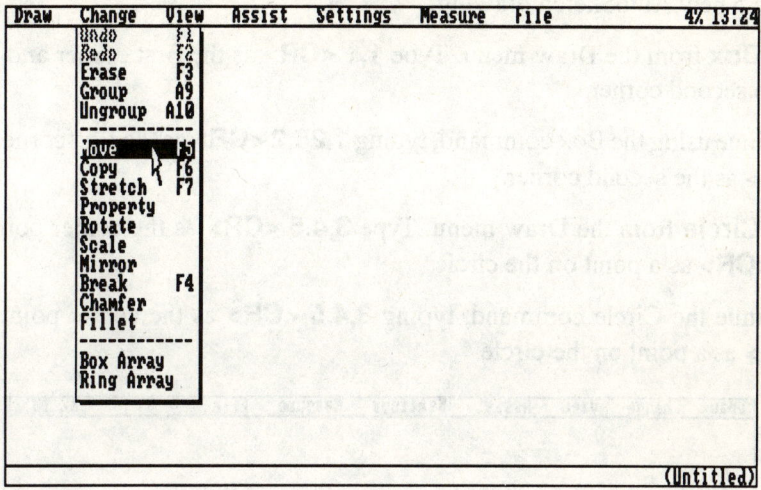

DESCRIPTION

The Move command, located on the Change menu, is used to reposition one or more objects on a drawing. When you select Move you select the object to move, specify a reference point, then specify a point for locating the reference.

There are three methods of specifying a point to relocate the reference:

- Pick the point on the screen, or type its coordinates.
- Type relative coordinates for the move, specifying both an X and Y displacement.
- Type polar coordinates, where the reference point serves as the origin for the polar coordinate system.

The point you pick as a reference point does not have to be part of the object, but it can be.

APPLICATIONS

Move is used to relocate a single entity or group of entities on a drawing. The Copy and the Move commands are similar. The major difference between the two commands is that the Move command repositions one or more selected objects from one place to another, while the Copy command duplicates one or more selected objects, leaving the original in place.

TYPICAL OPERATION

In this activity you draw the design for two trophies. The first consists of a rectangular base, with a ring on top. The second is similar, except that it adds a set of columns to the middle of the unit.

1. Begin a new AutoSketch drawing.

2. Pick **Box** from the Draw menu. Type **1,1 <CR>** as the first corner and **5,2 <CR>** as the second corner.

3. Continue using the Box command, typing **1.25,2 <CR>** as the first corner and **4.5,3 <CR>** as the second corner.

4. Pick **Circle** from the Draw menu. Type **3,4.5 <CR>** as the center point and type **3,3 <CR>** as a point on the circle.

5. Continue the Circle command, typing **3,4.5 <CR>** as the center point and **3,3.5 <CR>** as a point on the circle.

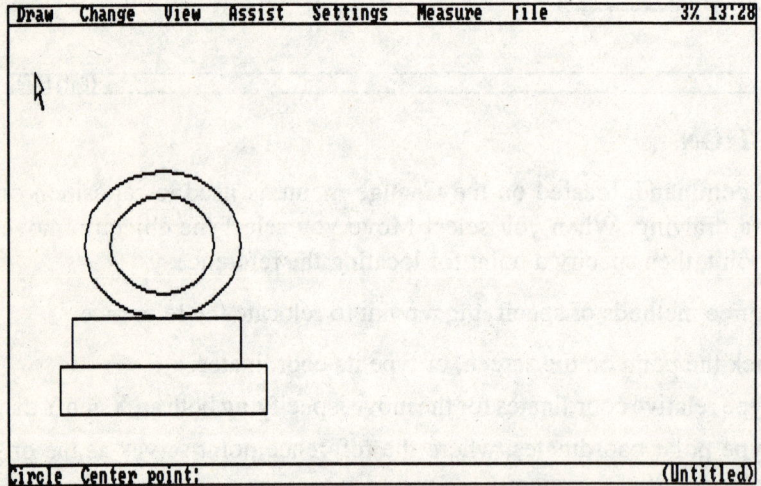

6. Pick **Copy** from the Change menu. Enclose the entire figure in a selection box. Type **1,1 <CR>** as the reference point and **8,1** as the placement point.

7. Pick **Move** from the Change menu. Enclose the top of the right figure in a crosses selection box as shown in the following illustration.

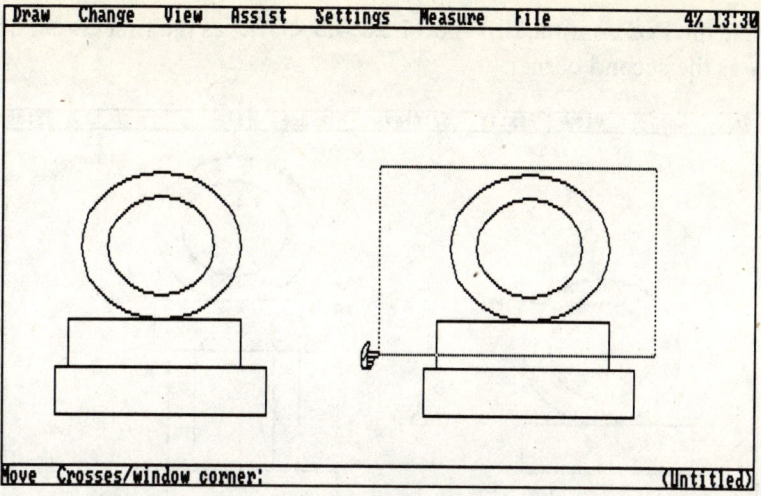

8. Pick a point near the center of the circles. (Precision does not matter.)

9. Type **P(2.5,90) <CR>** to specify the displacement in terms of polar coordinates—a move of three drawing units at a bearing of 90 degrees.

10. Pick **Redraw** from the View menu.

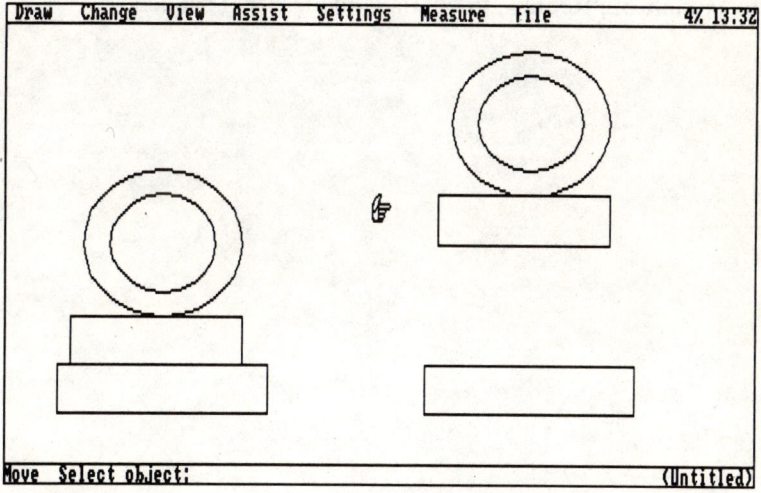

11. Pick **Box** from the Draw menu. Type **8.75,2 <CR>** as the first corner and **9.25,4.5 <CR>** as the second corner.

12. Continue the Box command. Type **11.25,4.5 <CR>** as the first corner and **10.75,2 <CR>** as the second corner.

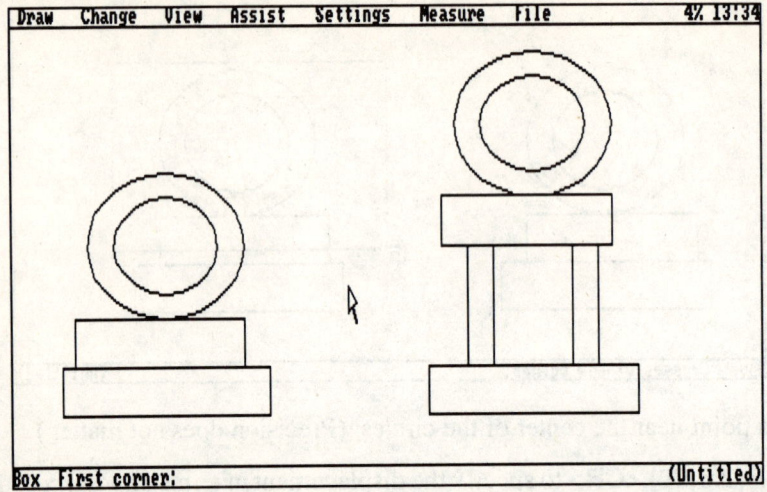

13. Pick **Quit** from the File menu and discard the drawing, or continue your work session by picking **New** from the File menu.

14. Turn to Module 52, Redraw, to continue the learning sequence.

Module 37
NEW

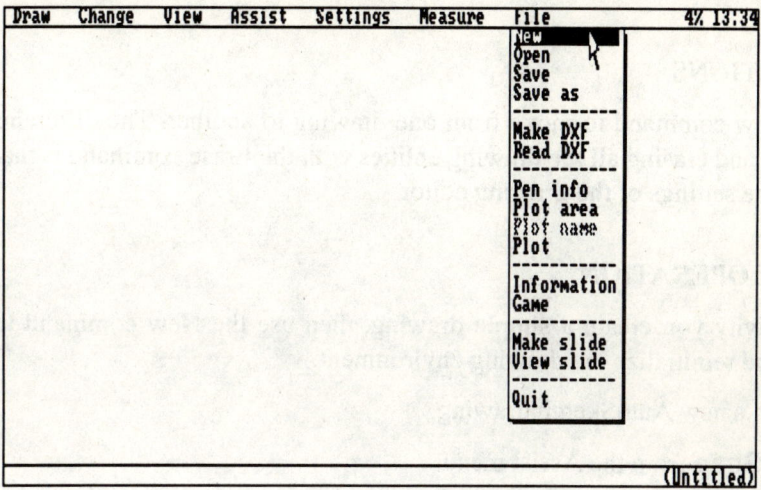

DESCRIPTION

Use the New command on the File menu to erase the contents of the drawing editor in preparation for beginning a new drawing. If you have not saved the most recent version of the drawing prior to selecting the New command, the following dialogue box appears.

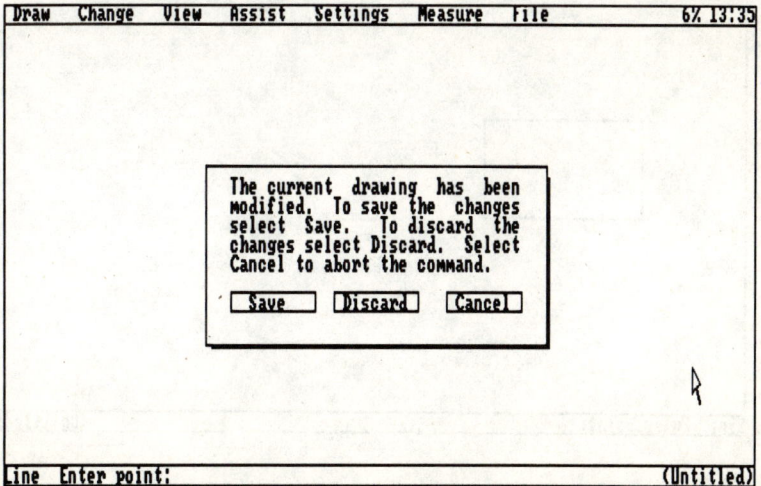

You may elect to save the drawing, discard the changes, or cancel the New command from this dialogue box.

In addition to clearing the drawing editor, the New command resets the values for the drawing aids on the Settings and Assist menus, providing you with a known starting environment for a new drawing.

APPLICATIONS

Use the New command to move from one drawing to another. The difference between using New and erasing all the drawing entities with the Erase command is that New also resets all the settings of the drawing editor.

TYPICAL OPERATION

In this activity you create a simple drawing, then use the New command to erase the drawing and reinitialize the drawing environment.

1. Begin a new AutoSketch drawing.

2. Pick **Snap** from the Assist menu.

3. Pick **Grid** from the Assist menu.

4. Pick **Line** from the Draw menu. Draw a rectangle as shown in the following screen. (Accuracy is not important.)

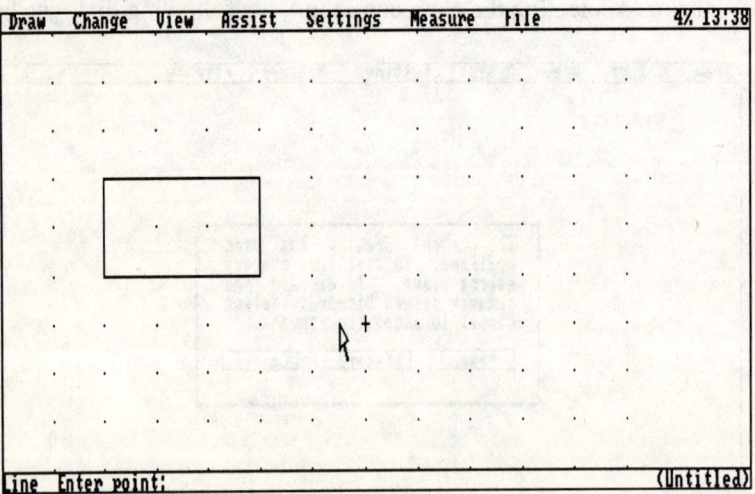

5. Pick **New** from the File menu.

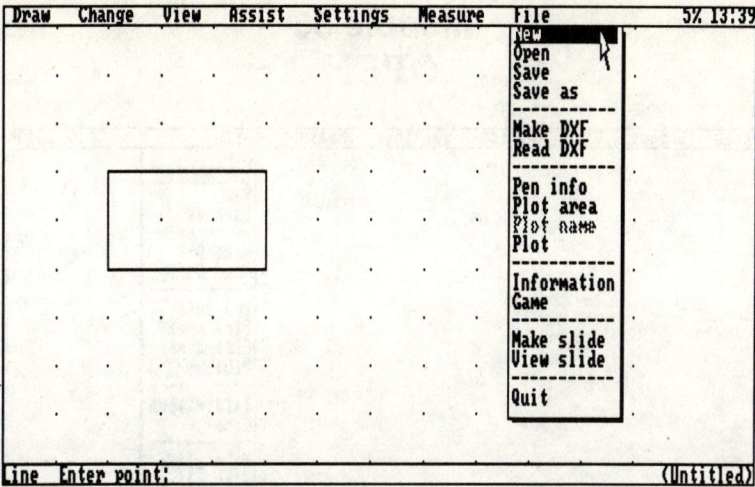

6. Pick **Discard** from the dialogue box.

7. Pick the **Assist** menu. Notice that the settings for Snap and Grid are deactivated. Further, the grid is removed from the drawing screen.

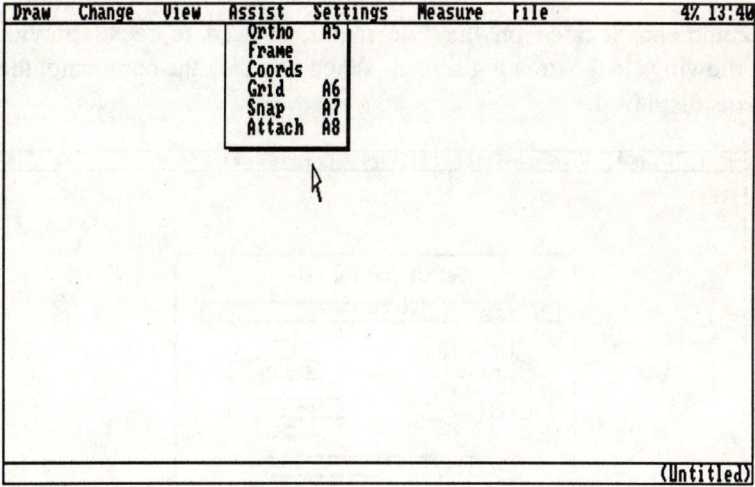

8. Quit AutoSketch, or turn to Module 8, Box, to continue the learning sequence.

Module 38
OPEN

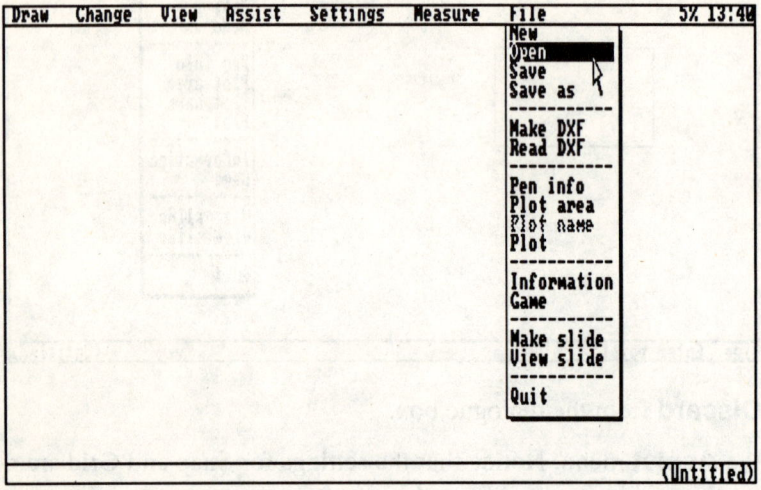

DESCRIPTION

The Open command, located on the File menu, is used to recall previously saved AutoSketch drawings to the drawing screen. When you pick the command, the following dialogue box is displayed.

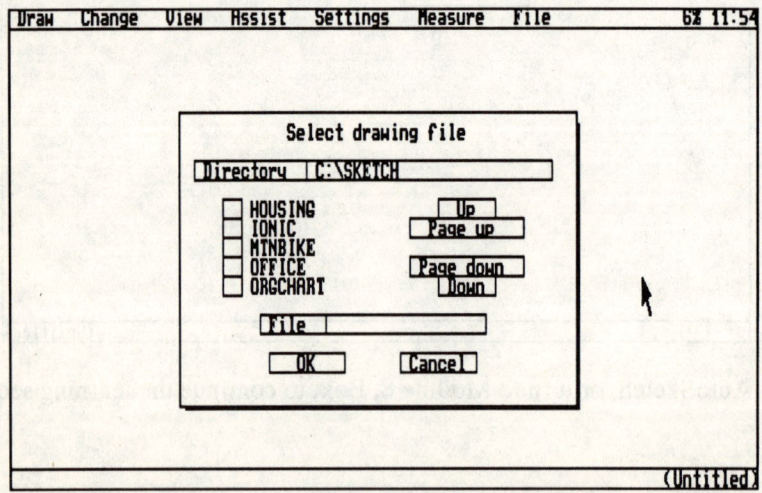

The first group of drawing files in the current directory are displayed in alphabetical order. Picking Up or Down scrolls the file display one entry in their respective direction. Picking Page up or Page down moves a screenful of files at a time. You may change drives and/or directories by picking the Directory selection box and typing a new drive and directory specification. You may either type the name of the desired drawing file in the File selection box, or pick the check box next to its name. Pick OK to load the file into the drawing editor.

APPLICATIONS

Use the Open command anytime you want to continue to work on a previously saved AutoSketch drawing.

TYPICAL OPERATION

In this session you reload the drawing you created in Module 55.

1. Pick **Open** from the AutoSketch File menu.

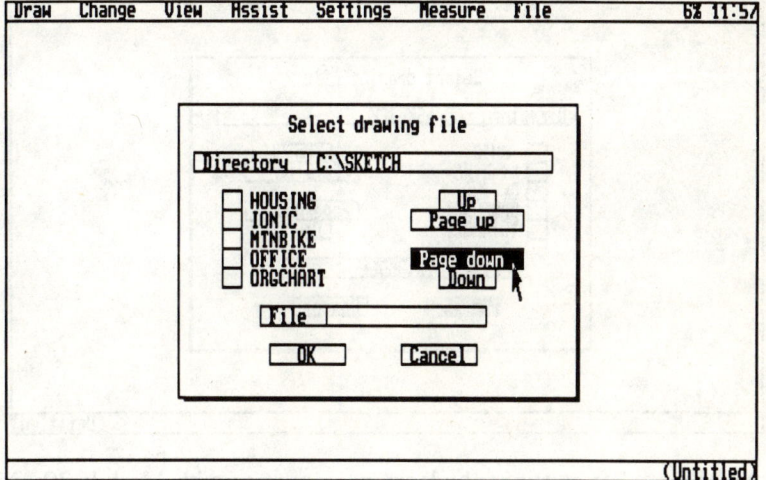

2. Pick **Page down, Down, Page up** and **Up** as required to bring TRIANGLE into view as a drawing file.

3. Pick the selection box adjacent to TRIANGLE.

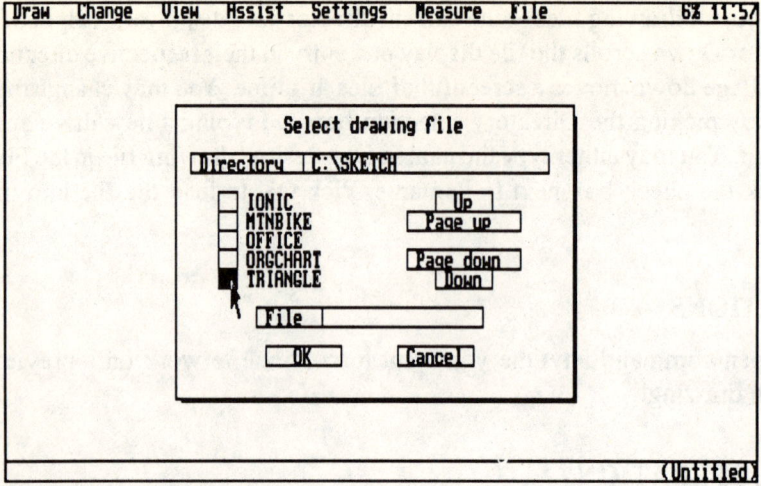

4. Pick **OK** in the dialogue box.

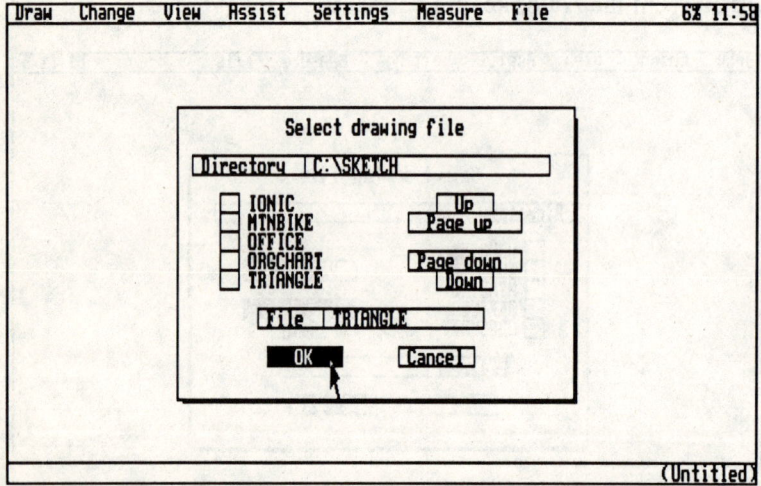

5. Quit AutoSketch, or continue the learning sequence with Module 39, Ortho.

Module 39
ORTHO

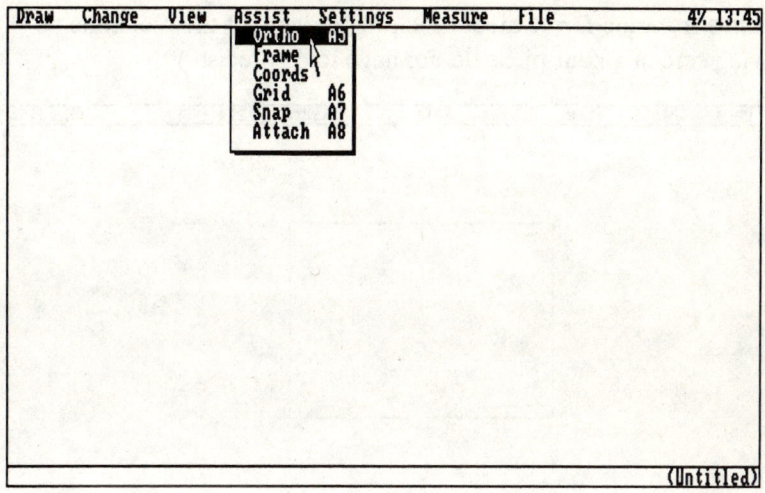

DESCRIPTION

The Ortho command, located on the Assist menu or activated by pressing Alt-F5, forces all lines and traces specified with the screen cursor to be either horizontal or vertical. It is not possible to draw a diagonal line when Ortho is selected.

APPLICATIONS

The Ortho command speeds the entry of points in a drawing which are aligned with the Snap grid, in other words, horizontal and vertical lines.

If your drawing has only a few diagonals, it is easiest to draw with Ortho on, pick the points on the horizontal and vertical lines, then toggle Ortho off and specify the diagonals.

Ortho can be selected in the middle of another command. For example, Ortho can be toggled on and off in the middle of drawing a series of lines with the Line command.

TYPICAL OPERATION

In this session you create a drawing by picking the points on the screen.

1. Begin a new drawing.

2. Pick **Snap** from the Assist menu.

3. Pick **Grid** from the Assist menu.

4. Pick **Ortho** from the Assist menu.

Draw a rectangle and its diagonal by picking the points on the screen. Notice that you must turn Ortho off to draw the diagonal.

5. Pick **Line** from the Draw menu. Pick the corners of the rectangle as shown in the following screen. (Your picks do not have to be precise.)

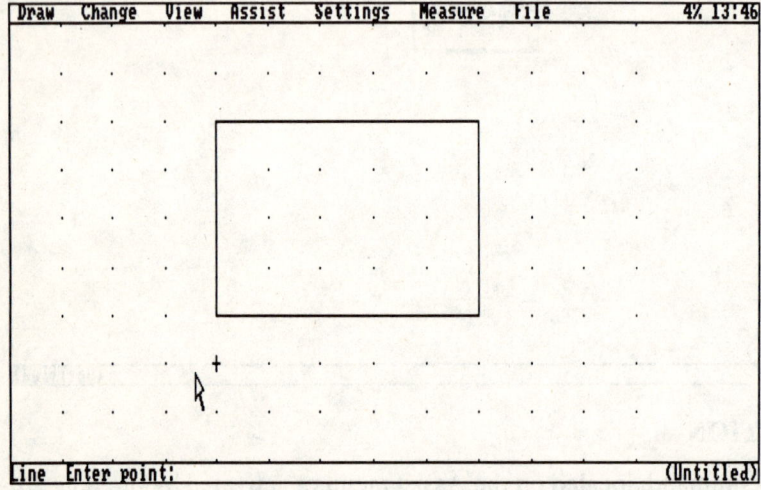

6. Press **Alt-F5** to toggle Ortho Off.

7. Pick the diagonal of the rectangle as shown in the following screen.

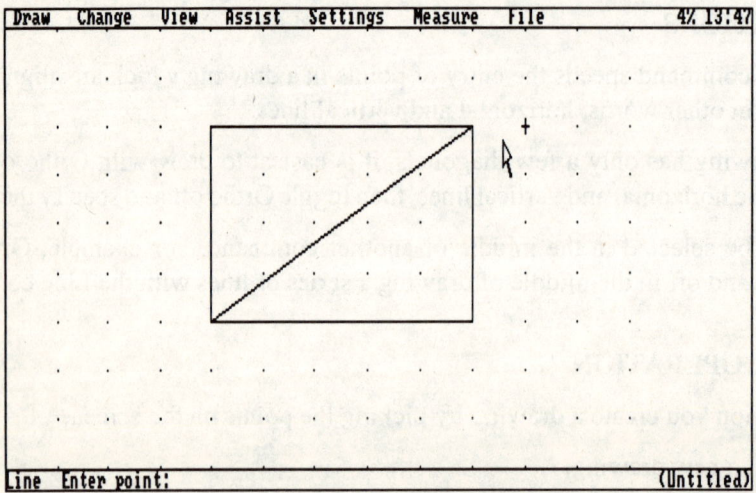

8. Quit AutoSketch, or turn to Module 12, Circle, to continue the learning sequence.

Module 40
PAN

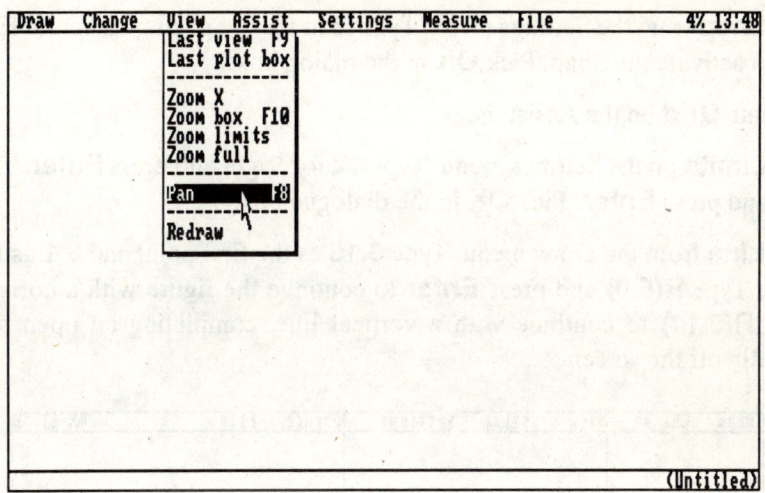

DESCRIPTION

The Pan command, located on the View menu, or activated by pressing F8, lets you reposition the drawing to a new position within the drawing window. You can move the drawing to the left, right, up, down, or diagonally.

To specify the Pan displacement, you first specify a reference point, then specify a point to where the reference point should move. You may either pick the points with the screen cursor or type the coordinates on your keyboard. If you type the coordinates, it is not necessary for either point to be visible on the screen. AutoSketch computes the displacement and angle between the two points and pans the drawing. When the Pan command operation is complete, the first specified point is moved to the second point.

APPLICATIONS

When the portion of a drawing you want to view or edit is off the screen, use the Pan command to slide the desired portion of the drawing into view on your screen. Use the Zoom command when the magnification of the drawing must change. Use the Pan command when the size relationship of the drawing should not change.

TYPICAL OPERATION

In this session you create a figure that is partially off the screen. Then you use the Pan command to view the hidden portion of the drawing.

1. Begin a new drawing.

2. Pick **Snap** from the Settings menu. Type **.5** as the X Spacing and press **Enter**. Pick **ON** to activate the Snap. Pick **OK** in the dialog box.

3. Activate **Grid** on the Assist menu.

4. Pick **Limits** on the Settings menu. Type **12** for Right and press **Enter**. Type **20** for Left and press **Enter**. Pick **OK** in the dialogue box.

5. Pick **Line** from the Draw menu. Type **3,15** as the first point and **3,1** as the second point. Type **R(5,0)** and press **Enter** to continue the figure with a horizontal line. Type **R(0,14)** to continue with a vertical line, completing an open box that is partially off the screen.

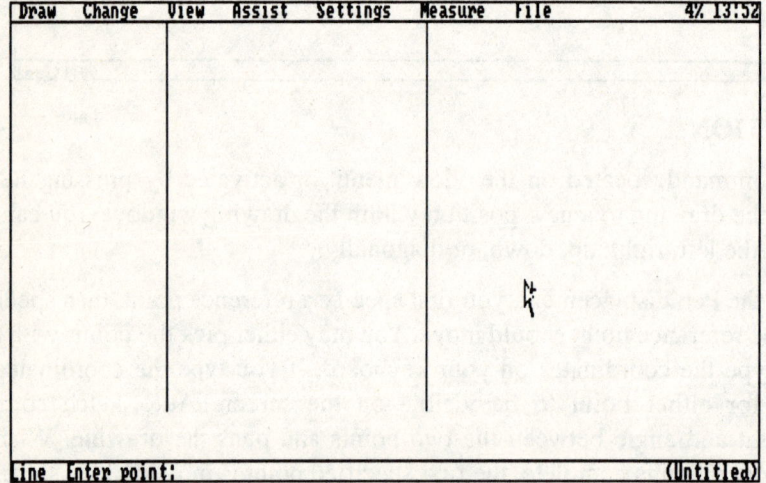

6. Pick **Pan** from the View menu. Type **3,15** as the first point and press **Enter**. Type **3,3** as the second point and press **Enter**.

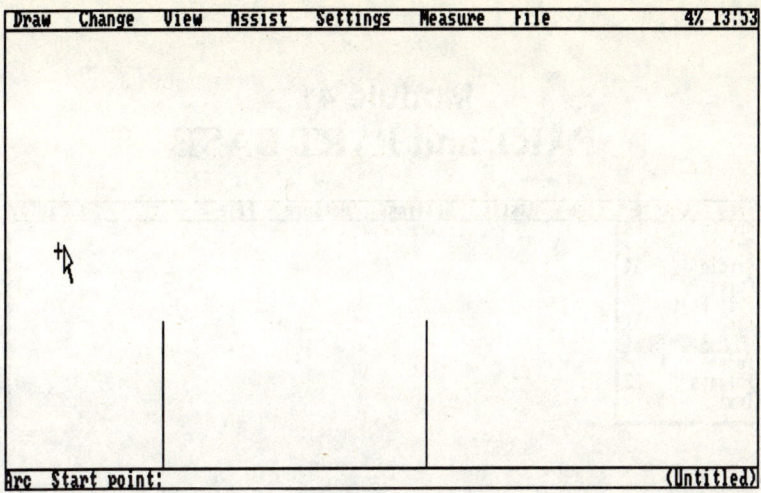

7. Pick **Arc** from the Draw menu. Type **8,15 <CR>** as the start point, type **5,5,17.5 <CR>** as a point on the arc, and type **3,15 <CR>** as the end point.

Your completed drawing appears similar to the following screen.

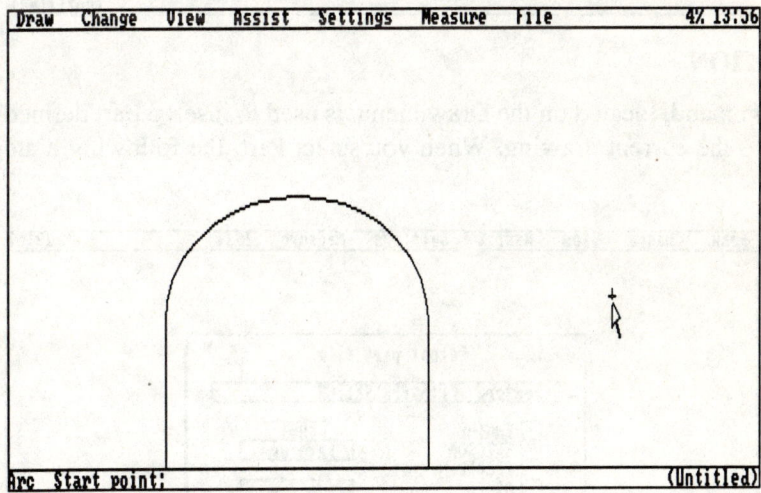

8. Quit AutoSketch, or turn to Module 28, Last View, to continue the learning sequence.

Module 41
PART and PART BASE

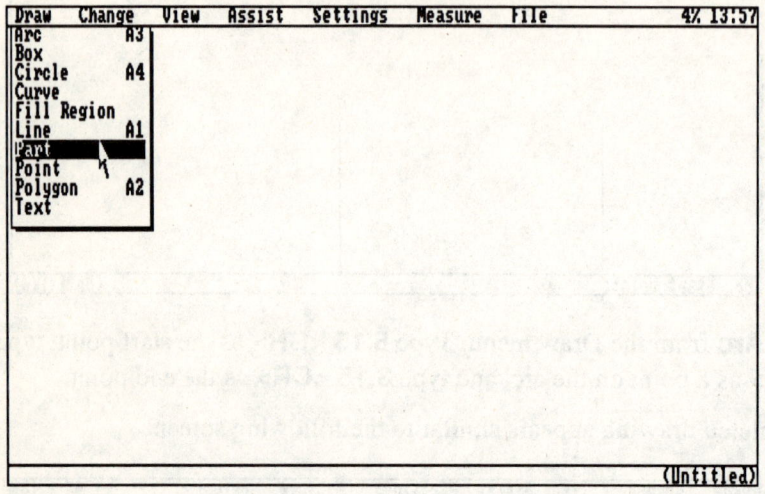

DESCRIPTION

The Part command, located on the Draw menu, is used to insert a part defined in another drawing into the current drawing. When you select Part, the following dialogue box is displayed.

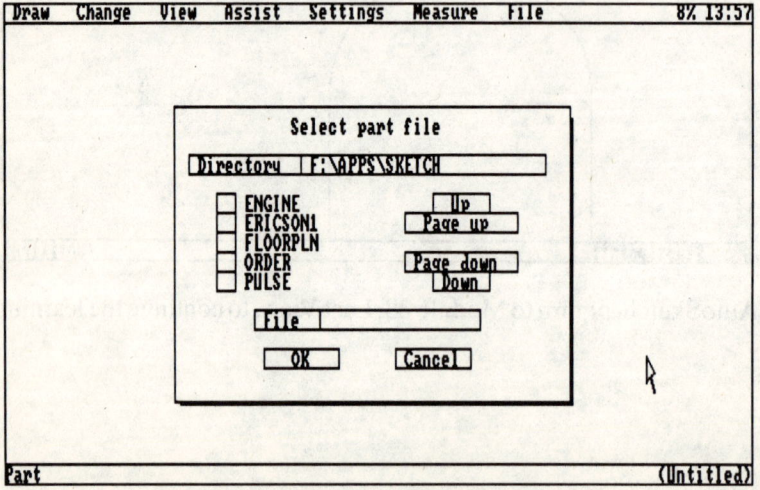

You select the drawing file that defines the part, then you either type or pick the position for insertion. Any AutoSketch drawing file can be used as a part. However, part drawings are normally constructed specifically for later insertion into other drawings.

It is not necessary to do anything special to a drawing to use it as a "part" for insertion in another drawing. When AutoSketch inserts the part, it uses the point (0,0) as the reference point for the part insertion. When you construct a drawing for use as a part, it is frequently useful to use a point on the part itself, other than the drawing origin, as the insertion reference point. To specify a different reference point, pick Part base from the Settings menu and pick the reference point prior to saving the part drawing on the disk.

APPLICATION

The Part command is used to insert parts from AutoSketch drawings into other AutoSketch drawings. This is an efficient way to repeat objects many times in a drawing. For example, you can draw the symbol of an electrical resistor and save it as a part. Then you can insert it as often as necessary on your electrical schematic diagram.

Use of the Part base command simplifies the positioning of parts in their receiving drawings. It is a good idea to establish a uniform standard for establishing the Part base on your part drawings. If you consistently use the center point or a particular corner of the drawing as the Part base, it precludes the need to remember different locations for different part references.

TYPICAL OPERATION

In this session you draw a symbol for an electrical outlet, then place several outlets along a wall.

1. Begin a new AutoSketch drawing.

2. Pick **Circle** from the Draw menu.

3. Type **1,1 <CR>** as the center point and **1.25,1 <CR>** as a point on the circle.

4. Pick **Zoom box** from the View menu. Enclose the circle in a box as shown.

5. Pick **Ortho** from the Assist menu.

6. Pick **Line** from the Draw menu. Draw two lines as shown in the following illustration.

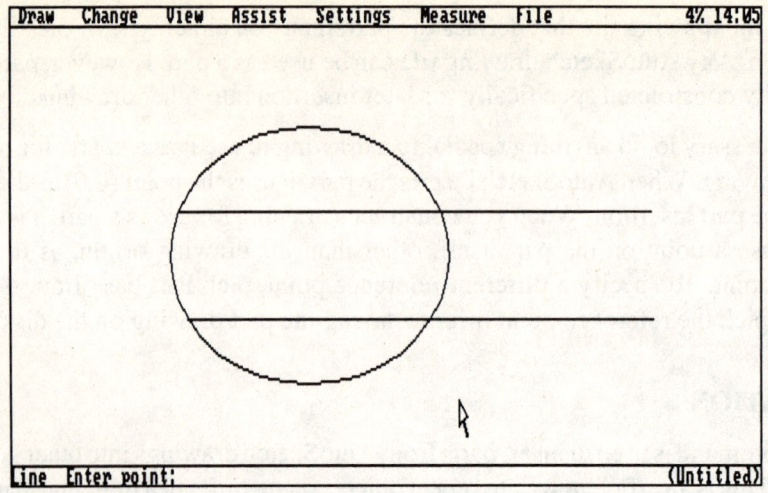

7. Pick **Part base** from the Settings menu. Type **1 <CR>** as the X coordinate and **1 <CR>** as the Y coordinate.

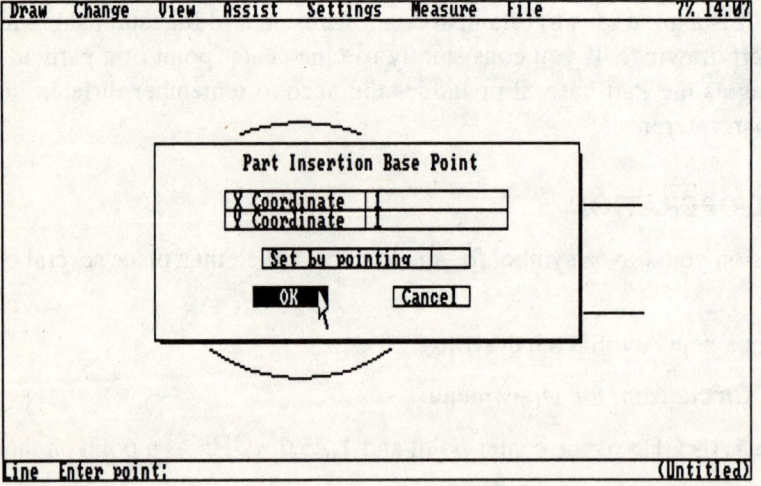

8. Pick **OK**.

9. Pick **Save as** from the File menu. Type **Socket** as the file name, press **Enter** and pick **OK**.

10. Select **New** from the File menu.

11. Pick **Box** from the Draw menu. Type **1,1 <CR>** as the first corner and **1.5,8 <CR>** as the second point.

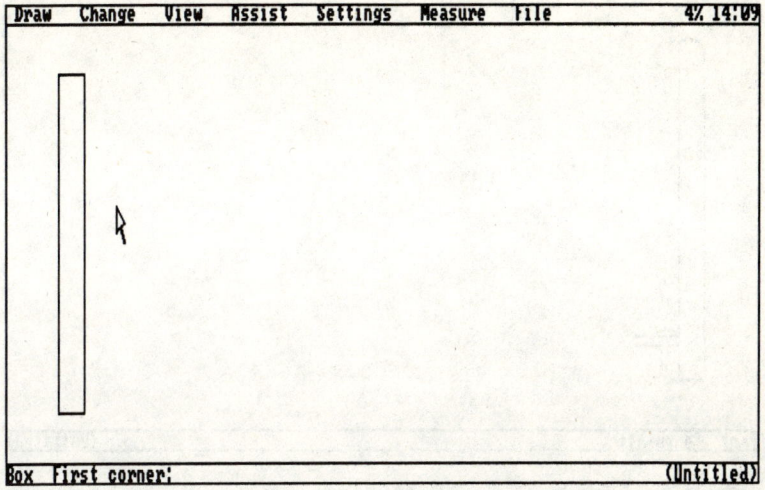

12. Select **Part** from the Draw menu. Select **Page down** in the dialogue box until the Socket drawing file is visible.

13. Pick the check box next to Socket.

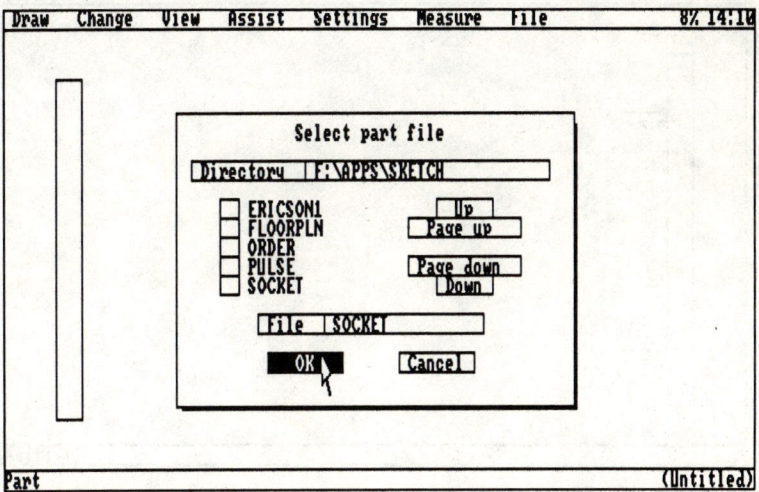

14. Pick **OK**.

15. Place the socket as shown in the following screen display.

16. Select **Part** from the Draw menu. Notice that Socket is now the default part file. Pick **OK**.

17. Place the socket against the wall as shown in the following illustration.

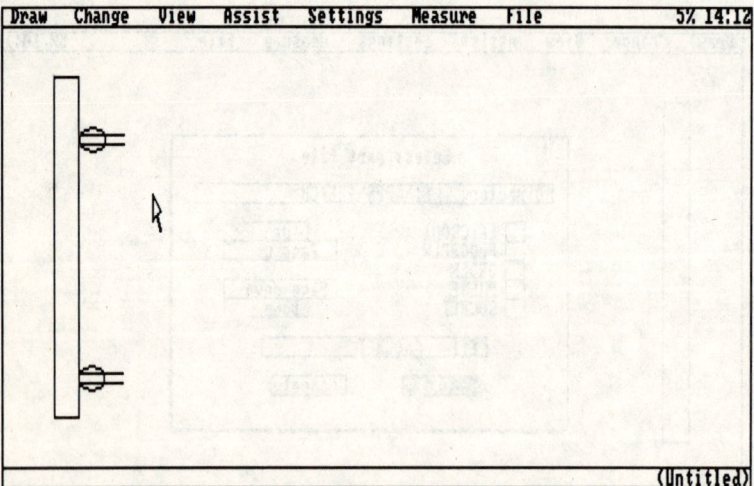

18. Pick **Quit** from the File menu and discard the drawing, or continue your work session by picking **New** from the File menu.

19. Turn to Module 62, Ungroup, to continue the learning sequence.

Module 42
PEN INFO

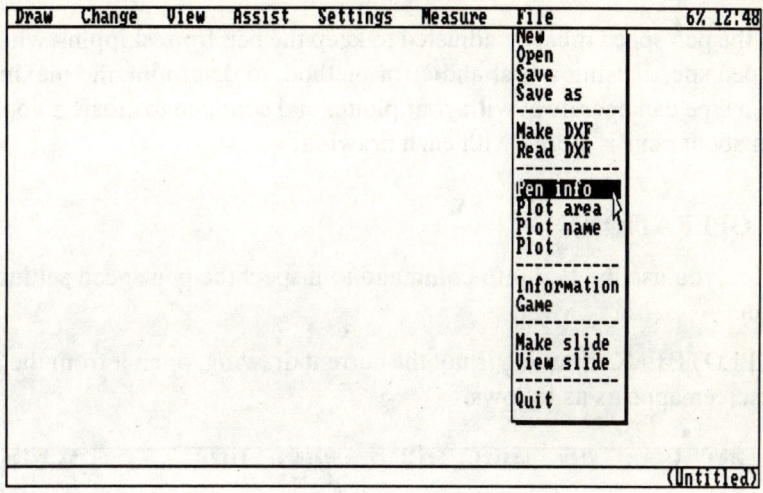

DESCRIPTION

To use Pen info, you must have configured a plotter in your AutoSketch installation; otherwise, the Pen info command is greyed out on the File menu. When you select the Pen info command, the following dialogue box appears.

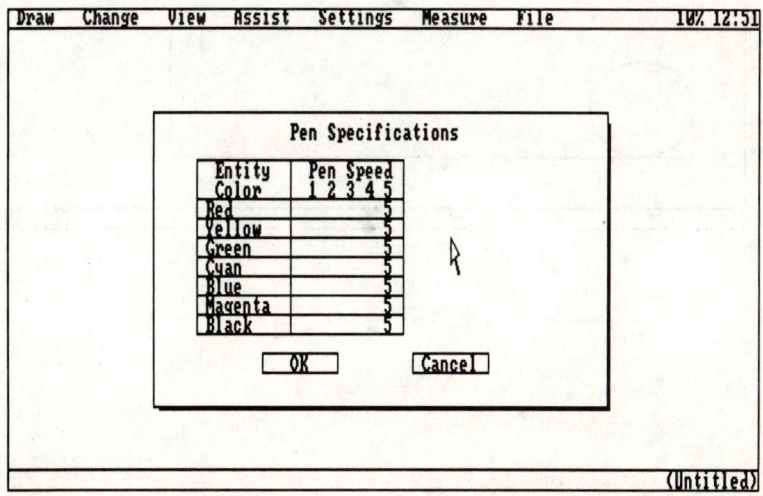

The colors that you draw with in AutoSketch can be matched with different pens if you have a multiple pen plotting device. The pen speed is also adjusted with this command. The speed can be set to the slowest speed of 1 or up to the fastest speed of 5.

APPLICATIONS

Sometimes the pen speed must be adjusted to keep the pen from skipping while plotting. Adjust the pen speed, using a trial and error method, to determine the maximum speed that each pen type can operate at with your plotter and continue to create a good line. The information about pens is stored with each drawing.

TYPICAL OPERATION

In this session you use the Pen info command to inspect the pen speed settings for your current plotter.

1. If the PLOTDEMO drawing is not the current drawing, open it from the File menu. Your screen appears as follows.

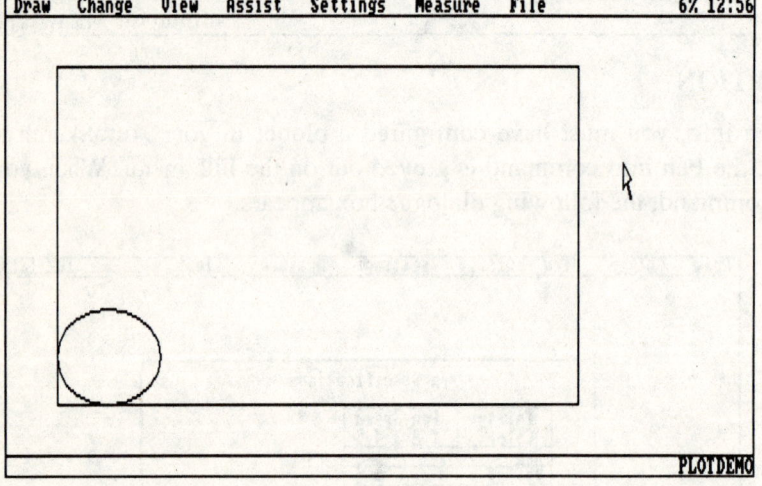

2. Select **Pen info** from the File menu. The following dialog box appears.

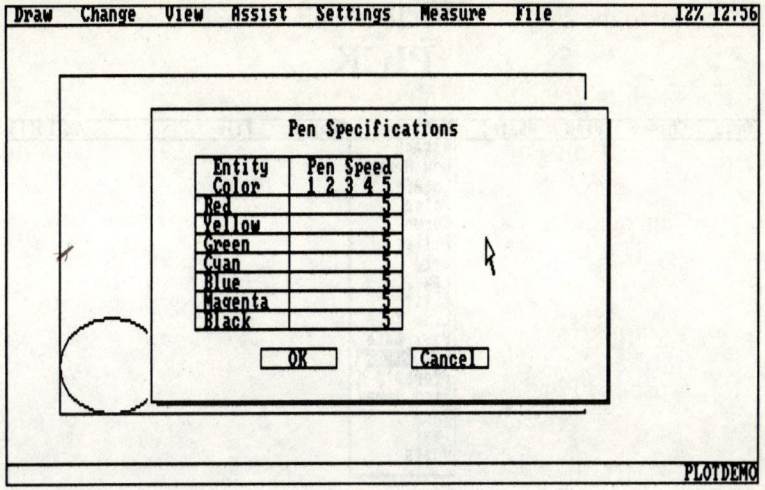

3. Select **OK**

4. Quit AutoSketch, or turn to Module 13, Color, to continue the learning sequence.

Module 43
PICK

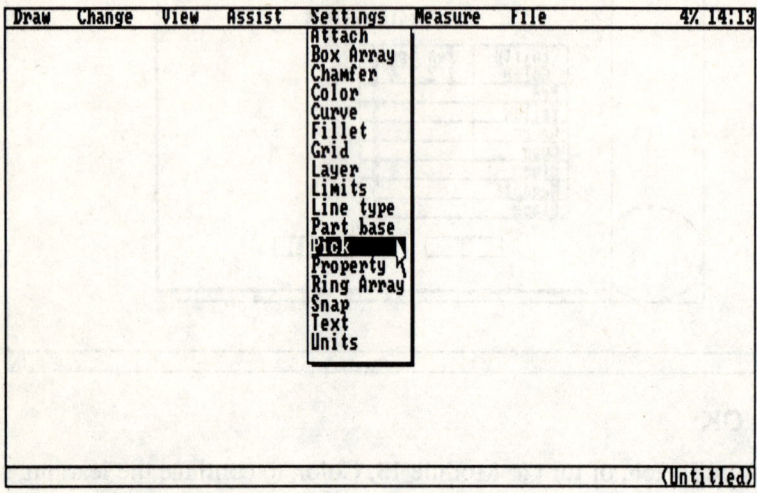

DESCRIPTION

The Attach command on the Assist menu allows you to selectively attach new drawing entities to existing entities if you pick "close" to them. The Pick command on the Settings menu defines the meaning of the word "close" in terms of percentage of screen height. When you select Pick from the Settings menu, the following dialog box is displayed.

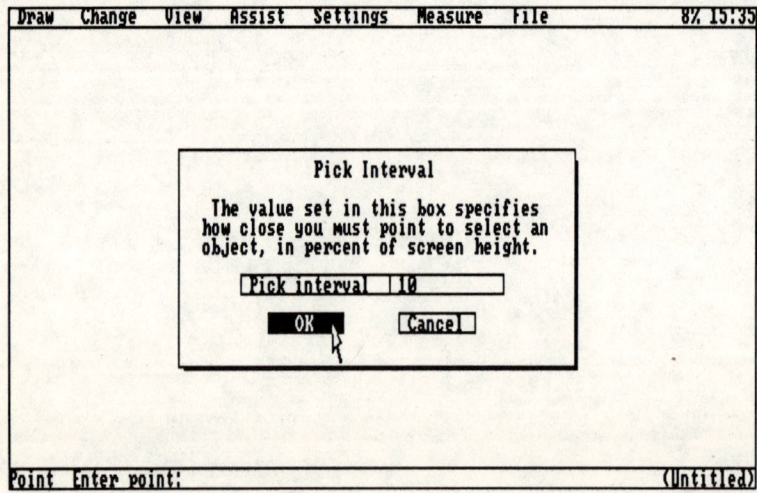

Type the new value, press Enter, or pick OK to accept it, then pick OK in the Pick dialogue box.

APPLICATIONS

The size of the Pick target is expressed as a percentage of screen height. The ideal target size is a function of hardware resolution, drawing complexity, and personal style. Selecting a target size that is too small requires additional effort in identifying points in the drawing with various Attach modes. Selecting a target size that is too large may make it impossible to isolate a single drawing entity within a complex drawing. Experiment with various sizes of targets to determine the best size (or sizes) for your needs.

TYPICAL OPERATION

In this session you change the size of the Attach target area with the Pick command.

1. Begin a new AutoSketch drawing.

2. Select **Line** from the Draw menu.

3. Type **2,2** as the first point and press **Enter**. Type **6,2** as the second point and press **Enter**.

4. Type **2,4** as the first point and press **Enter**. Type **6,4** as the second point and press **Enter**.

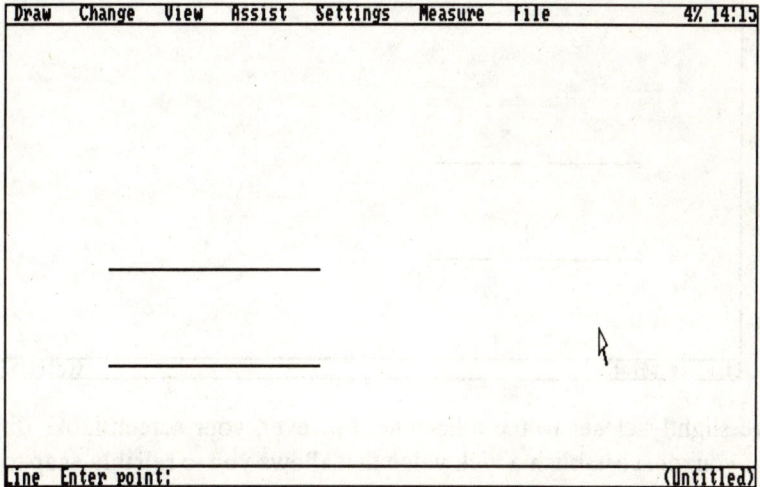

5. Select **Pick** from the Settings menu. Type **20** as the Pick interval and press **Enter**. Select **OK** in the dialogue box.

6. Pick **Attach** from the Assist menu.

7. Move screen cursor to a point between the lines as shown in the following screen, as close to being equally distant from the lines as possible.

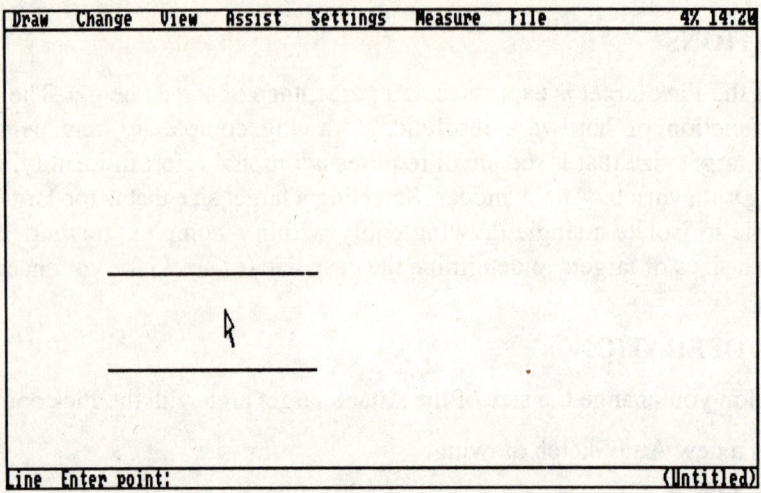

8. Pick the point. The first end of the line snaps to the end point of one of the existing lines. Your screen may look like the following.

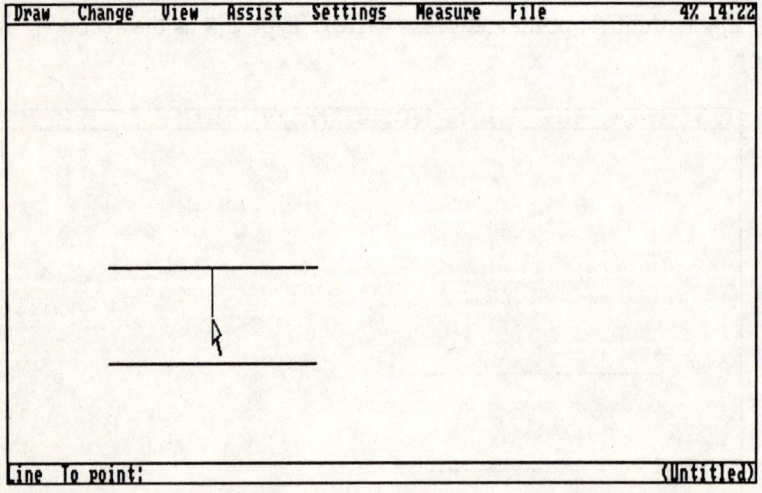

If you were slightly closer to the other line, however, your screen looks different. The point is that you must establish a Pick value that allows you to reliably snap to the desired objects. There is no one correct value, you must establish the value that makes your work easiest for each drawing situation.

9. Quit AutoSketch, or turn to Module 46, Point, to continue the learning sequence.

Module 44
PLOT and PLOT NAME

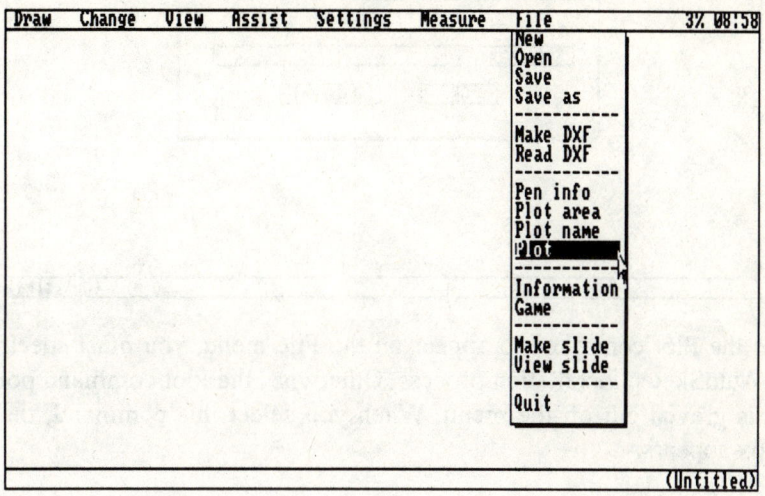

DESCRIPTION

Use the plotting commands — Pen info, Plot area, Plot name, and Plot from the File menu to transfer your completed drawing to paper. When you draw in AutoSketch, the drawing is created at full scale. The Plot command creates a paper drawing at any desired scale. Plot name places the information in a disk file.

PLOT NAME If you configured AutoSketch to plot to a file rather than to a plotter, the Plot name command is available from the File menu. Otherwise, the command name is greyed out on the menu. AutoSketch provides the DOS filename extension .PLT to identify a plot file. When you select the command Plot name, the following dialogue box appears.

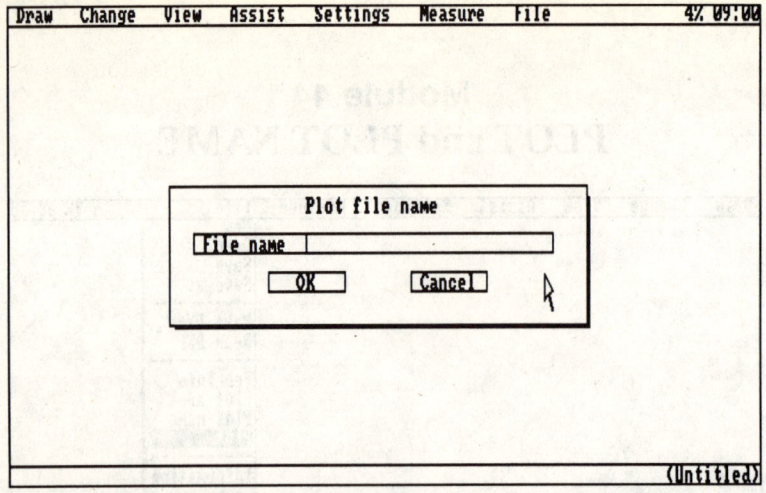

PLOT For the Plot command to appear on the File menu, you must specify a plotter during the AutoSketch installation process. Otherwise, the Plot command portion of the File menu is greyed out on the menu. When you select this command, the following dialogue box appears.

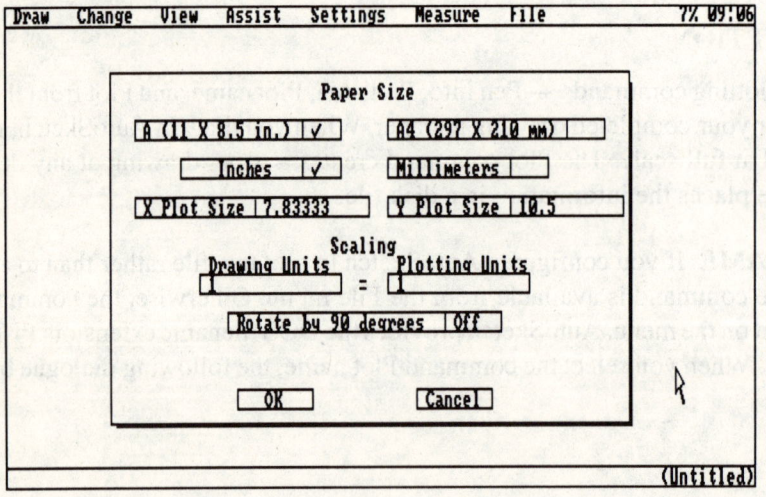

The current drawing is sent to the plotter or printer. If Plot boxes and Clip boxes are visible, they determine how plotting is carried out. The typical operation in this module will illustrates how these items work with the Plot command.

APPLICATIONS

The Plot command produces paper copies of drawings. The Plot command is useful for producing drawings to any desired scale and on any size paper that is appropriate to the plotter that you have installed on your computer. One example of how the Plot command is used in a real situation is in dealing with house plan drawings. The house plan is drawn in AutoSketch at full scale. If the drawing were plotted on paper at full scale it would be as large as the house it portrayed. The Plot command allows you to produce a plot at a reduced scale such as 1/4 inch equal to 1 foot. In other words, the plot of the house produced by the plotter would be 1/48th the size of the actual house because 1/4 inch divides 1 foot 48 times.

TYPICAL OPERATION

In this operation, you produce a simple drawing using the Line and Circle commands. You then use either the Plot or Plot name command to create the plotter output.

1. Begin a new AutoSketch drawing.

2. First, draw four lines on the screen. Pick **Line** from the Draw menu. Type **1,1 <CR>** as the first point and **1,8 <CR>** as the endpoint of the first line. Type **/LPOINT <CR>** to continue the second line and **11,8 <CR>** as the endpoint of the second line. Type **/LPOINT <CR>** as the starting point of the third line and **11,1 <CR>** as its endpoint. Type **/LPOINT <CR>** as the starting point of the fourth line and **1,1 <CR>** as its endpoint.

3. To draw a circle in the lower left-hand corner of the box, first pick **Circle** from the Draw menu. Then type **2,2 <CR>** as the center point and **1,2 <CR>** as a point on the circle.

4. Pick **Plot** from the File menu.

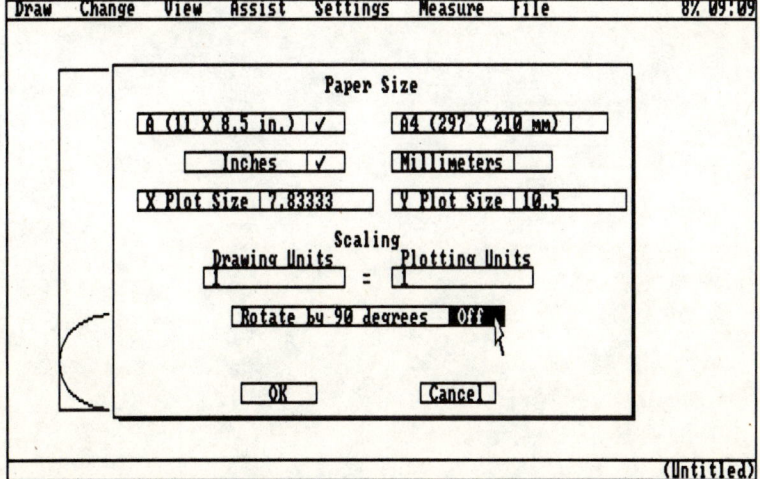

5. Pick **Off** in the Rotate by 90 degrees check box, changing the setting to "On." Then pick **OK**.

When the completed plot is produced on A size paper (11 X 8.5 inches) it does not produce a complete plot; one line is missing on the paper plot.

6. Save your drawing as PLOTDEMO. Continue the learning sequence with Module 45, Plot Area.

Module 45
PLOT AREA

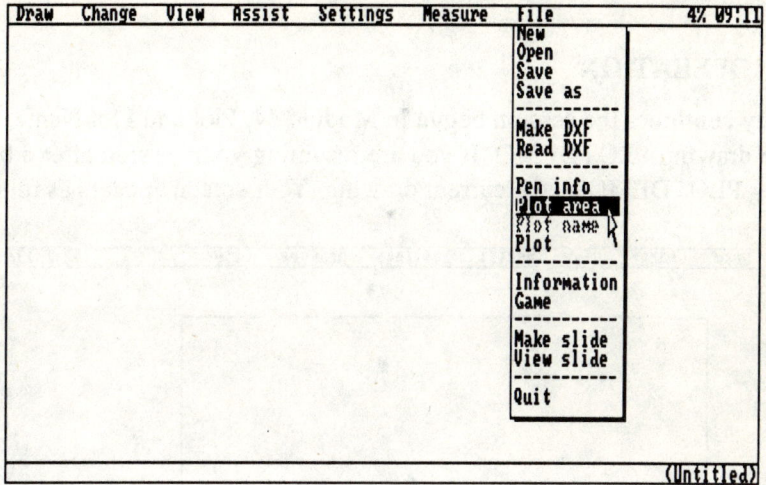

DESCRIPTION

To use the Plot area command, you must have specified a pointing device. Otherwise, the Plot area command is greyed out on the File menu. The Plot area command is the part of plotting in AutoSketch that requires the most experimentation for you to fully utilize its power. When you select the Plot area command from the File menu, the following dialog box appears.

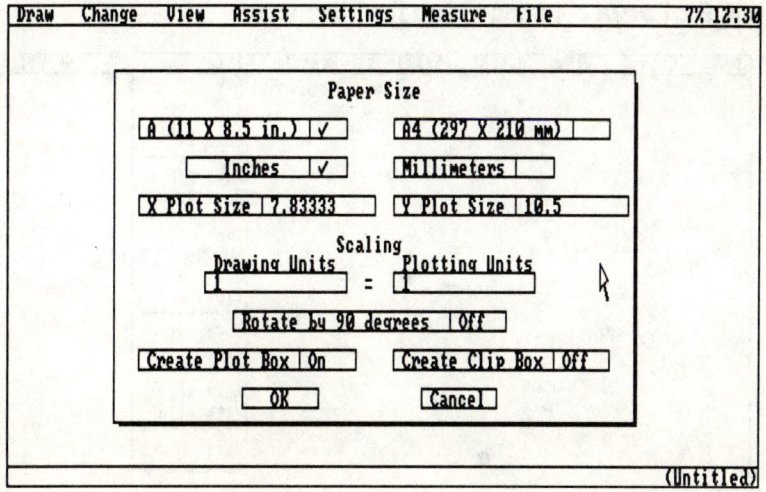

APPLICATIONS

You do not always want to plot the entire area covered by a drawing. For example, in laying out furniture for an office complex, it is sometimes useful to have individual prints of each office cubicle. In a complex drawing that includes subassemblies, it often useful to have drawings that include only single subassemblies.

TYPICAL OPERATION

This activity continues the session begun in Module 44, Plot and Plot Name, where you created the drawing PLOTDEMO. If you are resuming your session after a break, open the drawing PLOTDEMO as the current drawing. Your screen appears as follows.

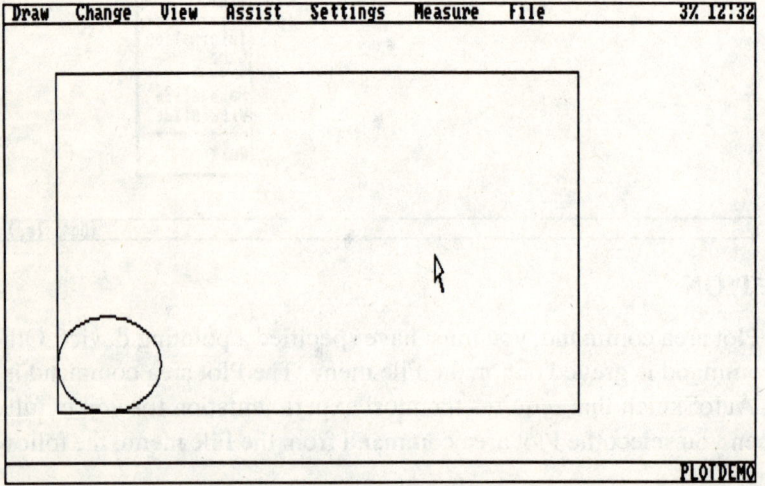

1. Pick the **Plot area** command from the File menu.

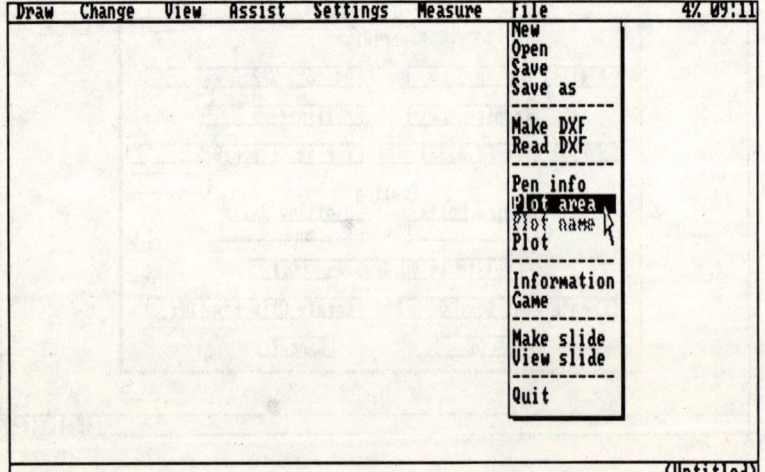

Check and compare the Paper size box shown here with the one shown on your screen. If they are not the same, make corrections to your box so that it matches the printed one.

2. Pick **OK**. Pick **Move** from the Change menu.

3. Pick the **Plot Box**. Be certain to select the Plot box and not a portion of the line or circle you have drawn. Type **11,0 <CR>** as the first point and **11.6,.63 <CR>** as the second point.

4. Pick **Redraw** from the View menu.

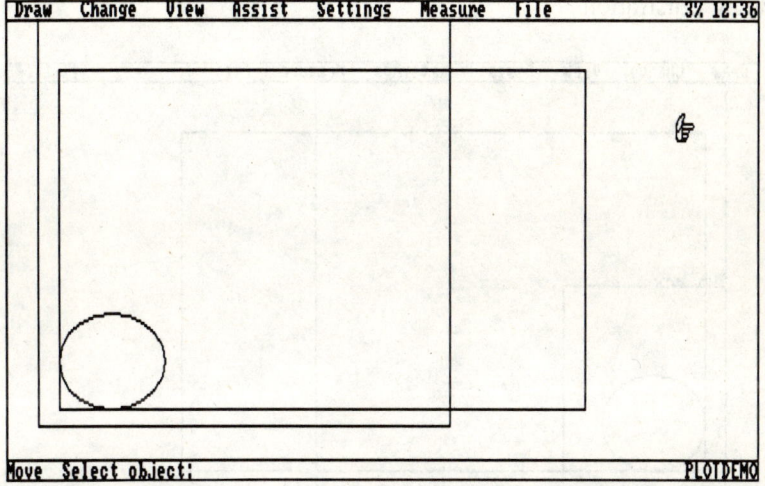

5. Pick **Plot** from the File menu. The complete drawing is plotted on the paper.

6. Pick **Plot area** from the File menu. Pick the **On** check box for Create Plot Box, turning it off. Pick the **Off** check box for Create Clip box, turning it on.

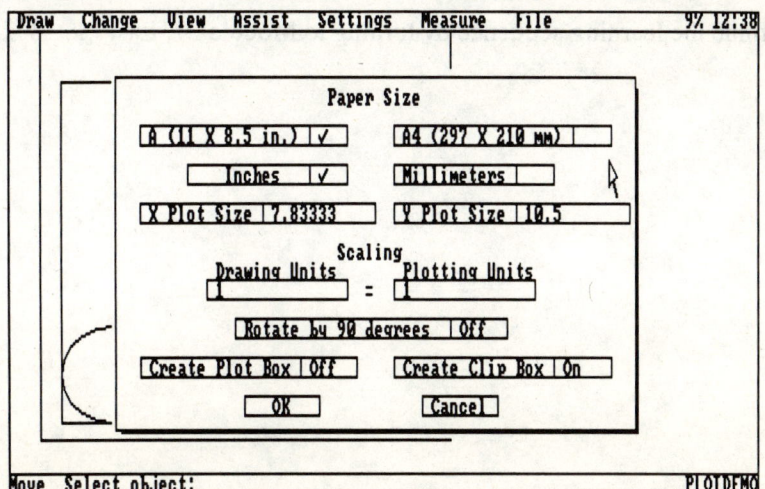

Check and compare the Paper size box shown here with the one shown on your screen. If they are not the same, make corrections to your box so that it matches the one printed above. After you are satisfied your settings are correct:

7. Pick **OK**.

8. Reduce the size of the Clip box by using the Scale command. Pick **Scale** from the Change menu. Type **11,.3 <CR>** to select the scale object, type **1,1 <CR>** as the base point and **1.2,1.2 <CR>** as the second point. You should now have a Clip box surrounding the circle in the lower left corner of the drawing, as shown in the following illustration.

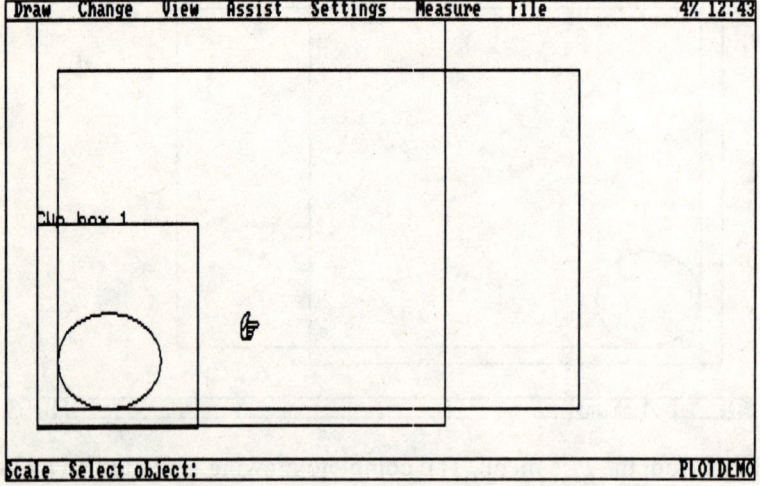

9. Pick **Plot** from the File menu. Then pick **OK**. You should now have a plot of the part of the drawing contained in the Clip box.

10. Continue the learning sequence by turning to Module 27, Last Plot Box.

Module 46
POINT

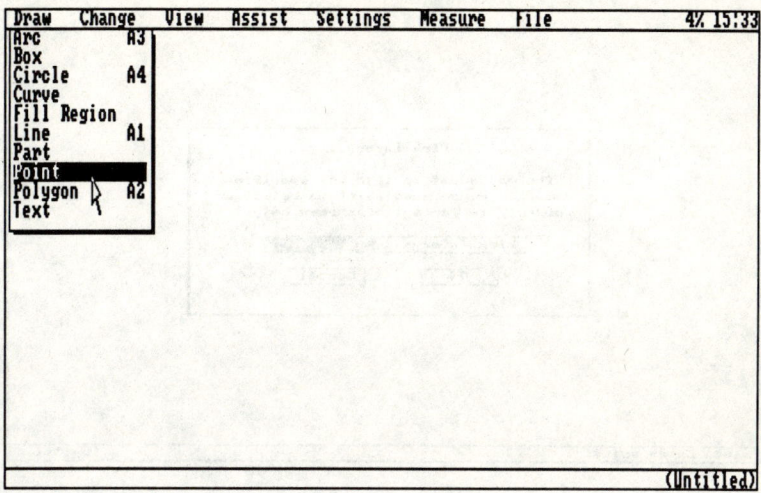

DESCRIPTION

The Point command, located on the Draw menu, places a point on the screen. Points are small marks that are placed on a drawing. The position of a point is selected by typing a location from the keyboard or by picking a location with the screen cursor.

It is important to note that a line is not made up of a series of points. A point is a distinct entity that has no length, width, or depth. When you plot a point, the width is controlled by the thickness of the plotter pen.

APPLICATIONS

Placing points on the screen with the Point command is often useful for establishing reference coordinates within a drawing. When working with the screen cursor, you can use the settings on the Attach menu to snap points you pick on the screen to a point. This gives you quick and precise access to a specific reference point on your drawing.

TYPICAL OPERATION

In this session you use the Point command to establish two reference points on your drawing screen. Next, you use Attach to jump from one point to the other.

1. Begin a new drawing.

2. Pick **Point** from the Draw menu. Type **1,1** and press **Enter**.

3. Type **5,5** and press **Enter**.

4. Select **Pick** from the Settings menu. Type **10** as the Pick interval and press **Enter**.

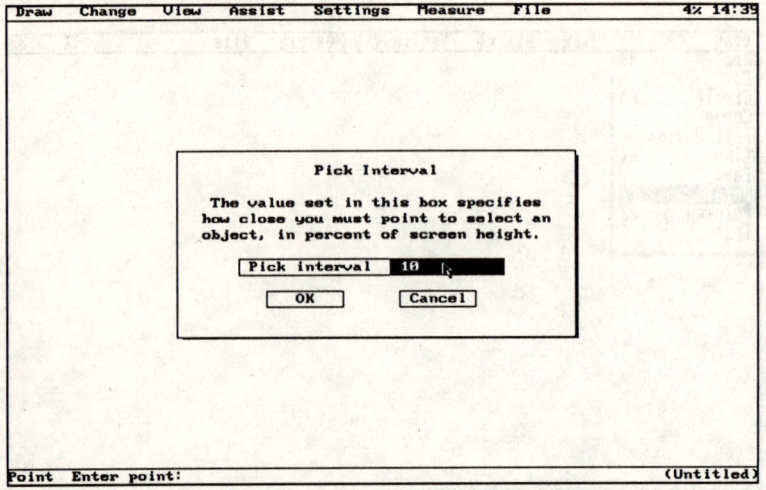

5. Pick **OK**.

6. Activate **Attach** on the Assist menu.

7. Pick **Line** from the Draw menu.

8. Pick close to the point 1,1.

9. Pick close to the point 5,5. Notice that the line endpoints jump to the points.

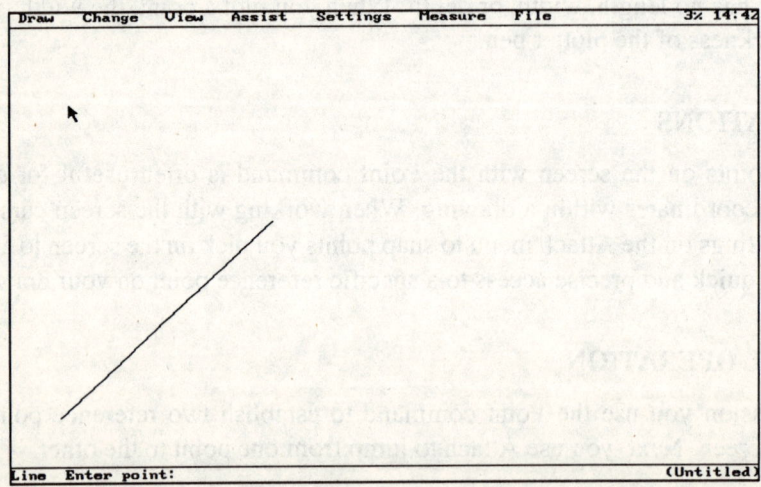

10. Quit AutoSketch, or turn to Module 18 to continue the learning sequence.

Module 47
POLYGON

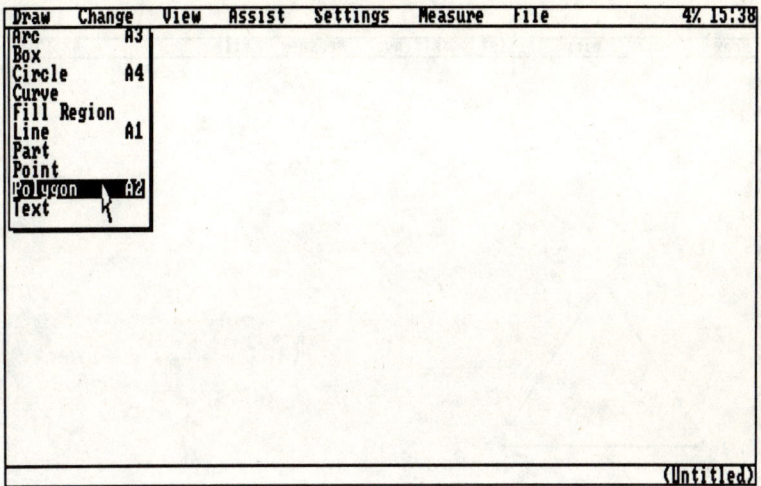

DESCRIPTION

The Polygon command, located on the Draw menu, or activated by pressing Alt-F2, lets you construct a series of connected lines that are treated as a single entity. The polygon may be open or closed. To complete the entry of points, either enter the last point twice, or pick the starting point, creating a closed polygon.

APPLICATIONS

When you construct a polygon with line segments, you must either pick each line segment, or enclose the entire polygon in a selection box to select the polygon. When you construct the figure as a polygon, you only need to select any one line segment to pick the entire polygon.

TYPICAL OPERATION

In this session you construct a system of two triangles. Then you take advantage of the selection of a polygon as a single entity to copy one of the triangles.

1. Start a new AutoSketch drawing.

2. Pick **Polygon** from the Draw menu.

3. Type **1,1** as the first point and press **Enter**.

4. Type **R(4,0)** and press **Enter** to construct the base.

5. Type **P(4,120)** and press **Enter** to construct the right side.

6. Pick **Attach** from the Assist menu.

7. Pick **1,1**, the start point of the polygon.

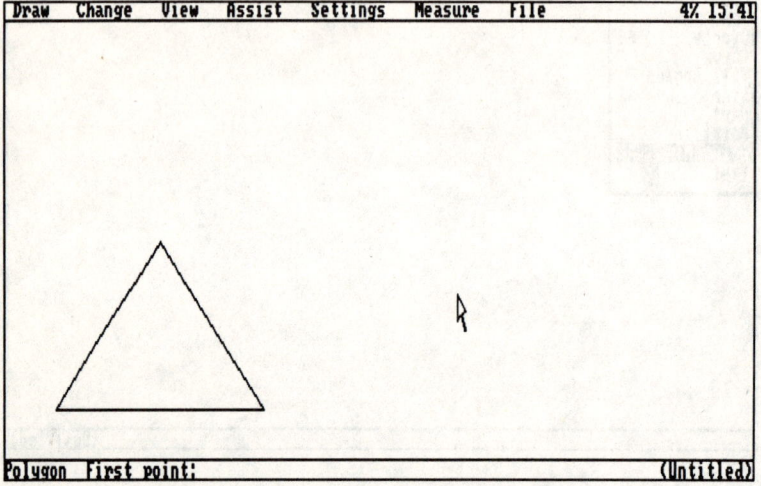

8. Pick the midpoint of the left side of the tringle.

9. Pick the midpoint of the right side of the triangle.

10. Pick the midpoint of the base of the triangle.

11. Pick the start point of the second triangle.

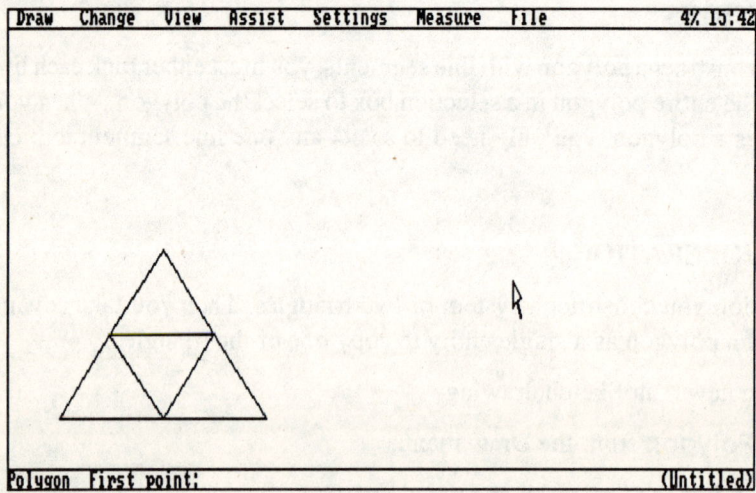

12. Pick **Copy** from the Change menu.

13. Pick the apex of the large, outer triangle once to select the triangle, then a second time as the reference point.

14. Drag the triangle and place it as shown in the following screen.

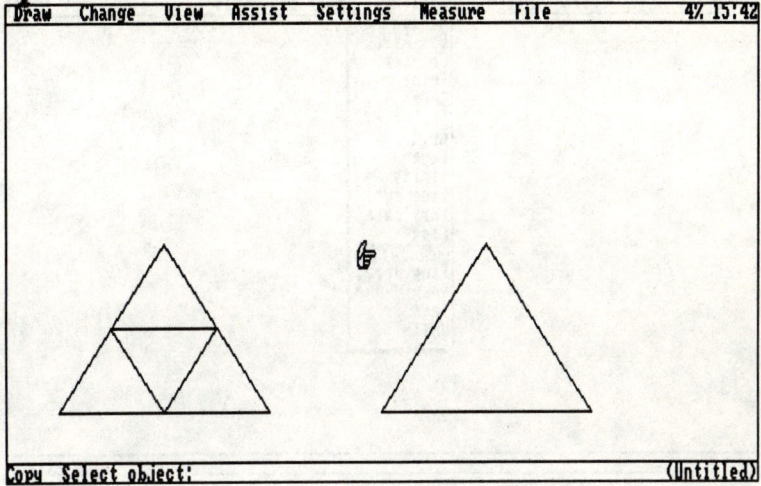

If the triangle had been constructed as separate line segments, it would have been necessary to have selected each line segment individually. Using a crossing window would have also selected the inner triangle.

15. Quit AutoSketch, or turn to Module 56, Scale, to continue the learning sequence.

Module 48
PROPERTY

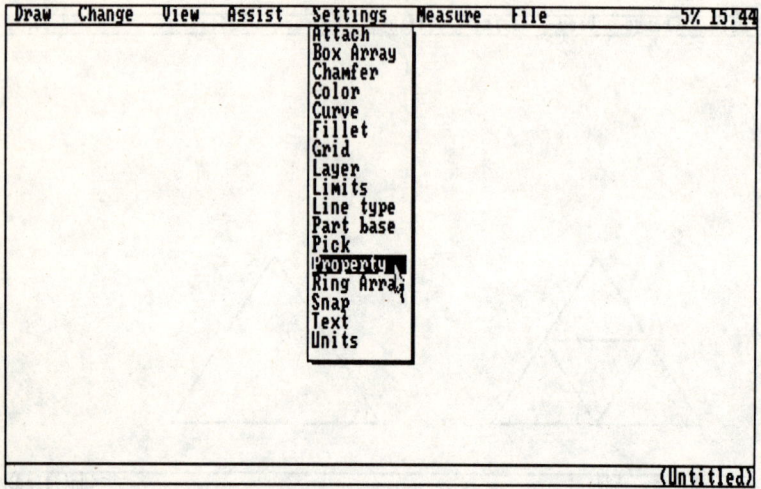

DESCRIPTION

The Propery command allows you to selectively change the color, layer, and line type of an object. First, pick the Property command on the Settings menu. The following dialogue box appears.

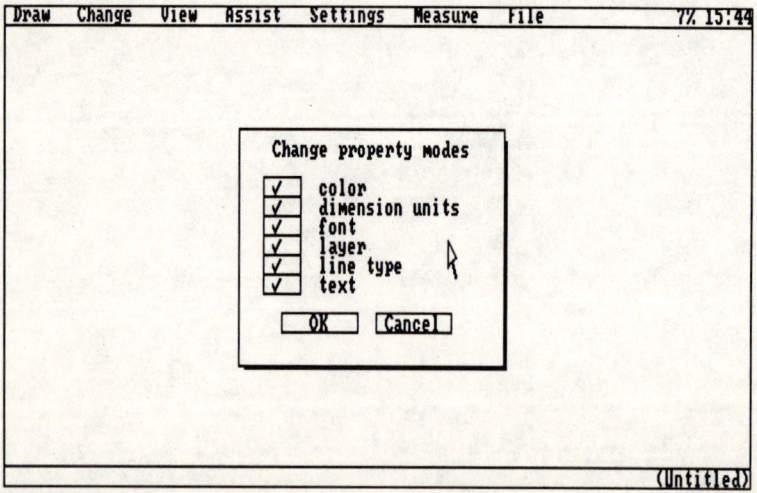

Pick the properties that you want to change. (A check mark next to the property indicates that the value will be changed.) Pick OK to close the dialogue box. Next, select the Property command from the Change menu. For each object that you select, the properties that you specify in the dialogue box become the current values and are used in drawing subject entities.

APPLICATION

If the world remained static, there would be little need for the Change command. However, changes are inevitable in the design process. You could make changes by deleting the incorrect portion of the drawing and creating a new, correct version. It is easier to use the Change command to modify the characteristics of the entity, retaining as much of the previous work as possible.

TYPICAL OPERATION

In this session you draw a box and a circle and then use variations of the Change command to modify them.

1. Begin a new drawing.

2. Pick **Circle** from the Draw menu. Type **6,4.5** as the center point and press **Enter**. Type **6,6** as a point on the circle and press **Enter**.

3. Pick **Box** from the Draw menu. Type **5,4** as the first corner and press **Enter**. Type **7,6** as the second corner and press **Enter**.

4. Pick **Layer** from the Settings menu. Pick **2** as the current layer. Then pick **OK**.

5. Pick **Line type** from the Settings menu. Pick **Dashed** on the dialogue box, then pick **OK**.

6. Pick **Property** from the Settings menu. By default, each property is checked. Pick **Change color** and **Change layer**, removing the associated check marks.

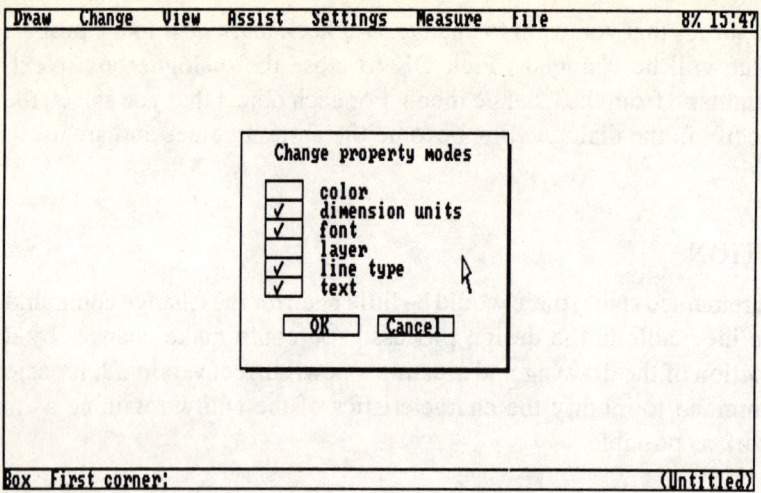

7. Pick **OK**

8. Pick **Property** from the Change menu.

9. Pick the circle. The line type changes to a dashed line.

10. Pick **Property** from the Settings menu.

11. Pick **Layer**.

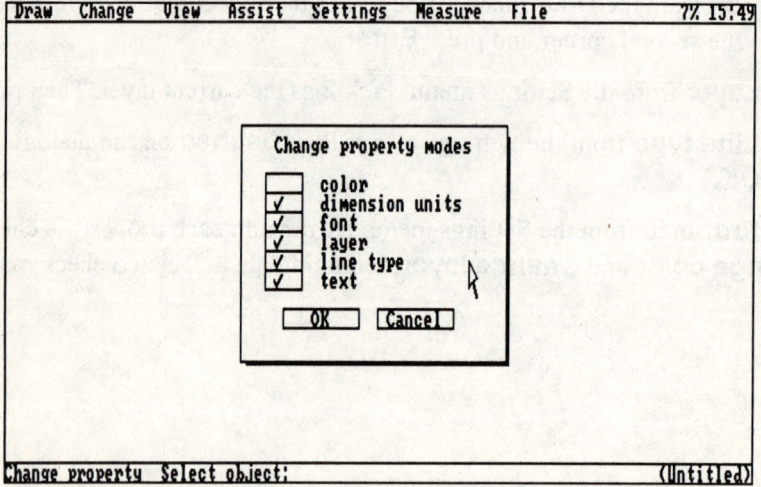

12. Pick **OK**.

13. Pick **Property** from the Change menu.

14. Pick the box. The Line type changes to a dashed line.

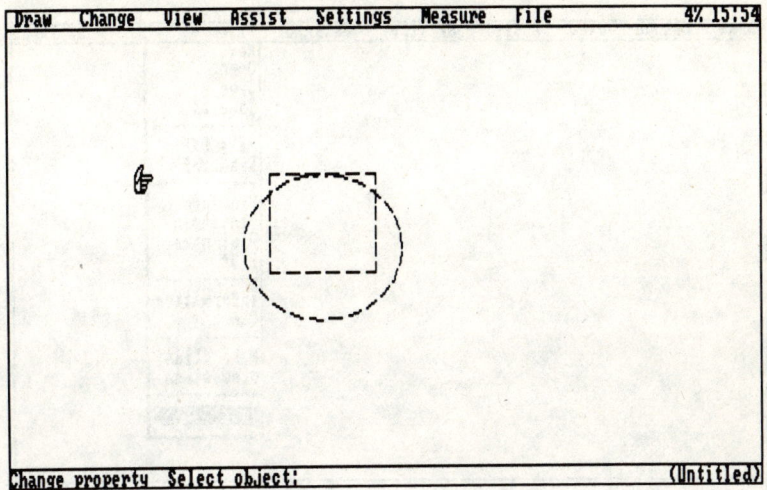

15. Pick **Save as** from the File menu, type **Property** as the File name, press **Enter**, then pick **OK**.

16. Quit AutoSketch, or turn to Module 57, Show Properties, to continue the learning sequence.

Module 49
QUIT

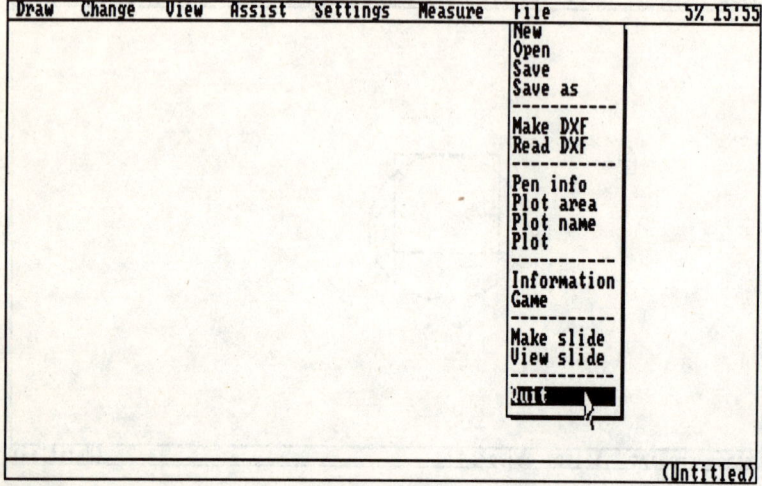

DESCRIPTION

The Quit command, located on the File menu, leaves the drawing screen and returns to DOS.

If the drawing has been modified, you must specify whether you want to Save or Discard the changes, or Cancel the Quit command, as shown in the following screen.

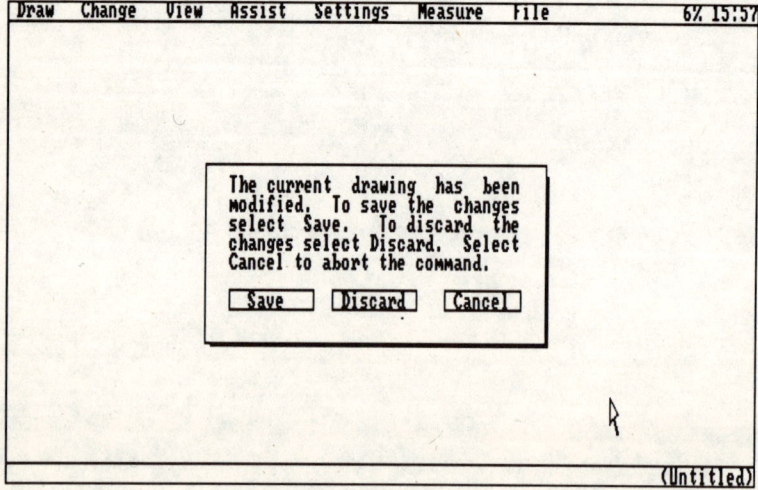

APPLICATIONS

Use the Quit command when you are done working with AutoSketch and want to use other computer applications. Use the New command to completely erase the existing drawing and reset the drawing environment.

TYPICAL OPERATION

In this operation the QUIT command is used to exit the drawing screen.

1. Begin a new drawing.

2. Pick **Line** from the Draw menu.

3. Type **1,1** and press **Enter**.

4. Type **4,4** and press **Enter**.

5. Pick **Quit** from the File menu.

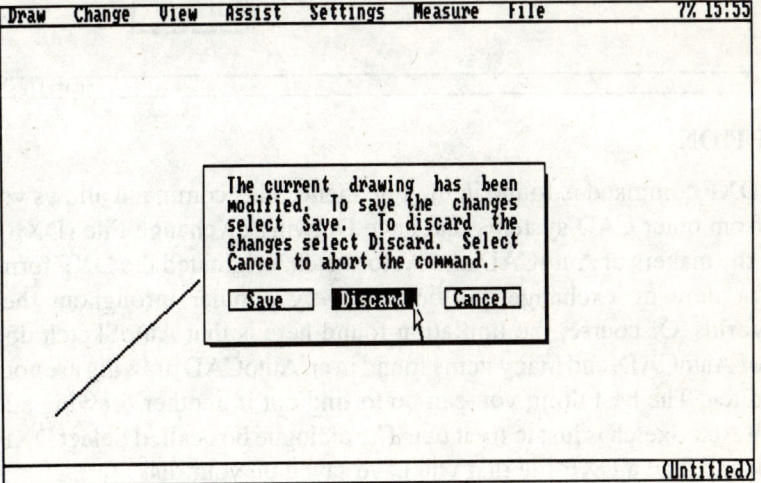

6. Pick **Discard**.

7. Turn to Module 26, Information, to continue the learning sequence.

Module 50
READ DXF

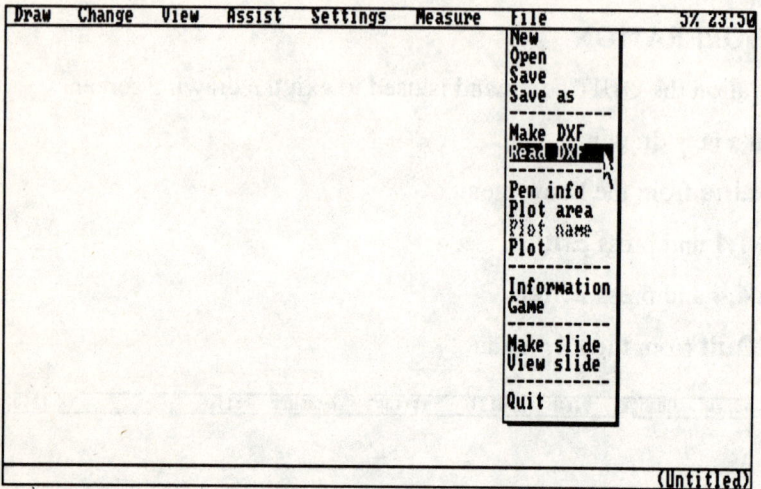

DESCRIPTION

The Read DXF command is found in the File menu. This command allows you to import drawings from other CAD systems that have Drawing eXchange File (DXF) capability. Autodesk, the makers of AutoCAD and AutoSketch, originated the DXF format, and this protocol for drawing exchange has become very popular throughout the CAD and graphics worlds. Of course, the limitation found here is that AutoSketch does not have the power of AutoCAD, and many items found in an AutoCAD drawing are not understood by AutoSketch. The best thing you can do to find out if another drawing's DXF output can work in AutoSketch is just to try it out. The dialogue box called Select DXF file allows you to pick and load a DXF file that you have saved on your disk.

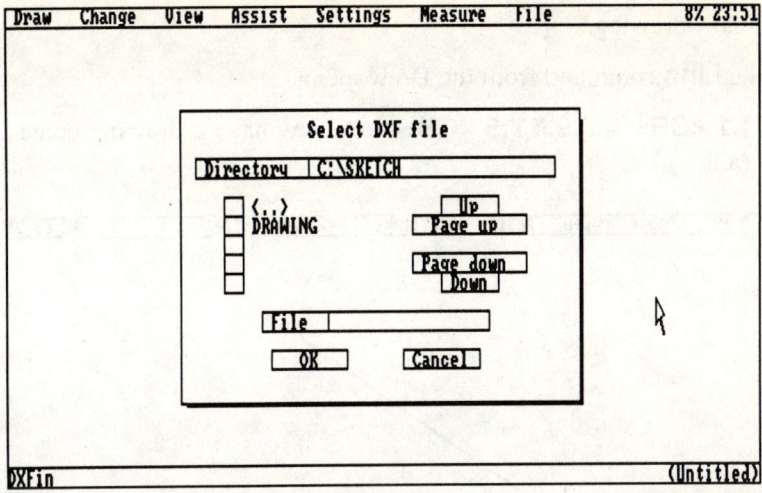

It is very clear that you must already have a DXF file saved on your disk to be able to use the Read DXF command. If you pick in the Directory box, you can then type in the directory and filename of the DXF file you want to read into AutoSketch. You can scroll through the DXF files that exist in the directory by using the Up, Page up, Page down, and/or Down boxes. If any directories are listed, they are surrounded by angle brackets (<>). If you want to pick the parent of the current directory, pick the item that appears as <..>.

Near the bottom of the dialogue box you see the File box. This is either empty or lists the last drawing opened. When you pick a new file it is automatically listed in the File box. After you have successfully picked the file you want to read into AutoSketch, pick the OK box at the bottom of the box.

APPLICATIONS

The Read DXF command is useful for taking drawings from other CAD systems such as AutoCAD and converting them into an AutoSketch drawing. If you only have AutoSketch capability at home and AutoCAD at your office, you can do some converting back and forth as long as you consider how much more powerful and complex AutoCAD is as compared to AutoSketch. It always works better to go from AutoSketch to AutoCAD than the other way around.

TYPICAL OPERATION

In this activity, you make a simple AutoSketch drawing and convert it to a DXF file using the Make DXF command. Then you use the Read DXF command to turn the file back into an AutoSketch drawing.

1. Start a new drawing.

2. Pick the **Line** command from the Draw menu.

3. Type **1.1 <CR>** and **9.5,7.5 <CR>**. You now have a drawing consisting of one entity (a line).

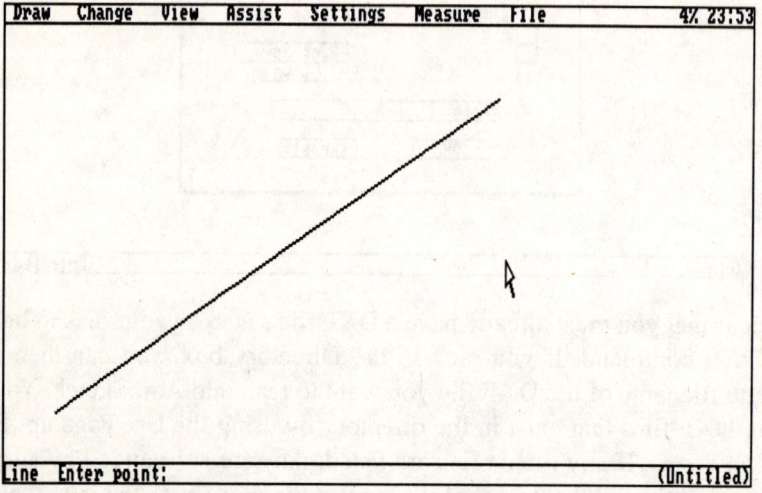

4. Pick **Make DXF** from the File menu.

5. Pick in the File name box and type **VECTOR <CR>**.

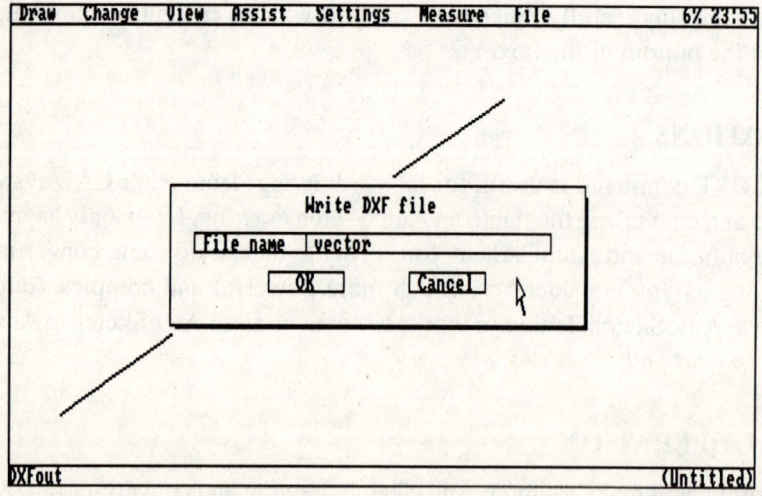

6. After you are satisfied that your dialogue box matches the one shown above, pick **OK**.

7. Pick **Quit** from the File menu.

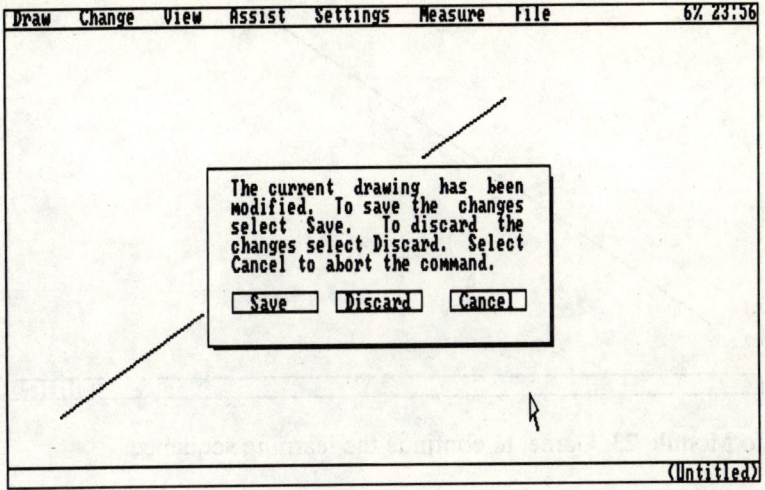

8. Pick **Discard** from the dialogue box to quit without saving the drawing as a .SKD file (we have already saved it as a .DXF file with the Make DXF command).

9. Restart AutoSketch and begin a new drawing again.

10. Pick **Read DXF** from the File menu.

11. Pick in the box next to the filename VECTOR. Notice that the word VECTOR is now in the File box.

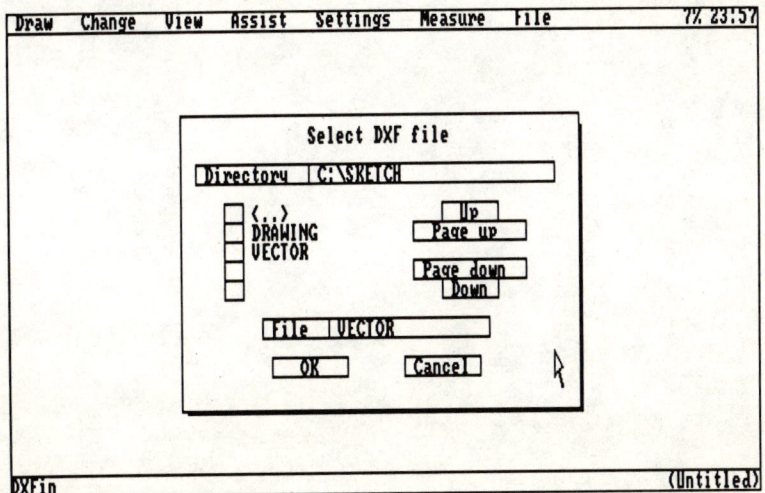

12. When you are satisfied with your dialogue box, pick **OK**.

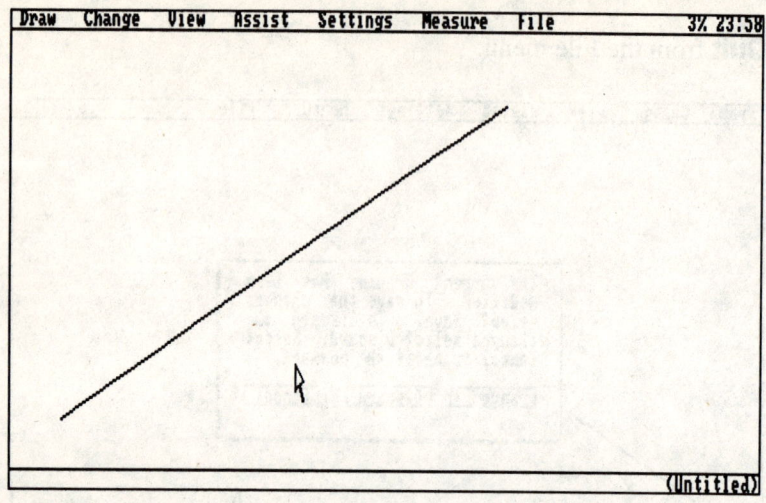

13. Turn to Module 23, Game, to continue the learning sequence.

Module 51
REDO

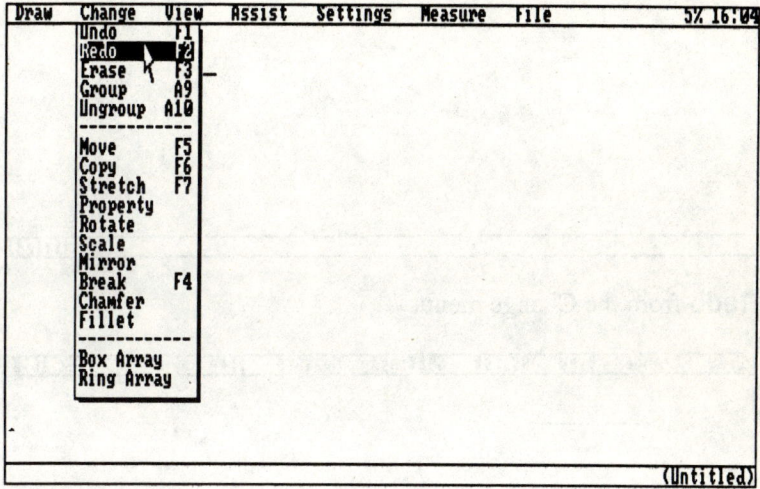

DESCRIPTION

The Redo command, located on the Change menu or activated by pressing F2, is used in combination with the Undo command to replace entities that have been undone. The Redo command is always used immediately following an Undo operation. Otherwise, it has no effect.

APPLICATIONS

The only application for Redo is to reverse an Undo operation. The Undo-Redo command pair gives you the freedom to experiment without worrying about permanent contamination of your work, especially when trying new construction techniques.

TYPICAL OPERATION

In this activity you use Redo to restore work that was erased in the previous module. Continue the work session you begin in Module 61, Undo. Your screen shows the following display.

```
Draw   Change   View   Assist   Settings   Measure   File          4% 16:05
┌─────────────────────────────────────────────────────────────────────────┐
│          ── ──                                                            │
│                                                                          │
│                               ↖                                          │
│                                                                          │
│                                                                          │
│                                                                          │
│                                                                          │
│                                                                          │
│                                                                          │
│                                                                          │
│                                                                          │
│                                                                          │
│                                                            (Untitled)    │
└─────────────────────────────────────────────────────────────────────────┘
```

1. Pick **Redo** from the Change menu.

```
Draw   Change   View   Assist   Settings   Measure   File          4% 16:04
┌─────────────────────────────────────────────────────────────────────────┐
│          ── ──                                                            │
│                                                                          │
│          ────                                                            │
│                               ↖                                          │
│                                                                          │
│                                                                          │
│                                                                          │
│                                                                          │
│                                                                          │
│                                                                          │
│                                                                          │
│                                                            (Untitled)    │
└─────────────────────────────────────────────────────────────────────────┘
```

2. Pick **Redo** again from the Change menu.

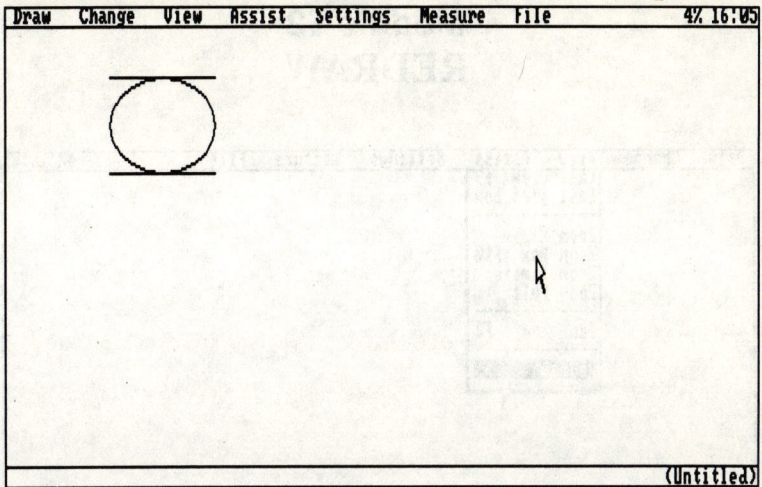

3. Quit AutoSketch, or turn to Module 15, Copy, to continue the learning sequence.

Module 52
REDRAW

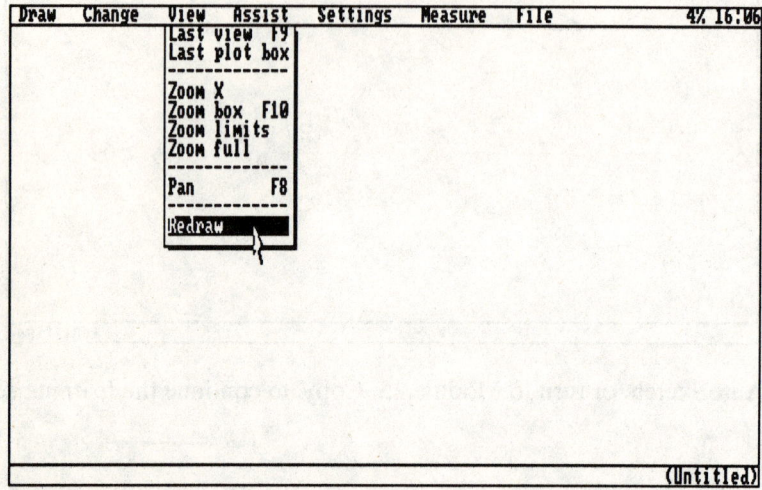

DESCRIPTION

The Redraw command, located on the View menu, refreshes your screen, eliminating blips and remnants of incomplete constructions and erasures.

When picking points on the screen, AutoSketch displays "blips" to designate the position of the point. These small crosses are not actually a part of the drawing; they are used only for visual reference. They are not saved on the disk nor do they appear in a plot. However, the blips can be distracting and are easily removed with Redraw.

APPLICATIONS

When you perform an Erase, Move, or Copy operation with the drawing Grid on, AutoSketch does not regenerate portions of the Grid that are removed. To clean up the drawing, use the Redraw command.

TYPICAL OPERATION

In this session you use Redraw to clean up the appearance of your screen.

1. Start a new AutoSketch drawing.

2. Pick **Box** from the Draw menu. Type **1,1** as the First corner and press **Enter**. Type **6,6** as the Second corner and press **Enter**.

3. Pick **Copy** from the Change menu. Pick the box. Type **1,1 <CR>** as the first reference point and type **6,1 <CR>** as the second point.

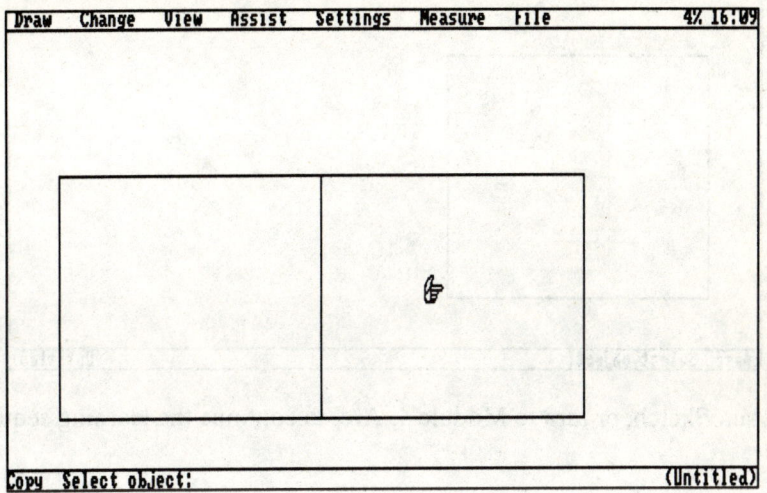

4. Pick **Erase** from the Change menu.

5. Pick the rightmost box anywhere but on the common side. The box is erased, along with the right side of the original figure.

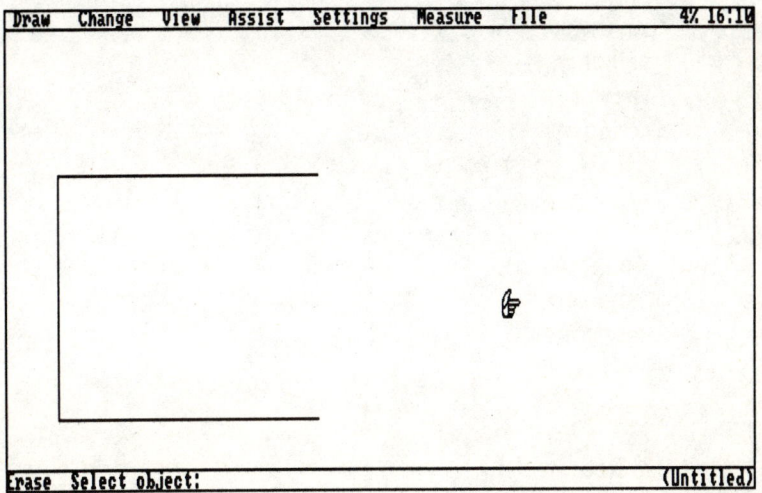

6. Pick **Redraw** from the View menu.

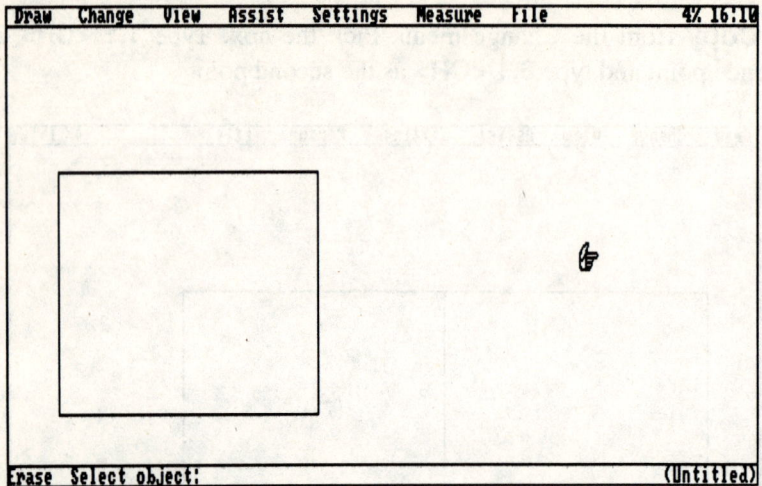

7. Quit AutoSketch, or turn to Module 4, Arc, to continue the learning sequence.

Module 53
RING ARRAY

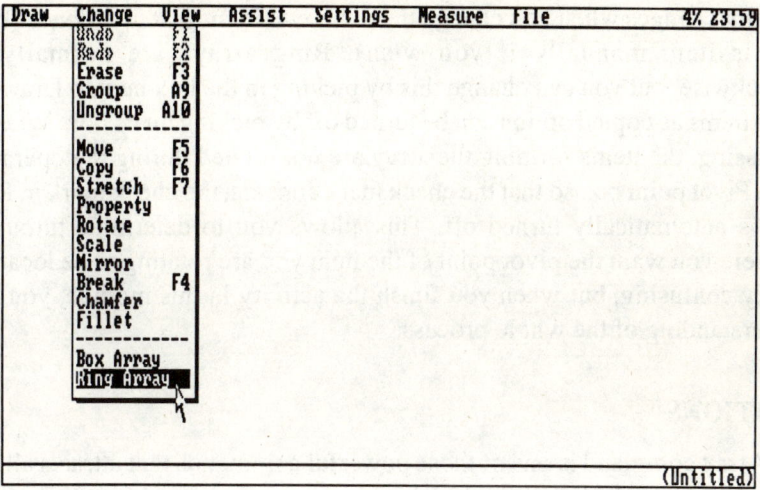

DESCRIPTION

The Ring Array command is located in the Change and Settings menu. The Ring Array is known as a polar array in some other CAD systems. This command produces multiple copies of objects in a circular pattern.

The Ring Array dialogue box is the key to controlling this command. You see this dialogue box when you pick Ring Array from the Settings menu.

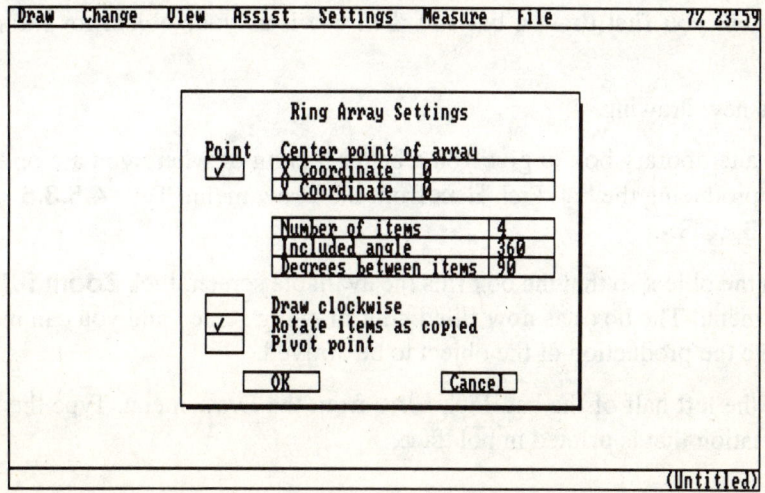

As you can see from this dialogue box, there are many settings that can be altered before completing a ring array. The center point of array setting is usually accomplished by pointing to its center during the actual production of the array. It is also possible to enter the X and Y values of the array center in this dialogue box, but it is usually not done in this way during practical use of the command. When using this command, you usually need to change the Number of items and the included angle. The Degrees between items automatically changes when you change the other two items just mentioned (but, you can change this item manually if you wish). Ring arrays are normally produced counterclockwise, but you can change this by picking in the box next to Draw clockwise. The Rotate items as copied option can be turned off by picking on its box. When the check mark is missing, the items forming the array are not rotated during the operation. If you pick on the Pivot point box so that the check mark appears, the check mark in Rotate items as copied is automatically turned off. This allows you to determine through picking, exactly where you want the pivot point of the item you are rotating to be located. This all sounds very confusing, but when you finish the activity in this module, you will have a better understanding of the whole process.

APPLICATIONS

The Ring Array command is one of those powerful commands that attracts all of us to use CAD in the first place. It eliminates the laborious process of drawing bolt circles and other circular patterns that designers and drafters need to do on a daily basis. As an example, if you were designing a new cast aluminum wheel for an exotic sports car, you would only need to draw one of the spokes and one of the lug nuts. The Ring Array would repeat the items drawn into a circular pattern automatically and presto, the most time consuming part of drawing the wheel is complete.

TYPICAL OPERATION

In this session, you first draw a bat and then use it as your object for the ring array operations.

1. Start a new drawing.

2. Draw a temporary box to give you a better feeling of where you are on the screen while producing the bat. Pick **Box** from the Draw menu. Type **4.5,3.5 <CR>** and **7.5,6.5 <CR>**.

3. Zoom the object so that the box fills the available screen. Pick **Zoom full** from the View menu. The box has now filled your drawing screen and you can more easily observe the production of the object to be arrayed.

4. Draw the left half of the bat. Pick **Line** from the Draw menu. Type the following information that is printed in boldface:

Line Enter point: **6,5.1 <CR>**
Line To point: **5.95,5.1 <CR>**
Line Enter point: **/LPOINT <CR>**
Line To point: **5.9,5.2 <CR>**
Line Enter point: **/LPOINT <CR>**
Line To point: **5.9,4.95 <CR>**
Line Enter point: **/LPOINT <CR>**
Line To point: **5.45,5.1 <CR>**
Line Enter point: **/LPOINT <CR>**
Line To point: **5.4,5 <CR>**
Line Enter point: **/LPOINT <CR>**
Line To point: **5.45,4.65 <CR>**
Line Enter point: **/LPOINT <CR>**
Line To point: **5.55,4.8 <CR>**
Line Enter point: **/LPOINT <CR>**
Line To point: **5.65,4.5 <CR>**
Line Enter point: **/LPOINT <CR>**
Line To point: **5.75,4.65 <CR>**
Line Enter point: **/LPOINT <CR>**
Line To point: **5.85,4.45 <CR>**
Line Enter point: **/LPOINT <CR>**
Line To point: **5.9,4.6 <CR>**
Line Enter point: **/LPOINT <CR>**
Line To point: **6,4.6 <CR>**

5. Now mirror the object to complete the bat. Pick **Mirror** from the Change menu. Type **5,4 <CR>** and **6.5,5.5 <CR>**. Type **6,5.1 <CR>** and **6,4.6 <CR>**.

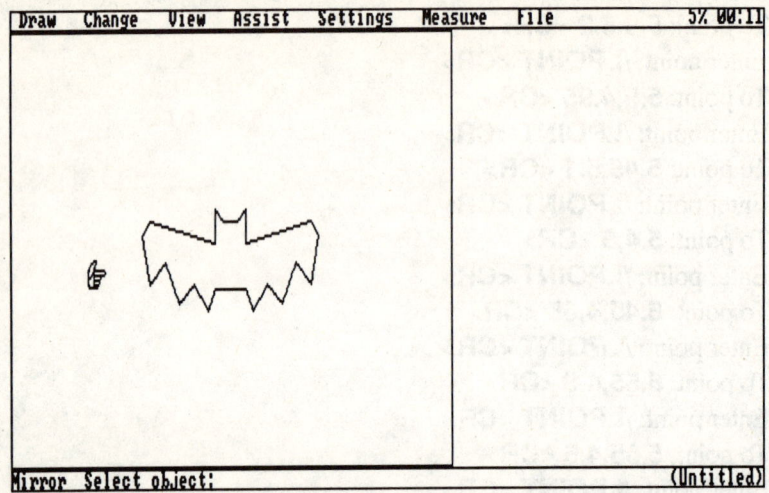

6. Erase the temporary box. Pick **Erase** from the Change menu. Type **7.5,6.5 <CR>** to select the box to be erased.

7. Now zoom the screen to the dimensions of its limits. Pick **Zoom limits** from the View menu. It now becomes very clear why we zoomed in to a smaller area of the screen to draw the bat. Without zooming, you would not have been able to observe the drawing activities very easily.

8. Now produce a ring array counterclockwise with the object rotating as it is arrayed. Pick **Ring Array** from the Settings menu. Pick in the Number of items box. Type **10 <CR>**. Pick in the Included angle box. Type **180 <CR>**.

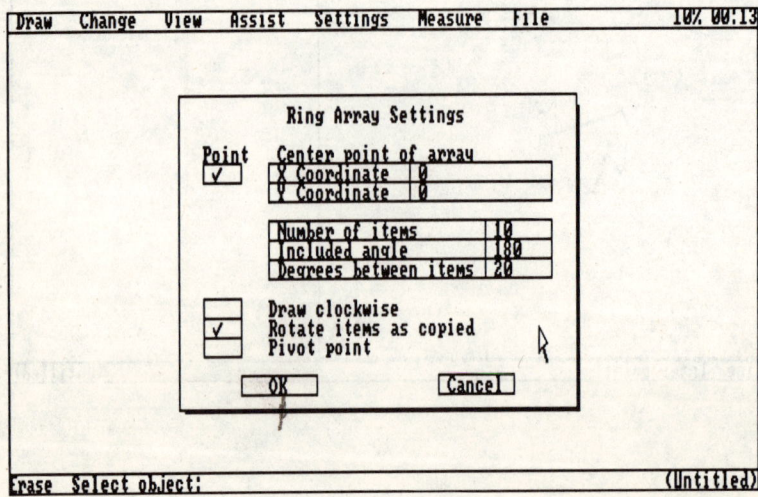

9. Check to make sure that your changes result in a dialogue box that is set as shown above. After you are satisfied, pick **OK**.

10. Pick **Ring Array** from the Change menu. The object is selected by placing a box around it. Type **5,4 <CR>** and **7,6 <CR>**.

11. Pick the center point of the array by typing **3.5,5 <CR>**. Finish the operation by picking **Accept**.

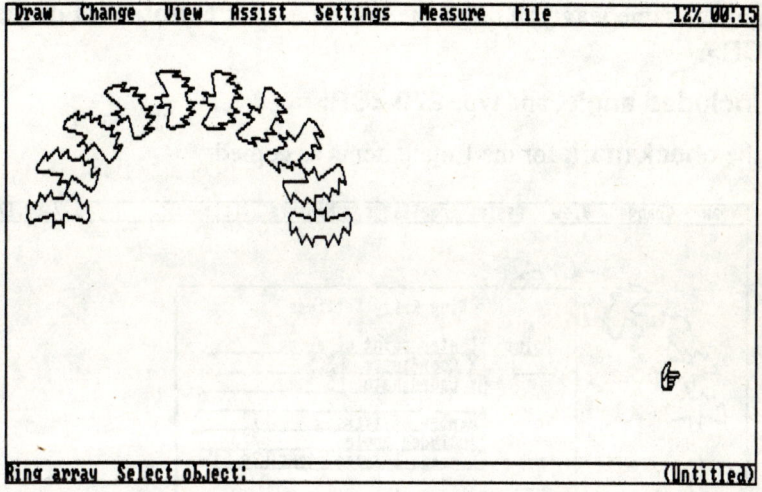

Real scary, right?

12. Now produce a counterclockwise array without rotating as it is generated. Pick **Ring Array** from the Settings menu.

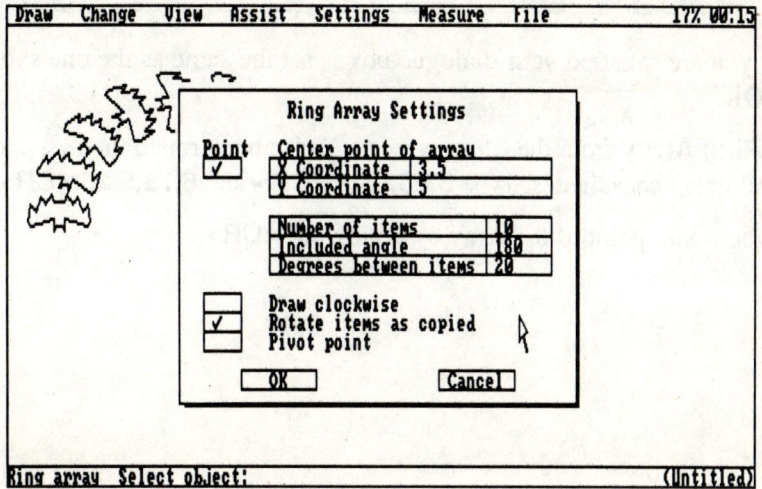

NOTE

Notice that the dialogue box now contains the X and Y coordinates of where we picked for the center of the last array produced. When you pick on the screen for the next center, this is automatically updated. The box also contains all the information needed to produce the last array that was completed.

13. Now change the information in the Ring Array Settings dialogue box. Do these changes the same way you did it the last time. Pick **Number of items**, and type **12 <CR>**.

14. Pick **Included angle**, and type **270 <CR>**.

15. Pick the **check mark** for the Rotate items as copied.

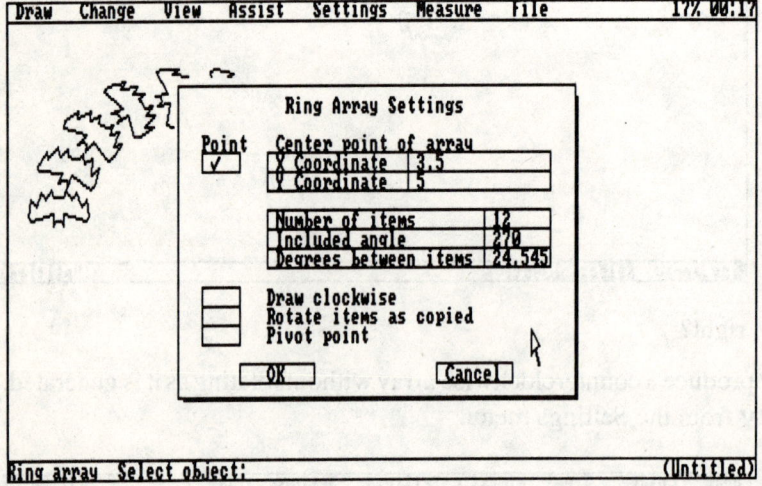

16. After you are satisfied your dialogue box is set the same as the one shown above, pick **OK**.

17. Pick **Ring Array** from the Change menu. Pick a box around the first bat by typing the following coordinates. Type **5.25,4.25 <CR>** and **6.75,5.25 <CR>**.

18. Pick the center point of the array by typing **9,4 <CR>**.

19. Pick **Accept**.

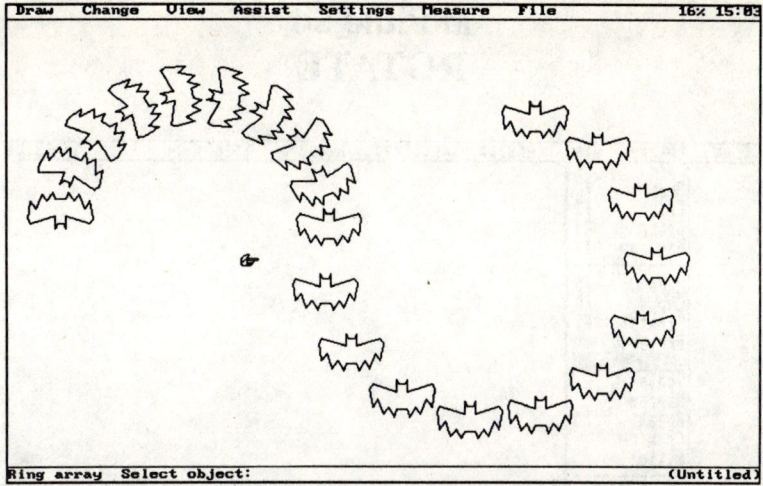

20. As you can see from this activity, the Ring Array command is a very powerful drawing tool. Do some more experimenting with this command, keeping in mind that it can increase your drawing productivity more if you understand it well.

21. Turn to Module 32, Line Type, to continue the learning sequence.

Module 54
ROTATE

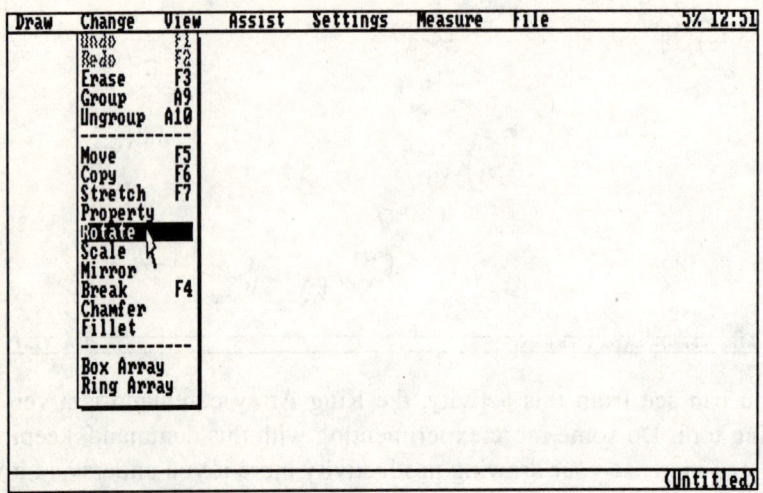

DESCRIPTION

The Rotate command on the Change menu rotates an object or group of objects around a point. First, you select the objects to rotate using any object selection method. Next, you pick a base point. The base point may be anywhere on the drawing. It does not have to be on or inside the object to rotate. You may rotate an object around itself, or you may rotate it around some external point. The amount of the rotation is specified in two ways.

Number	You can type the measure of an angle using polar coordinates.
Drag	You can drag the angle. The dragging is relative to the base point you previously specified.

APPLICATIONS

Object rotation lets you rotate selected portions of a drawing without having to define the objects as a group and insert the group with rotation. This saves steps and allows the original objects to remain single entities, rather than become part of a group.

TYPICAL OPERATION

In this session you create a logo, rotating it to several orientations.

1. Start AutoSketch and select **Open** from the File menu. Open the drawing SCALE that you created in the Scale module.

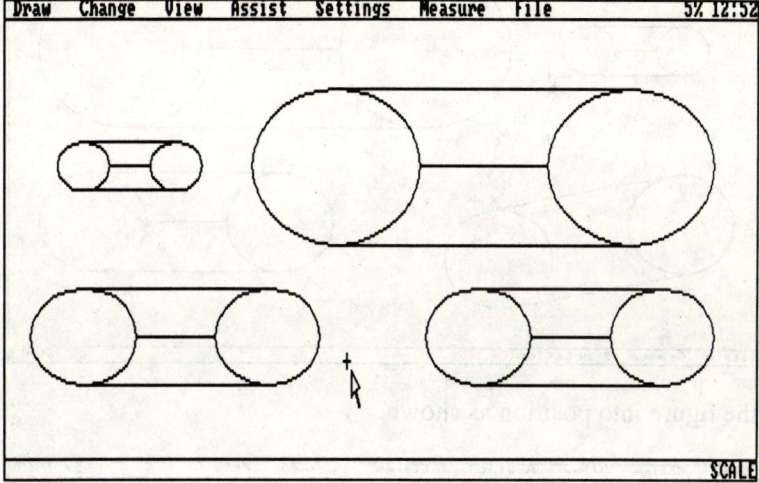

2. Pick **Rotate** from the Change menu. Enclose the lower left figure in a selection box. Pick the center of the left circle as the rotation point. Drag the figure to the position in the following screen.

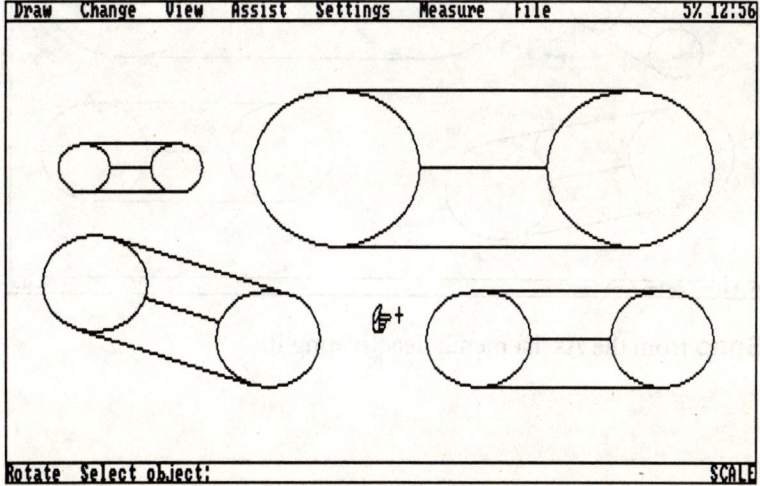

3. Enclose the upper left figure in a selection box. Pick the center of rotation to the left of the figure, as shown in the following screen.

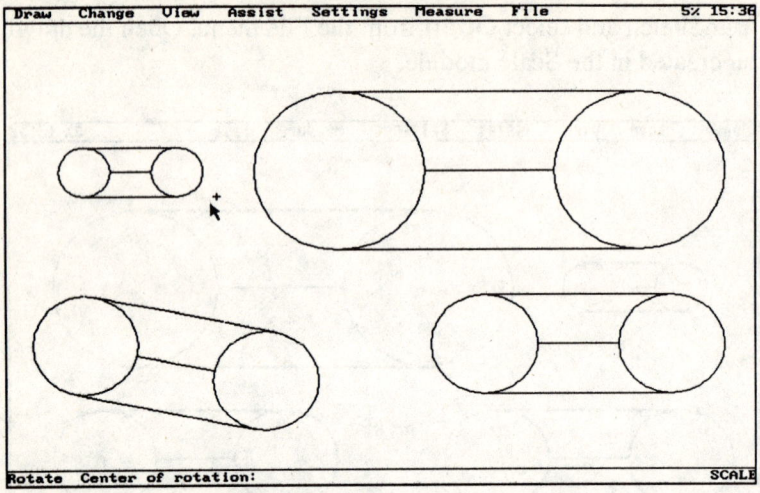

4. Drag the figure into position as shown.

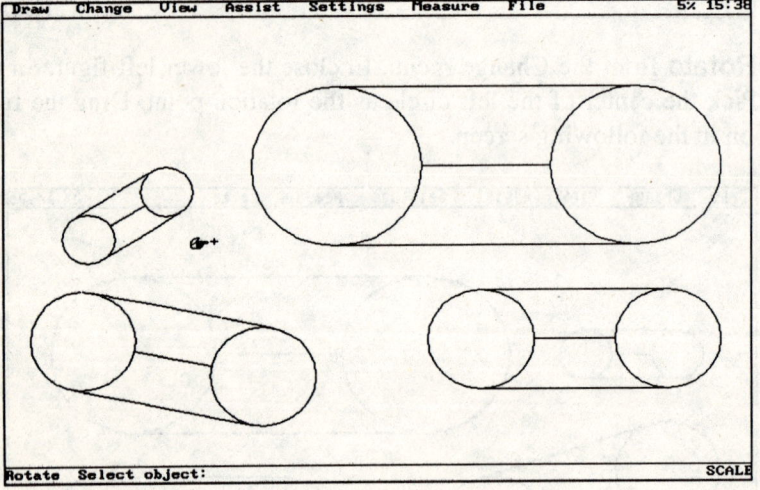

5. Pick **Snap** from the Assist menu, deactivating it.

6. Enclose the lower right figure in a selection box. Pick the center of rotation at the 4 o'clock position on the left circle as shown. Type **P(1,317)** and press **Enter** to specify the rotation in the Polar coordinate system.

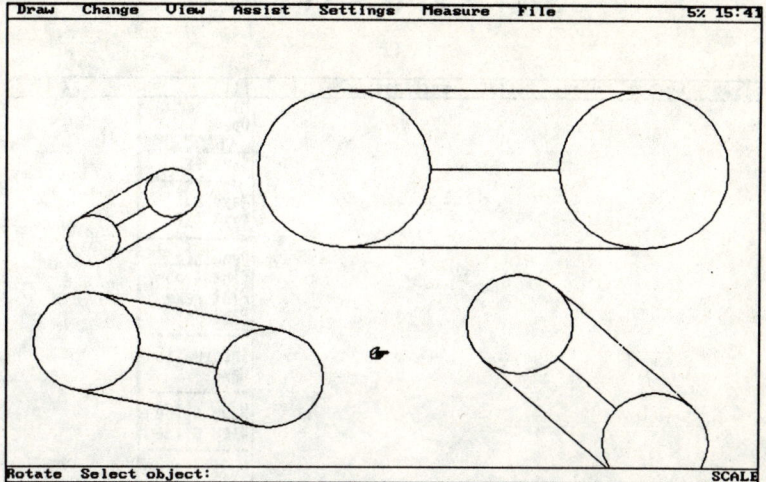

7. Pick **Quit** from the File menu, or turn to Module 35, Mirror, to continue the learning sequence.

Module 55
SAVE and SAVE AS

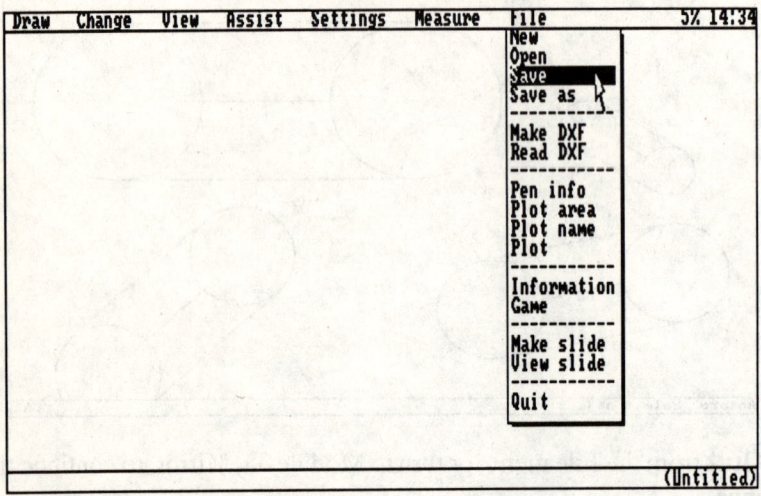

DESCRIPTION

The Save command, located on the File menu, allows you to save your AutoSketch drawing using its current name. The Save as command allows you to specify the name for a newly created file, or to change the name for a modified version of an existing file. When you pick Save as, the following dialogue box is displayed.

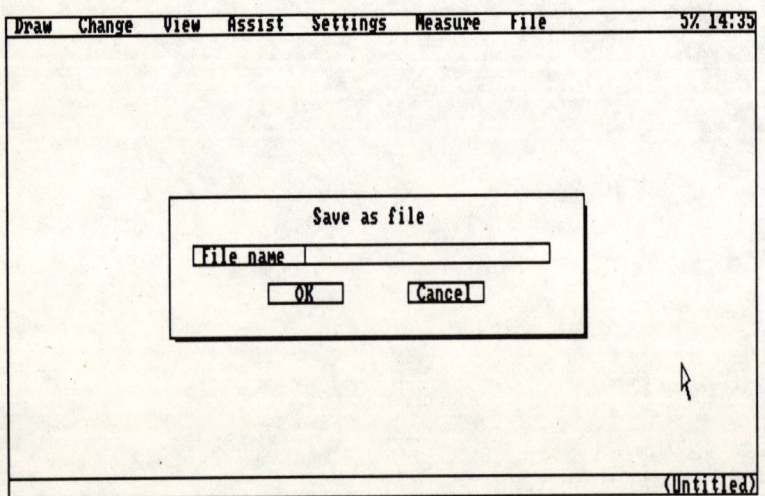

Pick the File name box to the right of the words "File name," type the desired file name, accept the file name by pressing Enter or picking OK, then pick OK to accept the save operation.

The Save command does not display a dialogue box. It saves the drawing using name used when the drawing file was opened, or the name assigned with the Save as command.

APPLICATIONS

The Save command provides protection against power failures, hardware failures, and human error. Saving your work often is an excellent insurance policy.

TYPICAL OPERATION

In this activity you draw a triangle and save the drawing on the disk.

1. Begin a new AutoSketch drawing.

2. Pick **Line** from the Draw menu.

3. Type **1,1 <CR>** as the first point and **5,5 <CR>** as the second point.

4. Type **/LPOINT** as the first point and **10,1 <CR>** as the second point.

5. Pick **Save as** from the File menu.

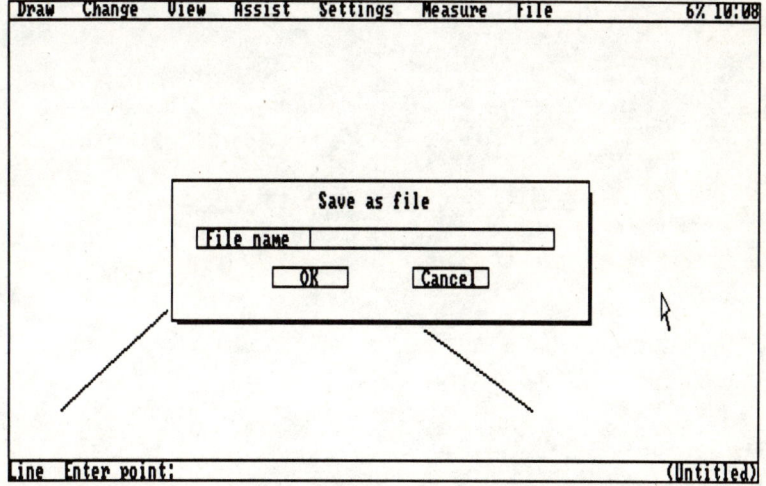

6. Pick the box to the right of File name, then type **TRIANGLE** as the file name, press **Enter**, and pick **OK** in the dialogue box.

7. Pick **Line** from the Draw menu. Type **10,1 <CR>** as the first point and **1,1 <CR>** as the second point.

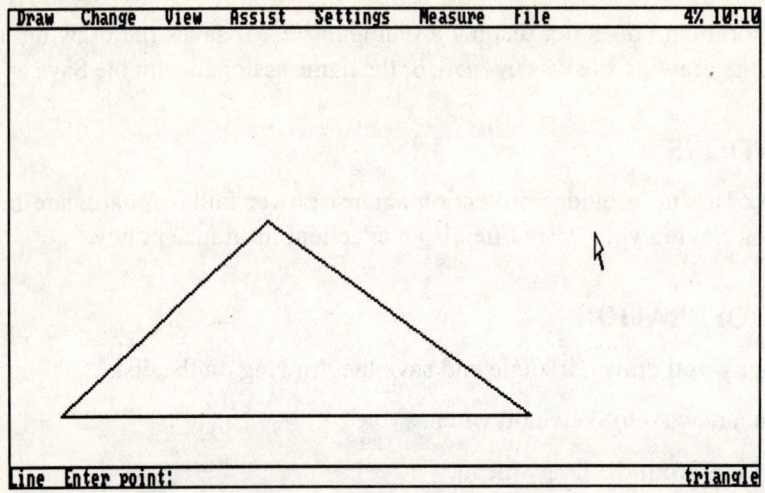

8. Pick **Save** from the File menu.

9. Quit AutoSketch, or turn to Module 38, Open, to continue the learning sequence.

Module 56
SCALE

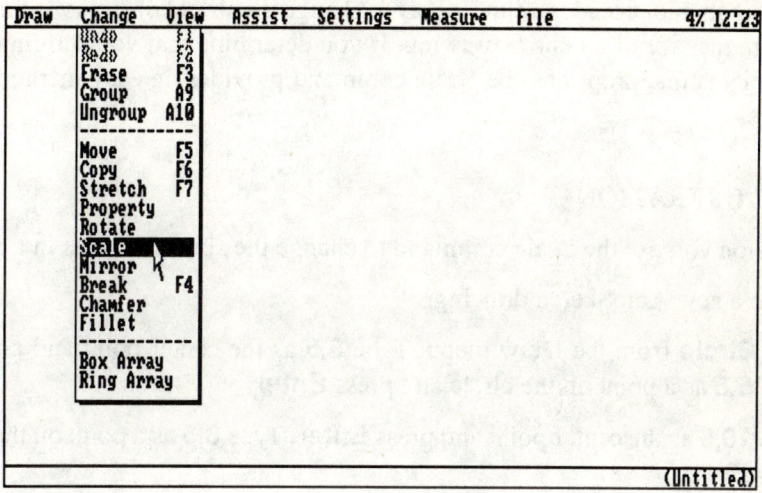

DESCRIPTION

The Scale command lets you re-size anything from an entity to an entire drawing. To use Scale, you select any group of entities in the drawing for scaling. If you wish, you can enclose the entire drawing in a window and re-scale it. Next, you select a base point. The location of the base point remains constant after the scaling operation is complete. The location of all other points are re-computed with reference to the base point. The last prompt requests the scale factor or reference.

After picking the base point, move the screen cursor away from the base point in any direction to drag the scale factor. The numeric scale factor is displayed at the bottom of the screen in increments of .1. A scale factor of 1 does nothing. A scale factor less than 1 reduces the size of the drawing. A scale factor greater than 1 increases the size of the drawing.

The dragging is relative to the base point you previously specified. Dragging less than one drawing unit away from the base point reduces the drawing, dragging more than one drawing unit away from the base point enlarges the drawing. It does not matter which direction you move from the base point. The Scale command relates to the distance you move, not the direction.

One way to add accuracy to your specification of the scale factor is to activate Snap before picking the scale factor points, where the snap interval is set to an appropriate value. You may also specify the scale factor by typing a relative point specification for the scale.

APPLICATIONS

The Scale command provides a simple way to change the size of objects within a drawing, or to change the size of an entire drawing. If you determine that your original choice of drawing units is inappropriate, the Scale command provides an easy method to change your choice.

TYPICAL OPERATION

In this session you use the Scale command to change the size of entities in a drawing.

1. Begin a new AutoSketch drawing.

2. Pick **Circle** from the Draw menu. Type **3,5** as the center point and press **Enter**. Type **5,5** as a point on the circle and press **Enter**.

3. Type **10,5** as the center point and press **Enter**. Type **8,5** as a point on the circle and press **Enter**.

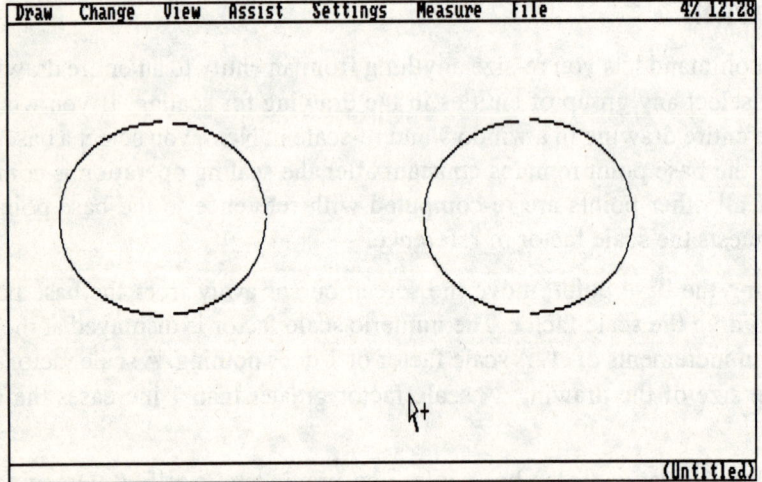

4. Activate **Snap** from the Assist menu.

5. Draw three lines connecting the circles as shown in the following screen.

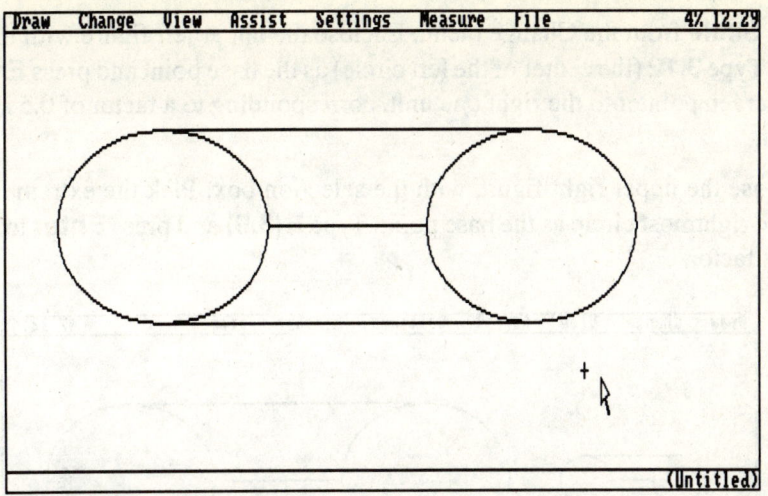

6. Pick **Limits** from the Settings menu.

7. Type **24** for Right and press **Enter**. Type **18** for Top and press **Enter**. Pick **OK**.

8. Pick **Zoom limits** from the View menu.

9. Pick **Copy** from the Change menu. Select the figure by enclosing it in a selection window. Type **3,5** as the base point and press **Enter**. Type **3,12** as the insertion point and press **Enter**.

10. Enclose both figures in a selection window. Type **3,5** as the base point and press **Enter**. Type **18,5** as the insertion point and press **Enter**.

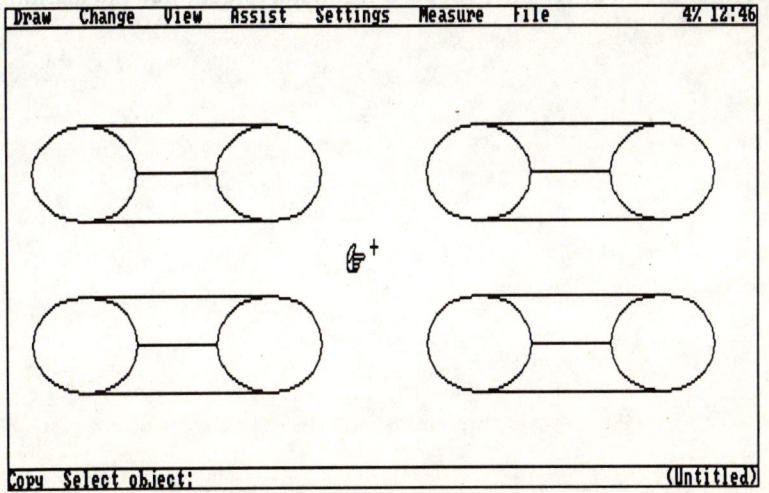

11. Pick **Scale** from the Change menu. Enclose the upper left figure with the selection box. Type **3,12** (the center of the left circle) as the base point and press **Enter**. Move the screen pointer to the right one unit, corresponding to a factor of 0.5 and pick the point.

12. Enclose the upper right figure with the selection box. Pick the extreme right point of the rightmost circle as the base point. Type **R(3,0)** and press **Enter** to specify the scale factor.

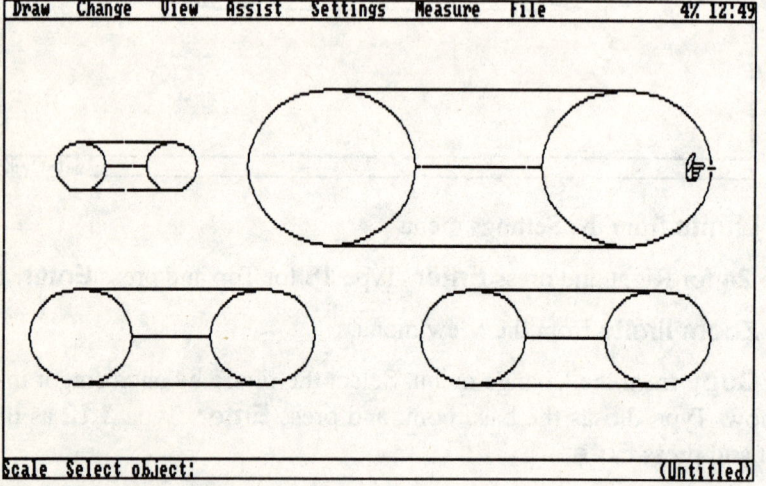

13. Save the drawing as SCALE.

14. Quit AutoSketch, or turn to Module 54, Rotate, to continue the learning sequence.

Module 57
SHOW PROPERTIES

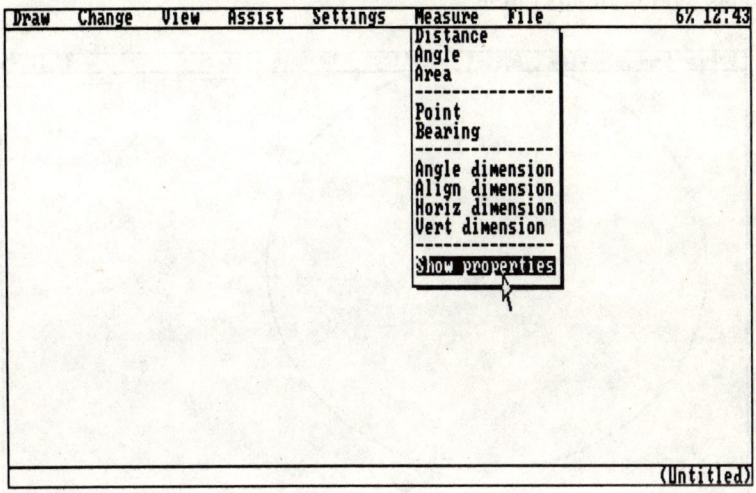

DESCRIPTION

The Show properties command, located on the Measure menu allows you to inspect the object type, layer, color, and line type of any drawing entity. When you select Show properties and pick an entity, the following dialogue box appears.

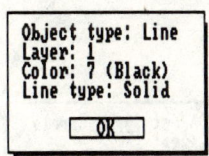

After inspecting the characteristics of the drawing entity, pick OK to return to your drawing activities.

APPLICATIONS

When working with multiple layers, colors, and linetypes, it is easy to become confused about the properties of an object—especially if you use a monochrome monitor. Use the Show properties command to inspect the object type, color, layer, and line type. Use the Property command on the Settings menu to change the values of these characteristics.

TYPICAL OPERATION

In this session you examine the properties of a drawing entity.

1. Begin a new AutoSketch drawing

2. Pick **Circle** from the Draw menu. Type **5,5 <CR>** as the center point and type **8,8 <CR>** as a point on the circle.

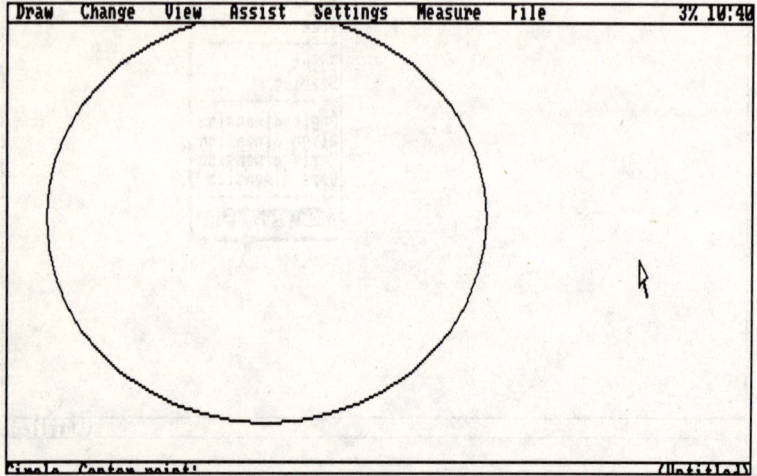

3. Pick **Show Properties** from the Measure menu. Then pick the circle.

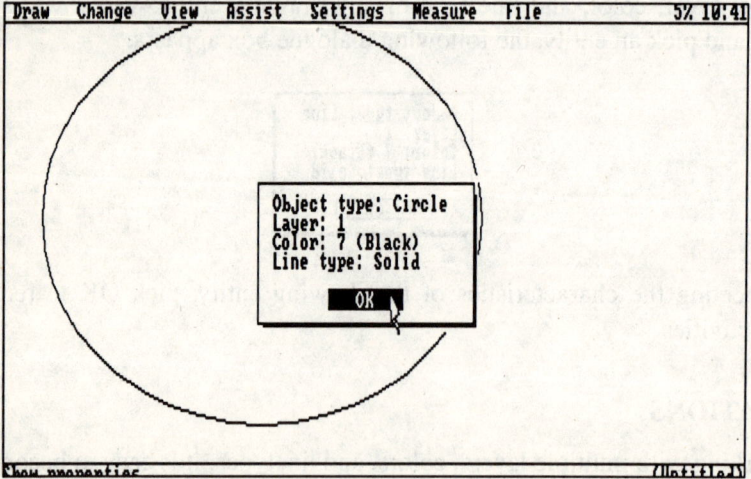

4. Pick **OK**.

5. Quit AutoSketch, or turn to Module 17, Dimension to continue the learning sequence.

Module 58
SNAP

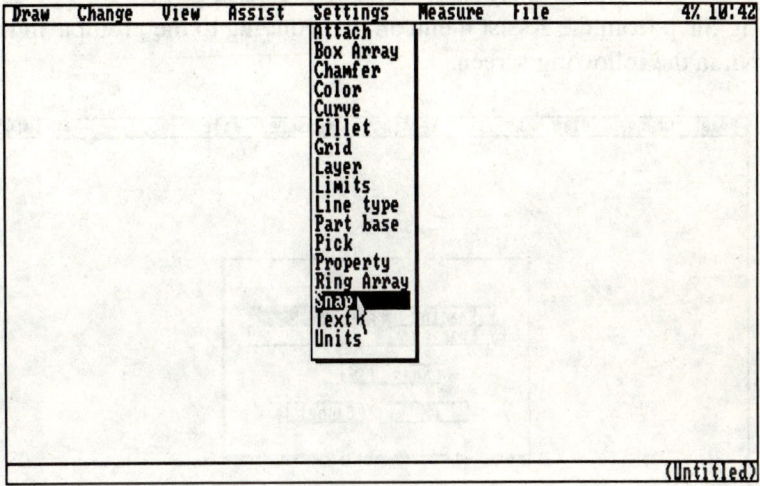

DESCRIPTION

Select Snap from the Settings menu to establish the Snap X Spacing and Y Spacing. The following dialogue box appears.

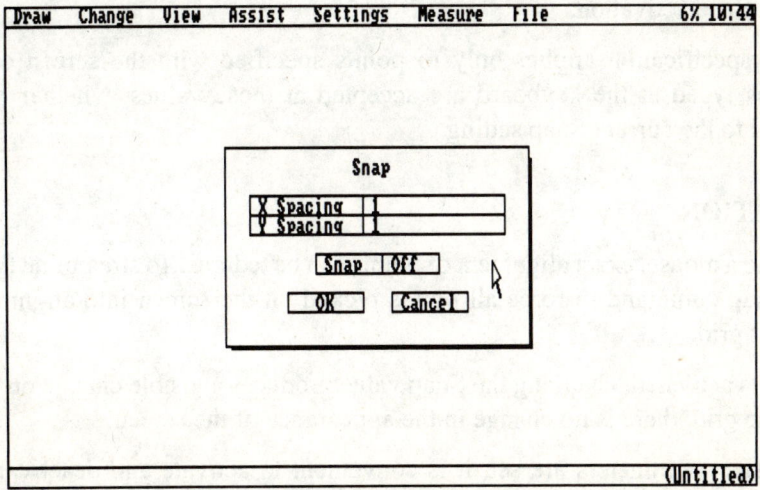

The default values of 1 for X spacing and Y spacing can by changed by picking the desired value box, typing the new value, and pressing Enter or picking OK. When you specify a value for X Spacing, the value is automatically carried forward to the Y Spacing setting. Typically, this is the way you work. If you want a different Y Setting, you may Pick Y Spacing, type the desired value, and press Enter or pick OK.

Turn Snap on or off from the Snap dialog box on the Settings menu, by pressing Alt-F4, or by picking Snap from the Assist menu and responding to the prompts in the dialogue box as shown in the following screen.

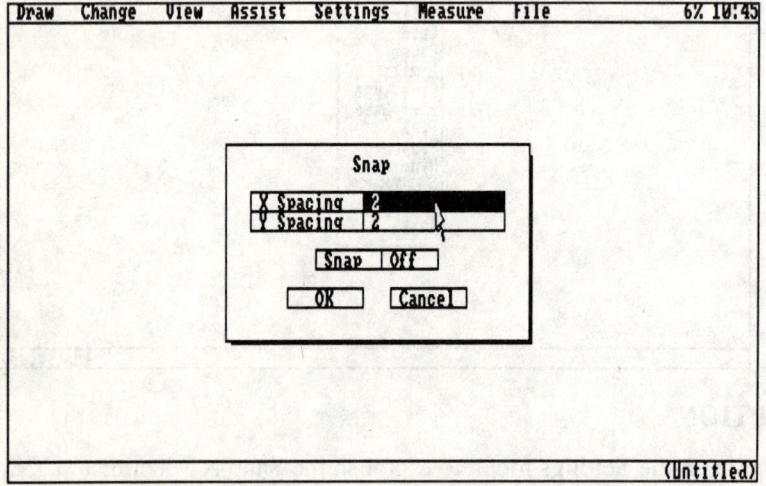

When you turn snap off, the values chosen for the X and Y spacing are retained for use at the next Snap activation.

The Snap specification applies only to points specified with the screen cursor. Any coordinates typed at the keyboard are accepted at those values, whether or not they correspond to the current Snap setting.

APPLICATION

When using a mouse, exact alignment of points can be tedious. To streamline this process, use the Snap command to force all points picked on the screen into alignment with a rectangular grid.

If the grid is activated, changing the Snap value produces a visible change on the screen. Without the grid, there is no change in the appearance of the screen.

Once the snap parameters are set, it is convenient to activate and deactivate Snap by pressing Alt-F4.

You can press Alt-F4 or pick Snap from the Assist menu to activate or deactivate Snap while performing another command. For example, in drawing a series of lines, you could turn Snap on to specify some of the points, and Snap off for other points, without having to terminate the Line command.

TYPICAL OPERATION

If a drawing is dimensioned in inches, and the smallest fractional unit is 0.25, the speed of entry of points is greatly increased by setting the snap to 0.25.

1. Begin a new drawing.

2. Pick **Snap** from the Settings menu.

3. Pick **X Spacing**, type **.25** and press **Enter**.

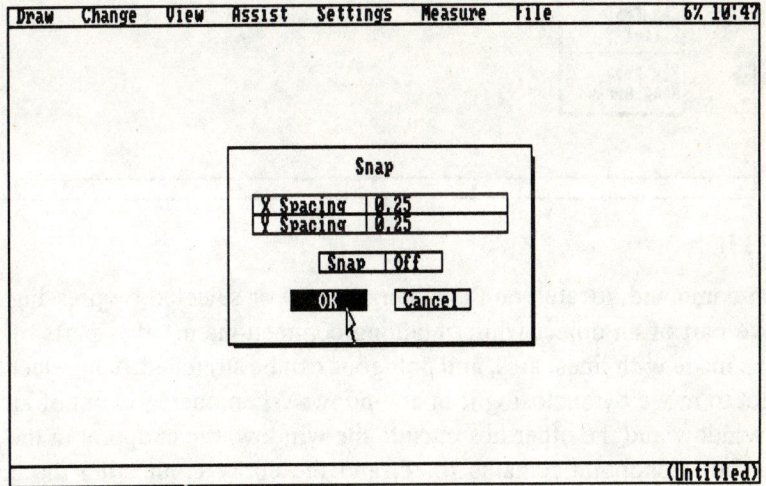

4. Pick **Off** to change the Snap to On, then pick **OK**.

There is no visible change on the screen unless the GRID command is also in use. However, it is now possible to only pick points which lie at the intersection of a rectangular grid .25 by .25 inches.

5. Move the screen cursor to check its response with the SNAP feature on.

6. Pick **Quit** from The File menu and discard the drawing, or continue your work session by picking **New** from the File menu.

7. Turn to Module 24, Grid, to continue the learning sequence.

Module 59
STRETCH

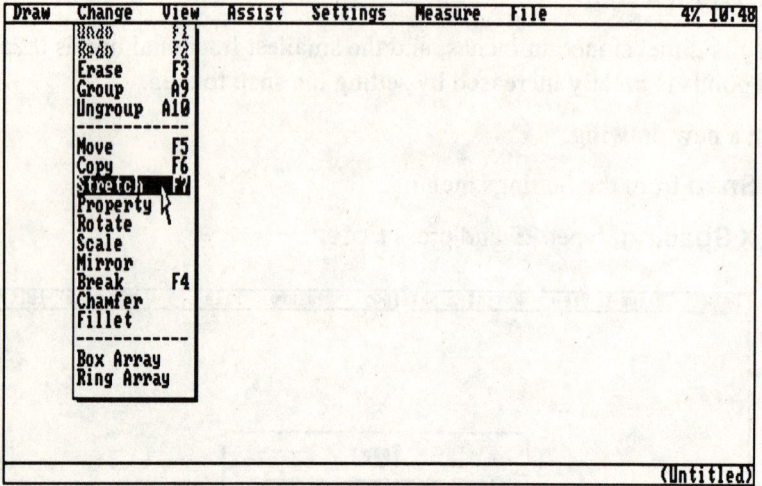

DESCRIPTION

The Stretch command, located on the Change menu or selected by pressing F7, allows you to move part of an object while retaining connections to other parts of the object. Connections made with lines, arcs, and polygons can be stretched. You select the portion of the object to move by enclosing it in a window. When one endpoint of an object lies inside the window and the other lies outside the window, the endpoint in the window is moved, the other endpoint remains fixed, and the entity connecting the endpoints is elongated. If the center of a circle is included in the selection box, the circle is moved. If the center is not included, the circle is ignored in the Stretch operation.

APPLICATIONS

The Stretch command lets you elongate any object constructed with lines, arcs, and polygons. If you wish to lengthen an object in the middle, but the endpoints must remain constant, use the Stretch command. For example, an automotive chassis can be stretched by moving the rear assembly back several inches. A floor plan can be stretched by moving part of the structure, stretching the connecting walls.

TYPICAL OPERATION

In this session you draw a chair. You then use Stretch to convert the chair into a couch.

1. Begin a new drawing.

2. Pick **Snap** from the Settings menu. Type **.5** as the X Spacing and press **Enter**. Pick **Off** to activate Snap, then pick **OK**.

3. Pick **Grid** from the Assist menu.

4. To draw the outline of the chair pick **Box** from the Draw menu. Type **.5,2.5** as the first corner, press **Enter**, type **3.5,5.5** as the second corner and press **Enter**.

5. To draw the cushion, pick **Polygon** from the Draw menu. Type **1,2.5** as the first point and press **Enter**. Type **1,4.5** as the second point and press **Enter**. Type **3,4.5** as the third point and press **Enter**. Type **3,2.5** as the final point and press **Enter**.

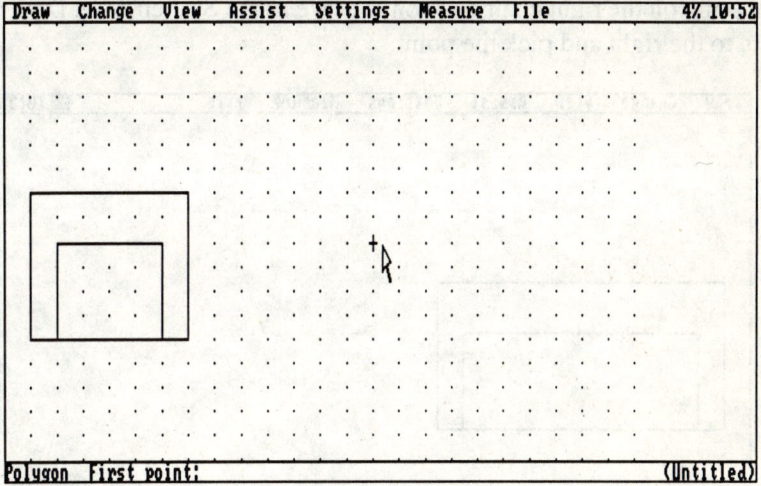

6. To stretch the chair into a couch, pick **Stretch** from the Change menu. Enclose one end cushion of the chair in the selection box as shown in the following screen.

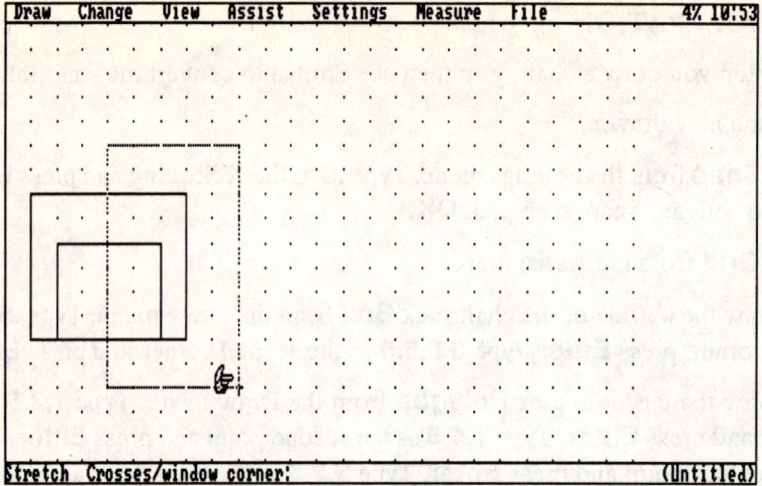

7. Pick a point on the right chair cushion to serve as the Stretch base. Drag the cushion 5 units to the right and pick the point.

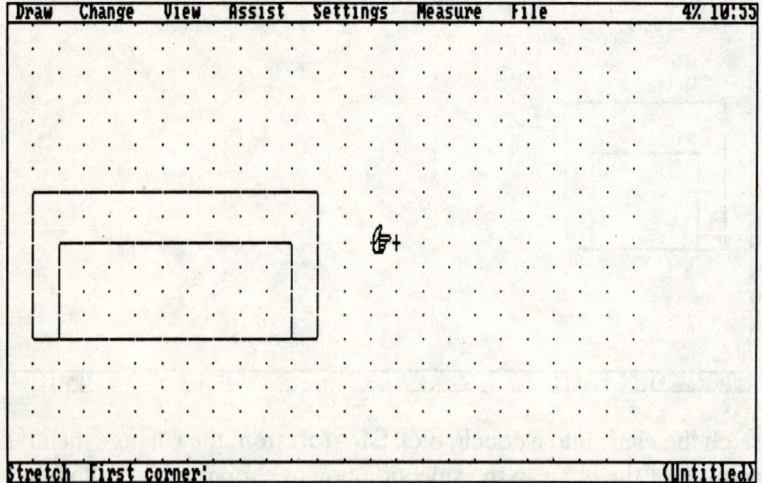

8. Quit AutoSketch, or turn to Module 16, Curve, to continue the learning sequence.

Module 60
TEXT

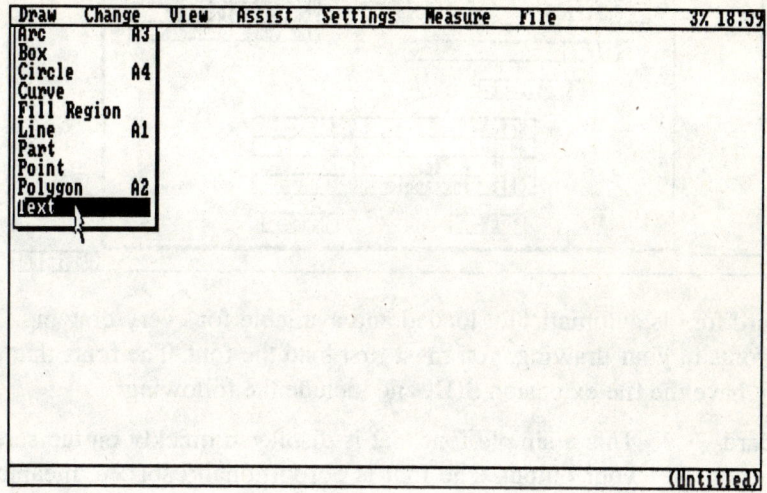

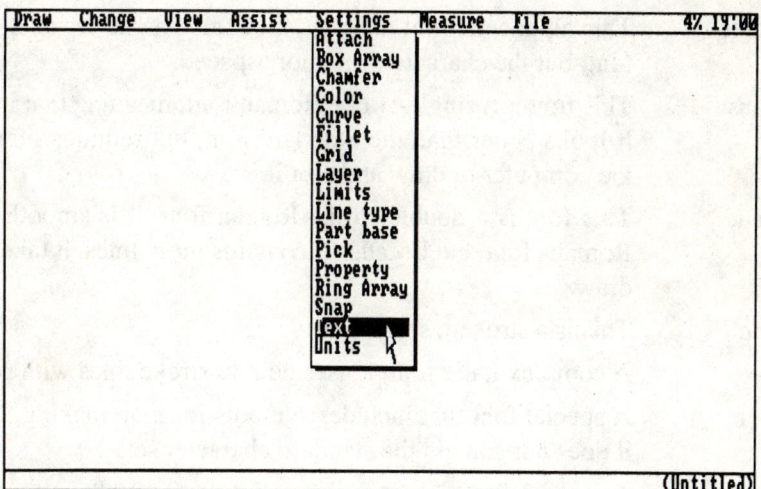

DESCRIPTION

Pick Text from the Settings menu to establish the font, height, angle, width, and angle for text. Pick Text from the Draw menu to actually place text in your drawing. When you pick Text from the Settings menu, the following dialogue box appears.

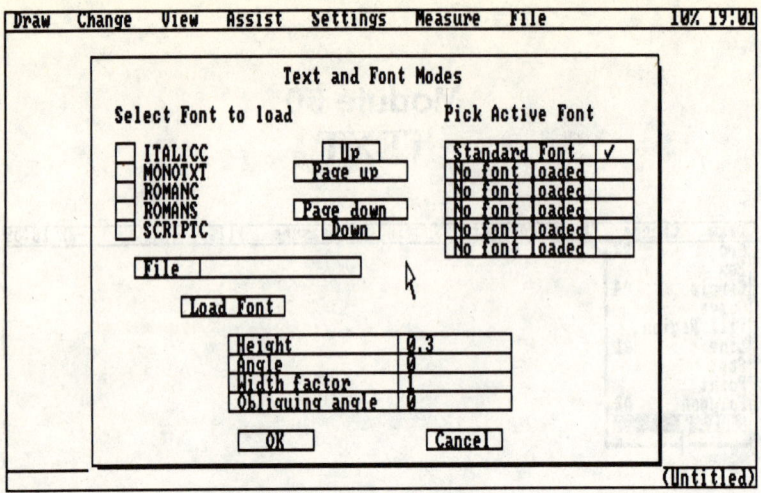

The Standard font is automatically loaded and available for every drawing. To include additional fonts in your drawing, you must first load the font. The fonts that come with AutoSketch have the file extension SHX and include the following:

Standard	This a simple font that is displayed quickly on the screen and in your output. The font is porportionally spaced, meaning that the letter I takes less horizontal space than the letter M.
Monotxt	This alphabetic font contains the same characters as the Standard font, but the characters are monospaced.
Romans	This font is a single-stroke Roman font, meaning that it has serifs. It looks better than the Standard font, but requires more time for the computer to draw and plot it.
Romanc	This font is a double-stroke Roman font. It is smoother than the Romans font, but because it contains more lines, it takes longer to draw.
Scriptc	This is a stroked, script font.
Italicc	A complex Italic font, it uses double-stroke lines with serifs.
Symap	A special font that includes symbols for map making. Notice that it does not contain the standard character set.
Symath	A special font that includes symbols for mathematics. Like the Symap font, it does not include the standard alphabetic characters.
Symusic	A symbol font containing musical symbols.

The following diagram shows the available fonts.

STANDARD   This is the standard text font.

MONOTXT   This is the monospaced font.

ROMANS   A simple roman font.

ROMANC   **A complex roman font.**

SCRIPTC   *A complex script font*

ITALICC   *A complex italic font.*

SYMAP   Mapping Symbols ▱△⋏⧖⟷⟷⊶⟷⊷⧓⥮

SYMATH   Math Symbols ℵ'‖|±∓×·÷=≠≡<>≦≧

SYMUSIC   Music Symbols ·♩♪♫○●♯♭♮▬▭×⌐𝄞𝄢♩:♯♯

To load a font, pick the check box corresponding to the desired font. Then pick Load Font.

The Symap, Symath, and Symusic fonts do not correspond to the Roman alphabet. The following shows the mapping of the symbol fonts to the alphabetic character set.

	A B C D E F G H I J K L M N O P Q R S T U V W X Y Z [\ ] ⌐ _ '
cyrillic	А Б В Г Д Е Ж З И Й К Л М Н О П Р С Т У Ф Х Ц Ч Ш Щ Ъ Ы Ь Э Ю Я
cyriltlc	А Б Ч Д Е Ф Г Х И Щ К Л М Н О П Ц Р С Т У В Ш Ж Й З Ь Ы Ъ Ю Э Я
greekc	А В Х Δ Е Φ Γ Н Ι ϑ К Λ М N О П Θ Р Σ Т Υ ∇ Ω Ξ Ψ Z [\ ] ⌐ _ '
greeks	А В Х Δ Е Φ Γ Н Ι ϑ К Λ М N О П Θ Р Σ Т Υ ∇ Ω Ξ Ψ Z [\ ] ⌐ _ '
syastro	☉ ☿ ♀ ⊕ ♂ ♃ ♄ ♅ Ψ ♆ ✶ ✳ ☊ ☋ ♈ ♉ ♊ ♋ ♌ ♍ ♎ ♏ ♐ ♑ = [\ ] ⌐ _ '
symeteo	· · · ● ▪ ▴ ∧ ∩ ‿ ⌣ ⌢ ' ' ' S ∿ ∞ ℞ ♄ — / ∣ \ ⟋ ⟍ / [\ ] ⌐ _ '

	a b c d e f g h i j k l m n o p q r s t u v w x y z { │ } ~ < >
cyrillic	а б в г д е ж з и й к л м н о п р с т у ф х ц ч ш щ ъ ы ь э ю я
cyriltlc	а б ч д е ф г х и щ к л м н о п ц р с т у в ш ж й з ь ы ъ э ю я
greekc	α β χ δ ε φ γ η ι ∂ κ λ μ ο π ϑ ρ σ τ υ ϵ ω ξ ψ ζ { │ } ~ < >
greeks	α β χ δ ε φ γ η ι ∂ κ λ μ ο π ϑ ρ σ τ υ ϵ ω ξ ψ ζ { │ } ~ < >
syastro	✳ ' ' ⊂ ∪ ⊃ ∈ → ↑ ← ↓ ∂ ∇ ⁀ ' ` ˘ × § † ‡ Ӡ ♌ ® © { │ } ~ < >
symeteo	│ \ ⟍ ⏤ ⟋ / │ ⟍ ⌣ ⌢ ⌣ ( ) ⁀ ⌐ ⟋ ⟍ ∾ ⊣ ℒ ℒ δ ϸ ℘ ℘ · { │ } ~ < >

AutoSketch and AutoCAD (release 9 and beyond) use the same fonts. If you need additional fonts for your AutoSketch work, you can use fonts from AutoCAD or from third-party software companies that create fonts that work with AutoCAD. If a font works with AutoCAD, it also works with AutoSketch.

Pick any text atributes that you want to change, type the new value, and pick the OK (or press Enter) or Cancel box for the entry. When you have made as many changes as you desire, pick OK on the dialogue box.

Text Height is measured in drawing units. You may specify any positive number of drawing units for text height. The height specification affects both text and dimensioning information.

The Angle, measured in degrees, defines the baseline angle for text. The default angle of 0 degrees specifies horizontal text. Change this value to 90 to create vertical text. The angle value, however, can be any value you choose to use.

The Width factor is a scaling factor that is applied to change the relative width of characters. The default width of 1 produces a character of medium width. A fractional value creates thin text, a value larger than 1 creates wide text. Negative values for width are not allowed.

The Obliquing angle defines the slant of the text with respect to the text baseline. The default value of 0 produces unslanted text. Negative values slant the text to the left, positive values slant the text toward the right.

To place text in the drawing, pick Text from the Draw menu. Then pick the starting point on the screen, or type the starting coordinates from the keyboard. The point specifies the bottom, or baseline, for the text. To enter multiple lines of text with a smooth left justification, press Ctrl-Enter. Press Enter to conclude the entry of a line or multiple justified lines of text.

Text is added to AutoSketch drawings with the Text command on the Draw menu. You control the style of the text with the Text command on the Settings menu.

AutoSketch uses control codes starting with double percent signs to add special symbols to your text.

%%o	Toggle overscore on/off
%%u	Toggle underscore on/off
%%d	Draw "degrees" symbol
%%p	Draw "plus/minus" symbol
%%c	Draw "circle diameter" dimensioning symbol
%%%	Force a single percent sign to be drawn
%%nnn	Draw special character number "nnn"

The single percent sign is handled as an ordinary character. There are, however, circumstances where this could be ambiguous (for example, turning off underscore immediately after a percent sign). In this case, you need the %%% symbol to force the printing of a single percent sign. For example:

Maximum Variation %%u5%%%%u. draws "Maximum Variation 5%."

You can produce two percent signs in a row with the sequence %%%%%.

APPLICATIONS

Use the Text command for placing descriptive information and labels in your drawing. Use the dimensioning commands to add numeric dimensions.

Be wary of text with extreme slants or extreme variations in height or width. Text must be readable to successfully communicate your ideas.

If you use more than five fonts in your drawing in addition to the Standard font, the performance of AutoSketch suffers. Try to limit your font selection to fewer choices.

TYPICAL OPERATION

In this session you place text in a drawing, varying the text attributes.

1. Begin a new AutoSketch drawing.

2. Pick **Text** from the Draw menu.

3. Type **1,8** as the start point and press **Enter**.

4. Type **If at first you don't succeed** and press **Ctrl-Enter**.

5. Type **get a bigger hammer** and press **Enter**.

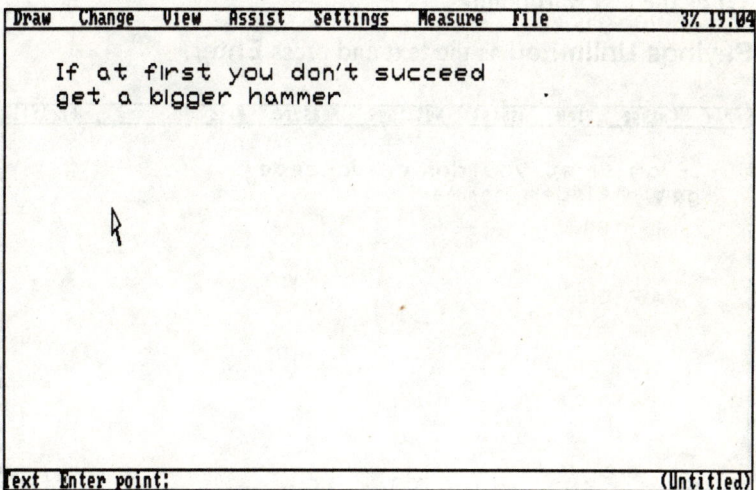

6. Pick **Text** from the Settings menu.

7. Pick **ROMANC** as the font to load.

8. Pick **Load Font**. Notice that ROMANC replaces the first instance of "No font loaded."

9. Pick **ROMANC** as the Active Font.

10. Pick the **Height** value, type **.75**, then pick **OK**.

11. Pick the **Obliquing angle** value, type **−15**, then pick **OK**.

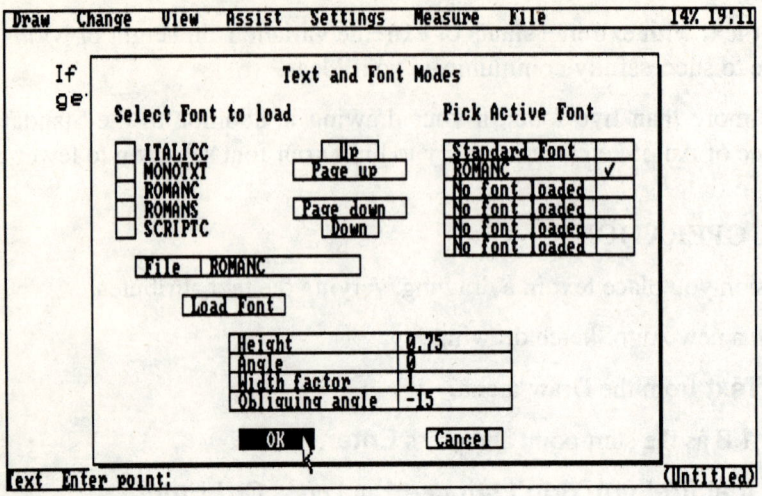

12. Pick **OK** in the dialogue box.

13. Type **1,1** as the text start point.

14. Type **Sayings Unlimited** as the text and press **Enter**.

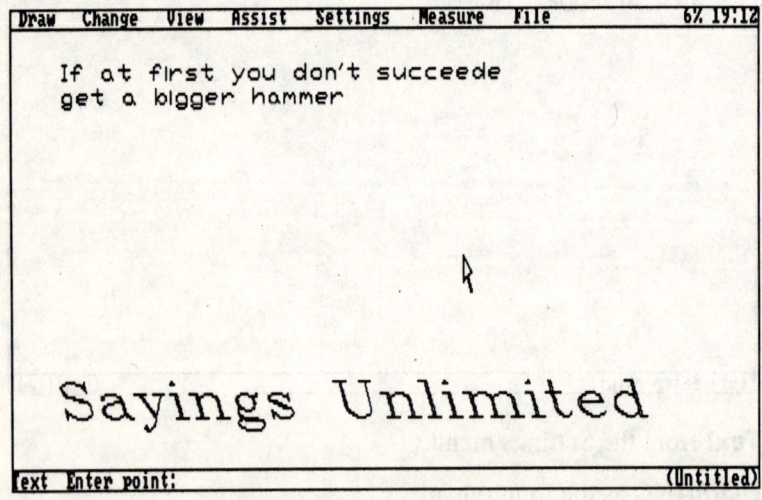

15. Quit AutoSketch, or turn to Module 21, Fillet, to continue the learning sequence.

Module 61
UNDO

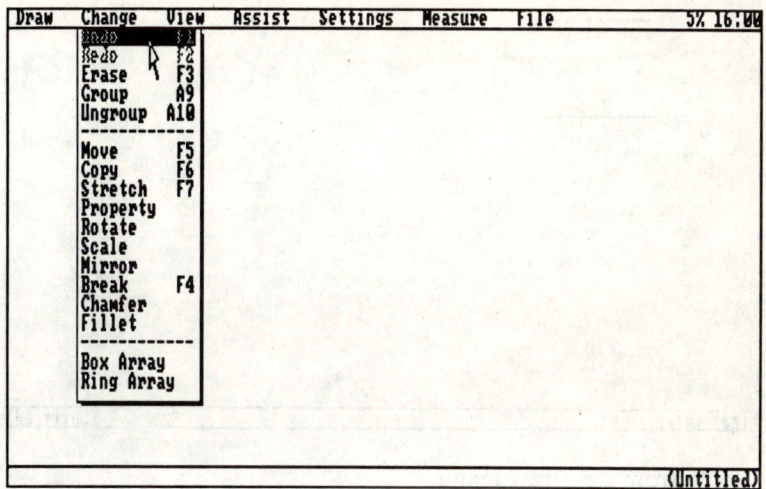

DESCRIPTION

The Undo command, located on the Change menu, reverses the most recent AutoSketch operation. Repetitive use of the Undo command can undraw an entire drawing.

APPLICATIONS

The Undo command is used to remove the last operation or operations performed. This is easier than using the Erase command to remove the last entity created. When you are experimenting with an operation, the Undo command is a convenient method for backing out undesired results.

If you accidentally Undo the wrong construction, you can use the Redo command to restore undone entities. Refer to Module 51 for a complete description of the Redo command.

TYPICAL OPERATION

In this activity you draw two lines and a circle. You then use the Undo command to remove the last two commands, leaving only the first line.

1. Begin a new drawing.

2. Pick **Line** from the Draw menu. Type **2,8 <CR>** as the first point and **4,8 <CR>** as the second point.

3. Type **2,6 <CR>** as the first point and **4,6 <CR>** as the second point.

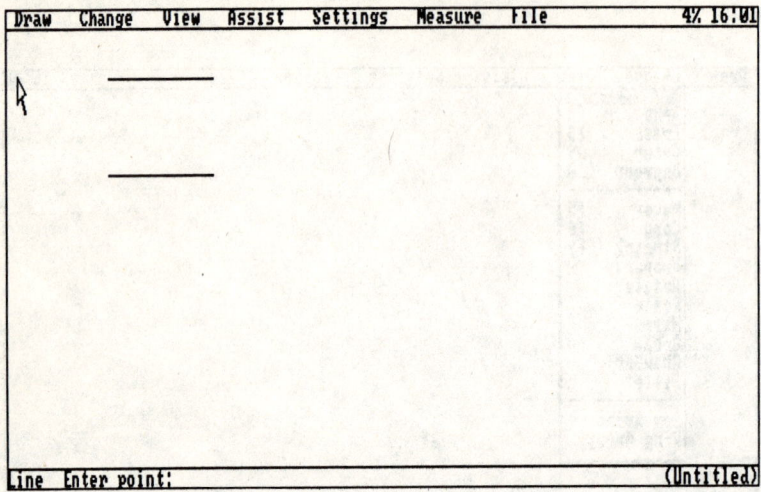

4. Pick **Circle** from the Draw menu.

5. Type **3,7 <CR>** as the center point and type **4,7 <CR>** as a point on the circle.

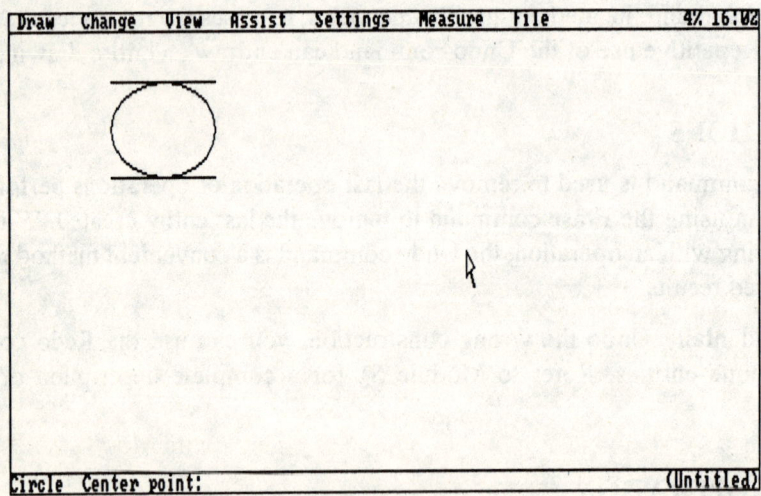

6. Pick **Undo** from the Change menu. (The gaps in the lines are visual artifacts. You learn to remove them in Module 52, Redraw.)

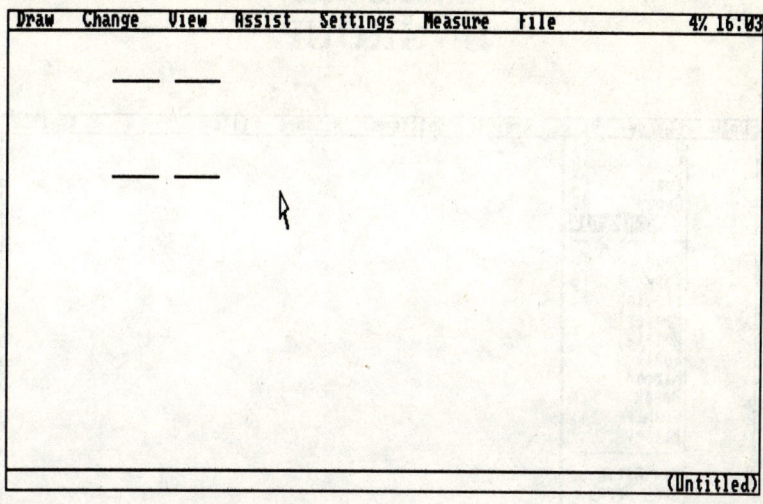

7. Pick **Undo** from the Change menu.

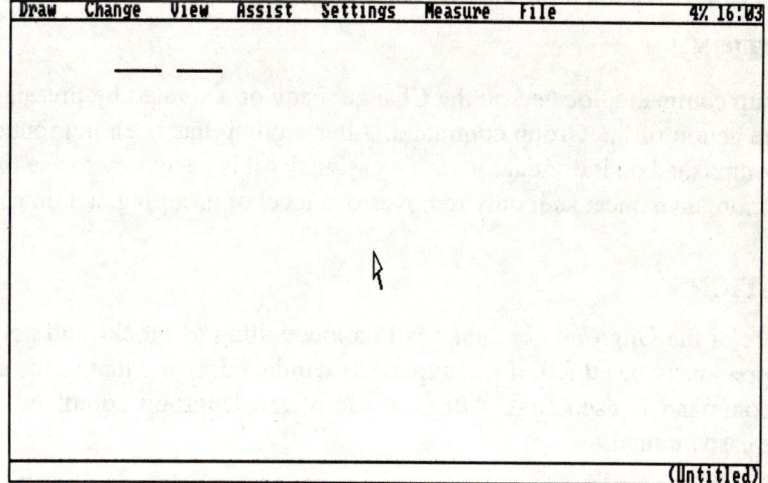

8. Do not stop. Continue the learning sequence directly with Module 51, Redo.

Module 62
UNGROUP

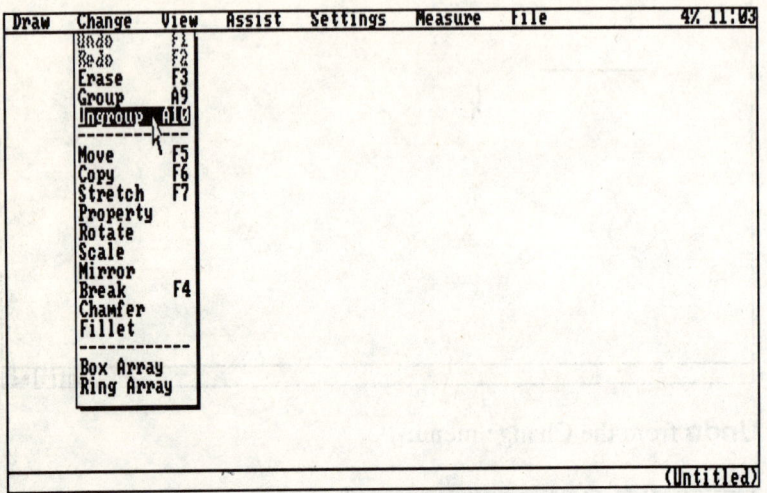

DESCRIPTION

The Ungroup command, located on the Change menu or activated by pressing Alt-F10, reverses the action of the Group command. After a group has been ungrouped, editing can be accomplished on individual parts. Occasionally it is necessary to use the ungroup command more than once, as it only removes one level of grouping at a time.

APPLICATIONS

The purpose of the Ungroup command is to allow editing of blocks and polylines that could not previously be edited. If a group exists within a drawing that needs editing, the Ungroup command is used first. After the use of the Ungroup command, individual entities are easily edited.

TYPICAL OPERATION

In this exercise you construct a use the Ungroup command to allow modification of individual drawing elements in a previously saved drawing.

1. Pick **Open** from the File menu. Pick **GROUP** as the drawing.

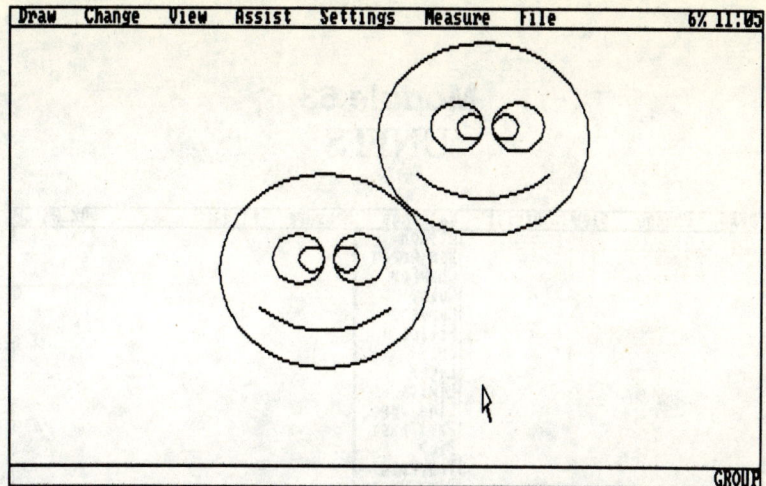

2. Select **Ungroup** from the Change menu.

3. Pick the original group of objects.

4. Pick **Erase** from the Change menu.

5. Pick the eyes of the Happy Face, erasing them.

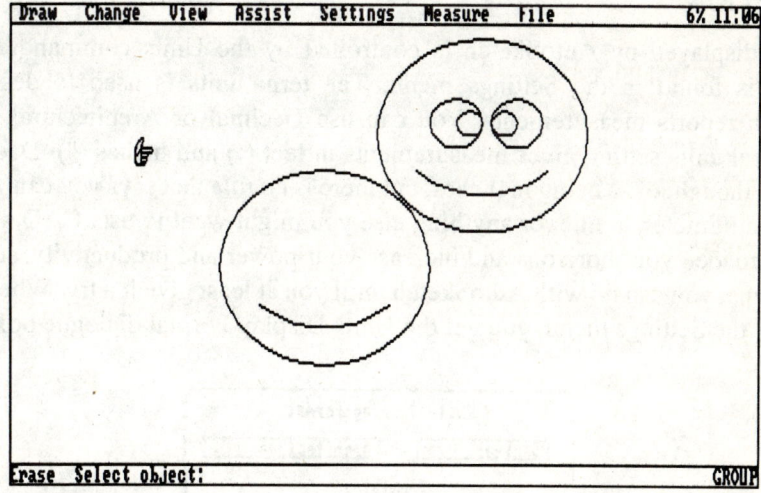

6. Quit AutoSketch, or turn to Module 44, Plot and Plot Name, to continue the learning sequence.

Module 63
UNITS

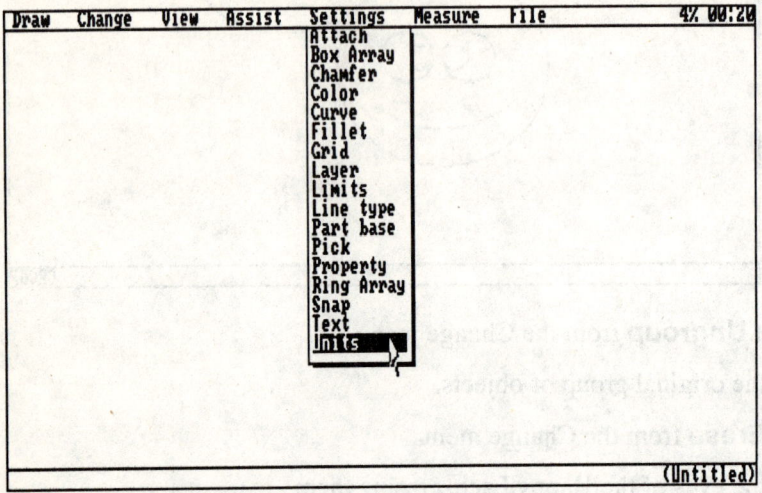

DESCRIPTION

The units displayed by AutoSketch is controlled by the Units command. The Units command is found in the Settings menu. The term units is used to describe how AutoSketch reports measurements. You can use Decimal or Architectural units. The Architectural units setting gives measurements in feet (') and inches ("). Decimal units are usually thought of as being in inches, but there is no rule that says you can't call a unit equal to a millimeter, a mile, or anything else you might want to use. CAD systems are meant to broaden your horizons and increase your power and productivity, so don't put limits on what you can do with AutoSketch until you at least give it a try. When you pick Units from the Settings menu, you get the Units Display Format dialogue box as shown below.

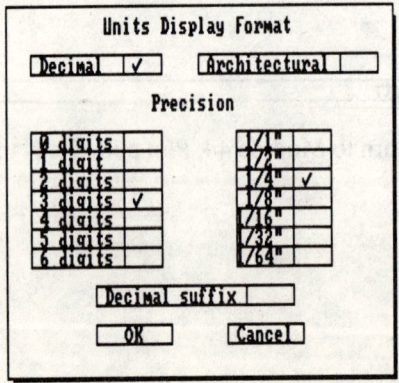

As you can see, the default setting for Units is Decimal with a precision of 3 digits past the decimal point. To change over to Architectural units, all that is necessary is to pick in the box next to Architectural. When you do this, the check mark next to the word Decimal is removed automatically. The default precision setting for Architectural is one-quarter of an inch. The Decimal suffix box is used to add things such as millimeters (mm) when dimensioning in decimal units. When you change the units format, all reporting that AutoSketch makes to you is displayed in that format with the exception of the Running Coordinates display. It always stays in the form of a decimal. If you need to know the coordinates on the screen in the Units format, you can use the Point command to get the report.

Use the following rules for entering feet and inches in a drawing:

- Use an apostrophe when specifying feet.
- Separate feet from inches with one intervening space or any printable character except a comma.
- Separate fractions of inches from whole inches by any printable character except a digit, double quote, slash, period, or comma.
- Separate the numerator from the denominator by a slash. The denominator must be a power of 2 (up to 1024).
- You can use a double quote after the inches value.

The following are examples of acceptable and equivalent ways of expressing the same value:

38.015625
3'–2 1/64"
3' 2–1/64
3'2+1/64

(All four examples mean exactly the same thing to AutoSketch.)

APPLICATIONS

The Units command is used when you want to change the units that AutoSketch is using. For instance, if you are drawing a house plan, it would be easier to give the builder a drawing dimensioned in feet and inches. When producing a drawing that needs to be dimensioned in millimeters, you could use decimal units with a Decimal suffix of mm. If you were drawing a map of your city or county, you could use decimal units equal to miles. The units of precision is very handy when dimensioning machine drawings in decimal units because you can change the amount of digits past the decimal point for differences in precision and tolerance.

TYPICAL OPERATION

One of the best ways to observe how the Units command works is to draw some lines and dimension them while changing units after each dimension is completed. In this activity you draw lines and dimension them using different settings for units.

1. Start a new drawing.

2. Pick **Coords** from the Assist menu to turn it on.

3. Pick **Snap** from the Settings menu to bring up the Snap dialogue box. Notice that snap spacing is set to 1. Pick **Off** to change it to On. Pick **OK** to leave the box. As you move your cursor around the screen, notice that it moves only in increments of 1 unit in the X or Y direction. You can observe the position of your screen cursor by looking at the coordinates display at the bottom of your screen as you move the cursor around.

4. Pick the **Line** command from the Draw menu.

5. Move the screen cursor to the coordinate 1.0000,7.0000 and pick that point.

6. Move the screen cursor to the coordinate 5.0000,7.0000 and pick that point.

7. Move the screen cursor to the coordinate 1.0000,5.0000 and pick that point.

8. Move the screen cursor to the coordinate 5.0000,5.0000 and pick that point.

9. Move the screen cursor to the coordinate 1.0000,3.0000 and pick that point.

10. Move the screen cursor to the coordinate 6.0000,3.0000 and pick that point.

11. Move the screen cursor to the coordinate 1.0000,1.0000 and pick that point.

12. Move the screen cursor to the coordinate 12.0000,1.0000 and pick that point.

```
Draw   Change   View   Assist   Settings   Measure   File        4% 00:24
┌─────────────────────────────────────────────────────────────────────┐
│                                                                       │
│        ──────────────                                                 │
│                                                                       │
│                                                                       │
│        ──────────────                                                 │
│                                                                       │
│                                                                       │
│        ───────────────                                                │
│                                                                  +  ʀ │
│                                                                       │
│        ─────────────────────────                                      │
│                                                                       │
│ Line  Enter point:              13.0000,3.0000          (Untitled)    │
└─────────────────────────────────────────────────────────────────────┘
```

13. Pick **Horiz dimension** from the Measure menu.

14. Move the screen cursor to the coordinate 1.0000,7.0000 and pick that point.

15. Move the screen cursor to the coordinate 5.0000,7.0000 and pick that point.

16. Move the screen cursor to the coordinate 3.0000,8.0000 and pick that point.

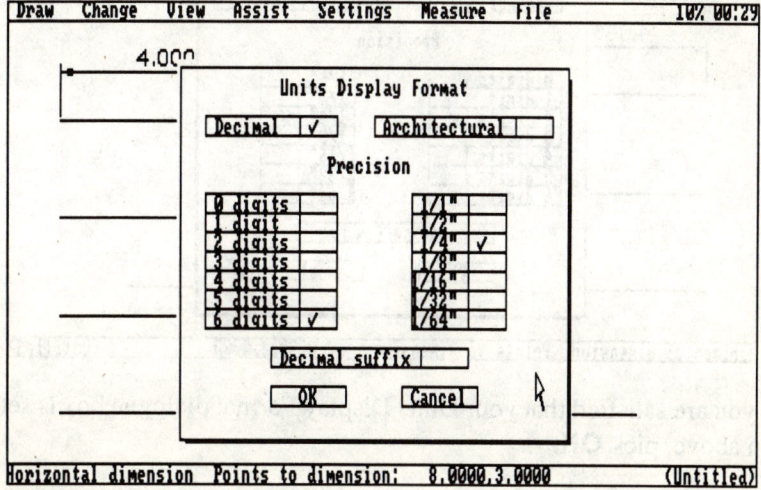

NOTE

As you can see, with the units set to their default, you get a decimal dimension with three digits past the decimal point.

17. Change the units by picking **Units** from the Settings menu. Pick the box to the right of 6 digits.

18. Pick **OK**.

19. Move the screen cursor to the coordinate 1.0000,5.0000 and pick that point.

20. Move the screen cursor to the coordinate 5.0000,5.0000 and pick that point.

21. Move the screen cursor to the coordinate 3.0000,6.0000 and pick that point.

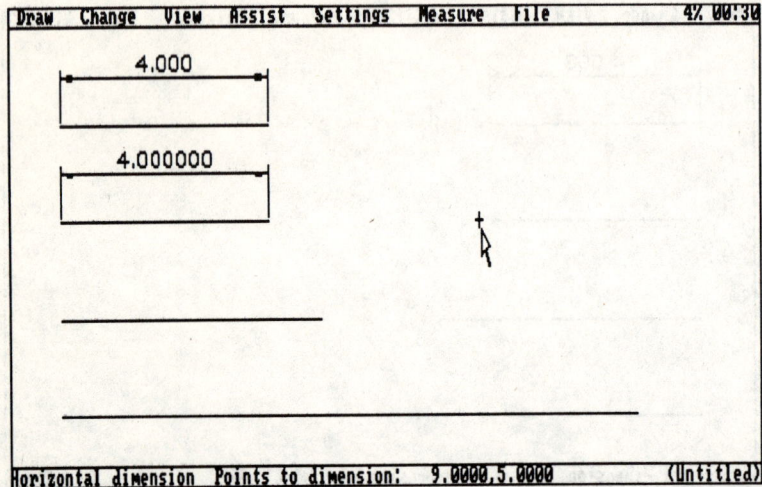

22. Change the units by picking **Units** from the Settings menu. Pick the box to the right of 2 digits and pick the box to the right of Decimal suffix and type **mm <CR>**.

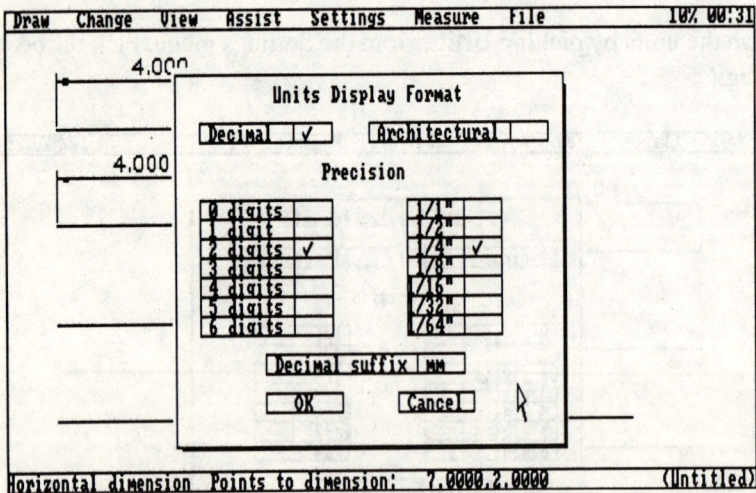

23. After you are satisfied that your Units Display Format dialogue box is set as the one shown above, pick **OK**.

24. Move the screen cursor to the coordinate 1.0000,3.0000 and pick that point.

25. Move the screen cursor to the coordinate 6.0000,3.0000 and pick that point.

26. Move the screen cursor to the coordinate 3.0000,4.0000 and pick that point.

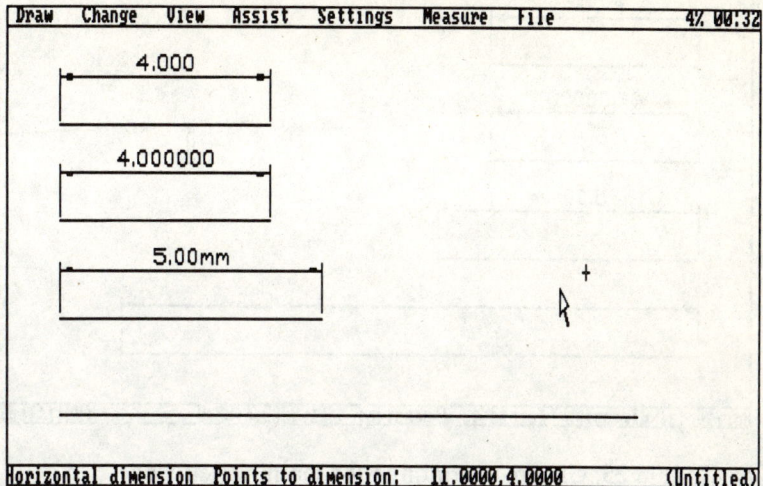

27. Change the units by picking **Units** from the Settings menu. Pick the box to the right of Architectural.

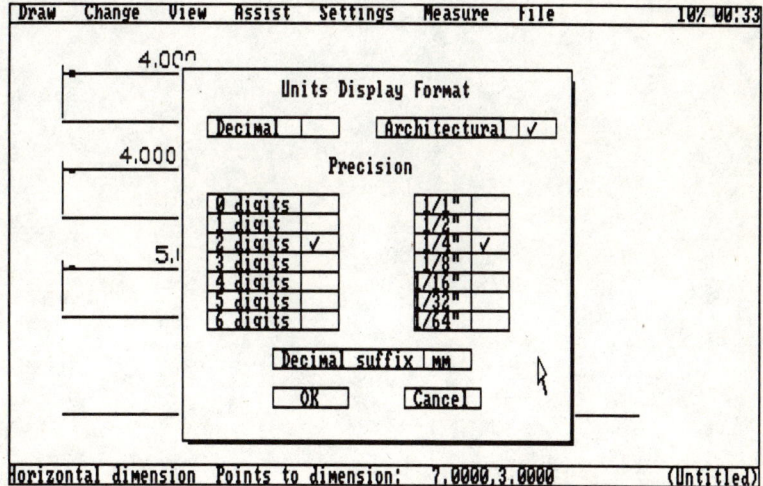

28. After you are satisfied that your Units Display Format dialogue box is set as the one shown above, pick **OK**.

29. Move the screen cursor to the coordinate 1.0000,1.0000 and pick that point.

30. Move the screen cursor to the coordinate 12.0000,1.0000 and pick that point.

31. Move the screen cursor to the coordinate 6.0000,2.0000 and pick that point.

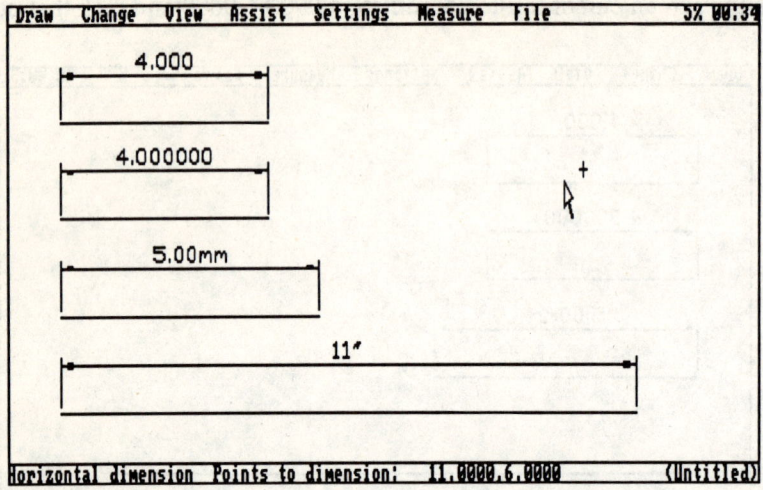

32. Turn to Module 25, Group, to continue the learning sequence.

Module 64
VIEW SLIDE

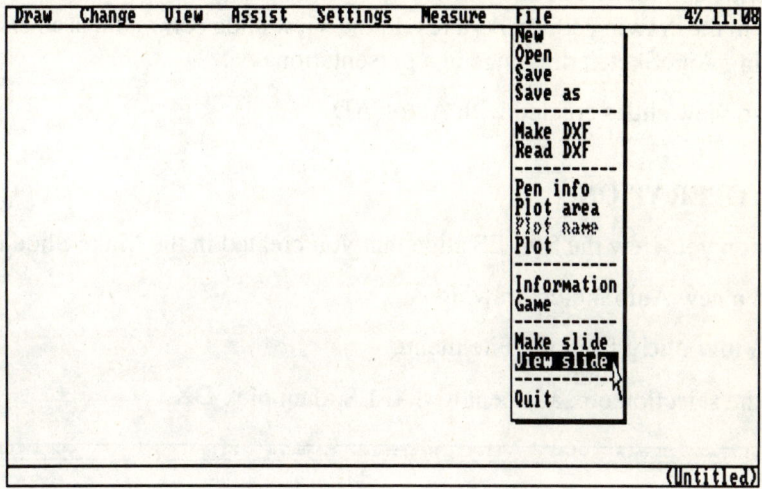

DESCRIPTION

The View slide command, located on the File menu, is used to view slides created with the Make slide command. When you select the View slide command, the following dialogue box appears.

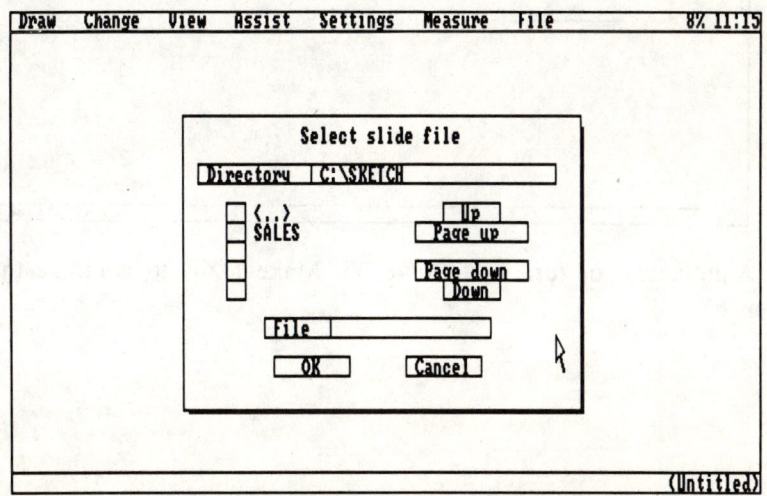

The slide selector dialogue box is similar to the Open dialogue box. Select the slide you want to view, then pick OK.

APPLICATIONS

The View slide command can be used to display drawings far more quickly than they can be redrawn in the drawing editor. As a result, the View slide command is an excellent tool for presenting AutoSketch drawings in a presentation.

You can also view slides created with AutoCAD.

TYPICAL OPERATION

In this session you view the SALES slide that you created in the Make Slide module.

1. Begin a new AutoSketch drawing.

2. Pick **View slide** from the File menu.

3. Pick the selection box adjacent to SALES, then pick **OK**.

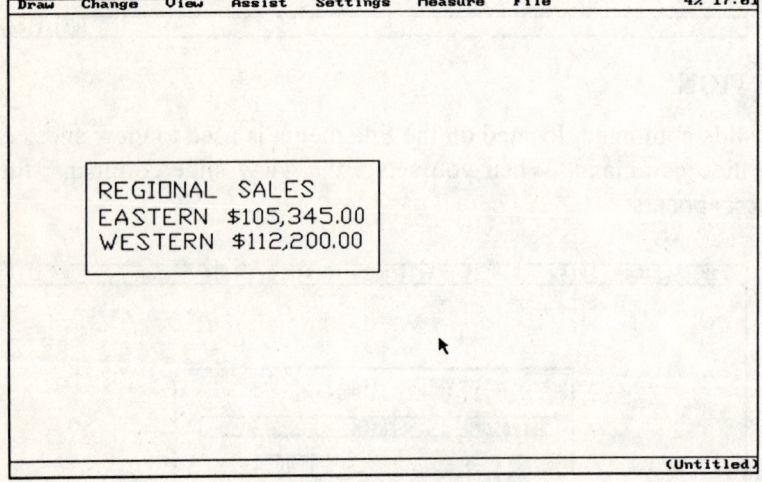

4. Quit AutoSketch, or turn to Module 33, Make DXF, to continue the learning sequence.

Module 65
ZOOM

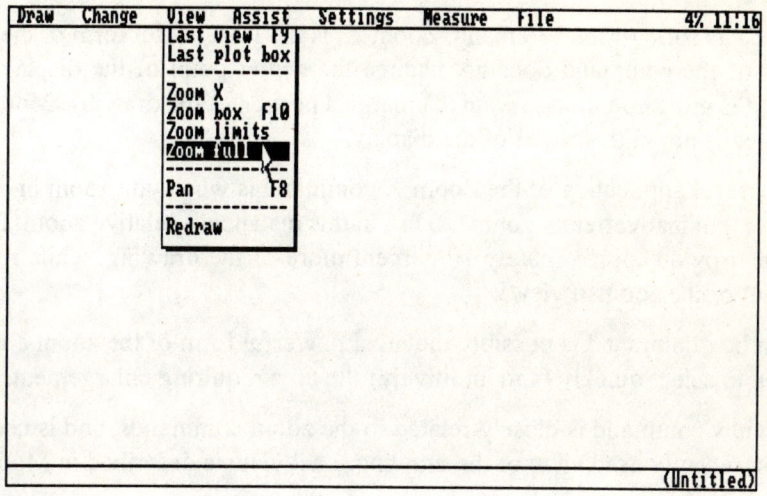

DESCRIPTION

The zoom commands, located on the View menu, let you enlarge and reduce drawing views. When making a large drawing you can "zoom in" on small objects in order to see hidden details. Each zoom command variation is described in the following list.

Zoom X	Type a number and press Return to specify a scale factor relative to the current view. A number greater than 1 increases the magnification; a decimal between 0 and 1 decreases the magnification.
Zoom box	Allows you to pick the lower left and upper right corner of the area (box or window) to be zoomed. You may pick the points in either order. You may also select Zoom box by pressing F10.
Zoom limits	The entire drawing is shown on the screen. The actual size depends on either the drawing limits (set with the LIMITS command) or the current extent of the drawing (if you have extended your drawing beyond the limits).
Zoom full	Fills the screen with the drawing elements. This is the maximum magnification capable of displaying all drawing elements.

Use of the zoom commands have no effect on the dimensions of the drawing. The commands affect only the screen display.

APPLICATIONS

The limited size and resolution of the screen make it impractical to create the individual elements of a large drawing when the entire drawing is displayed. Use the zoom commands to selectively expand portions of the drawing. When the selected portion of the drawing fills the screen, you can begin detail work.

The most basic form of the command, Zoom X, is the least useful form of the command. This form of the command does not change the center point of the display. In typical drawings, it is more common to want to enlarge a portion of the drawing. More often than not, this area is not in the center of the display.

The most useful application of the Zoom X command is when you zoom in on a portion of an object, but inadvertently zoom too far. In this instance, a relative zoom, for example 0.9, would provide approximately 10 percent more of the drawing, while retaining the center point of the zoomed view.

The Zoom box command is possibly the most powerful form of the zoom commands. It allows you to select quickly (and intuitively) the area requiring enlargement.

The Last view command is closely related to the zoom commands, and is used to return to the most recently used view of the drawing. Last view is described in Module 28.

TYPICAL OPERATION

This session lets you practice using the zoom commands by drawing a circle and changing its display size. Begin a new drawing.

1. Pick **Circle** from the Draw menu.

2. Type **2,2** as the center point and press **Enter**.

3. Type **2,3** as the point on the circle and press **Enter**.

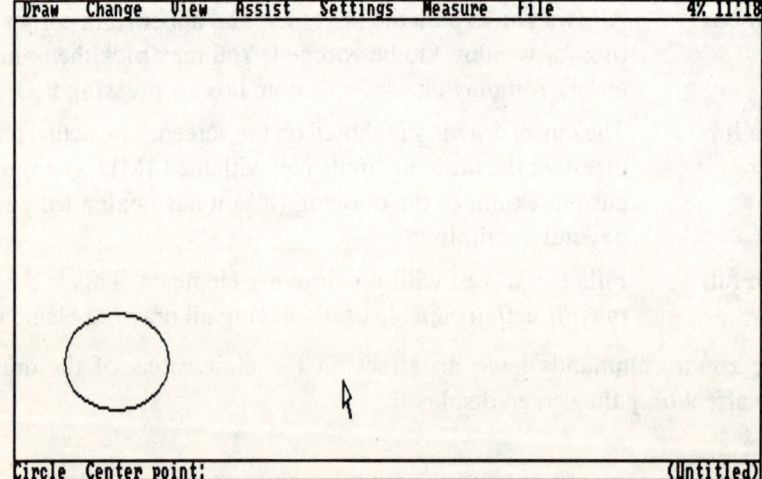

4. Pick **Zoom full** from the View menu.

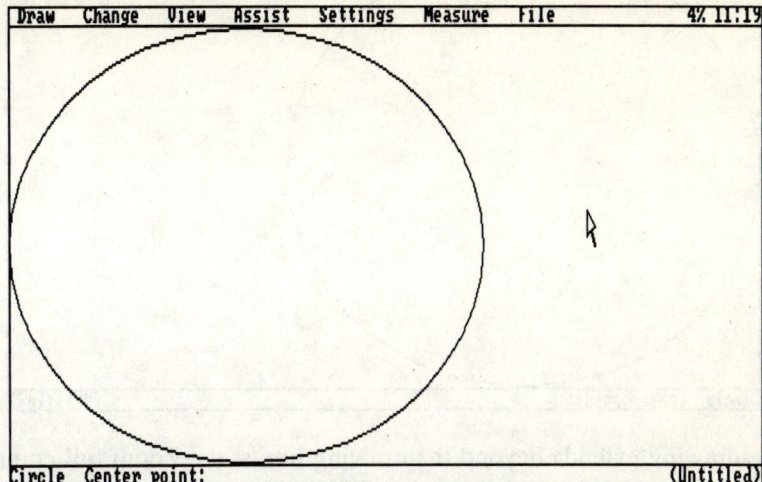

Notice that the circle expands to fill the screen.

5. Pick **Zoom limits** from the View menu. Notice that the previous display is restored.

6. Type **5,5** as the circle center point and press **Enter**.

7. Type **15,5** as the point on the circle and press **Enter**.

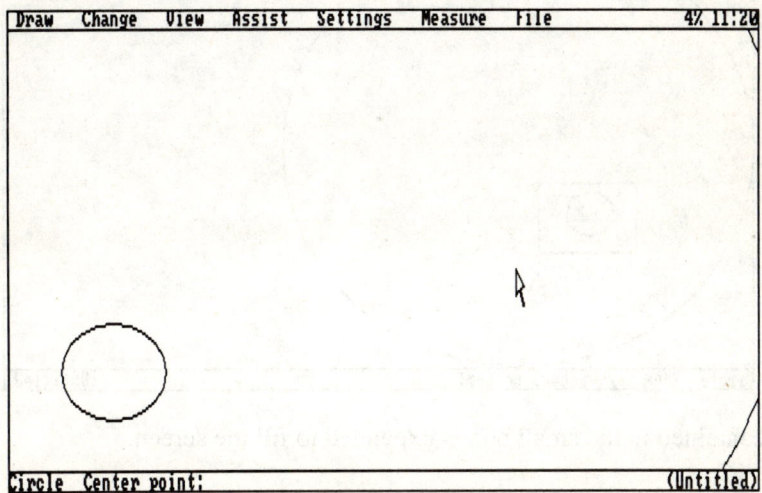

8. Pick **Zoom full** from the View menu. Notice that the large circle fills the display area.

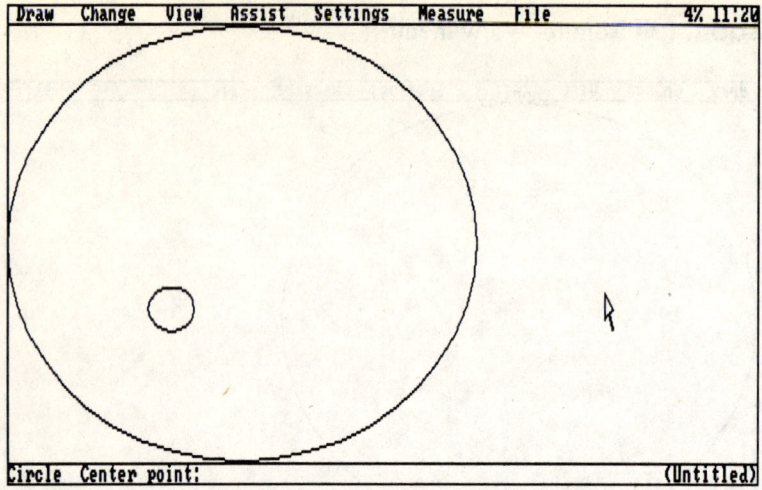

Because the drawing extends beyond the drawing limits, the Zoom full command uses the extents of the drawing instead of the drawing limits when performing this zoom.

9. Select **Zoom box** from the View menu.

10. Pick the corners of the box as shown in the following screen.

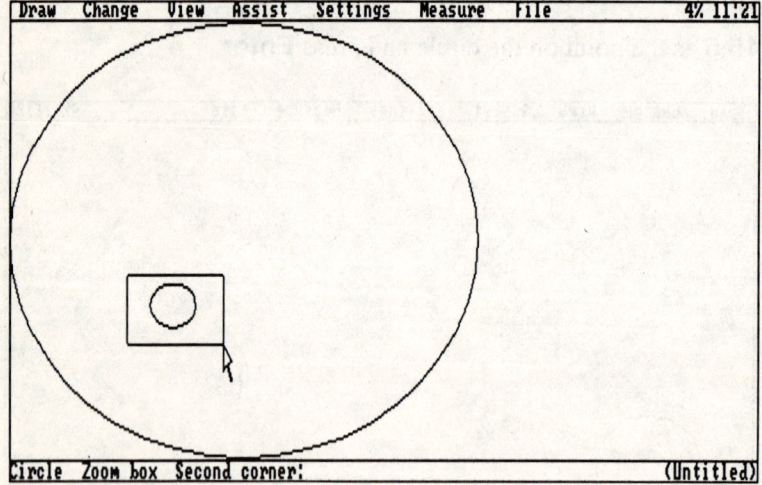

The view contained in the small box is expanded to fill the screen.

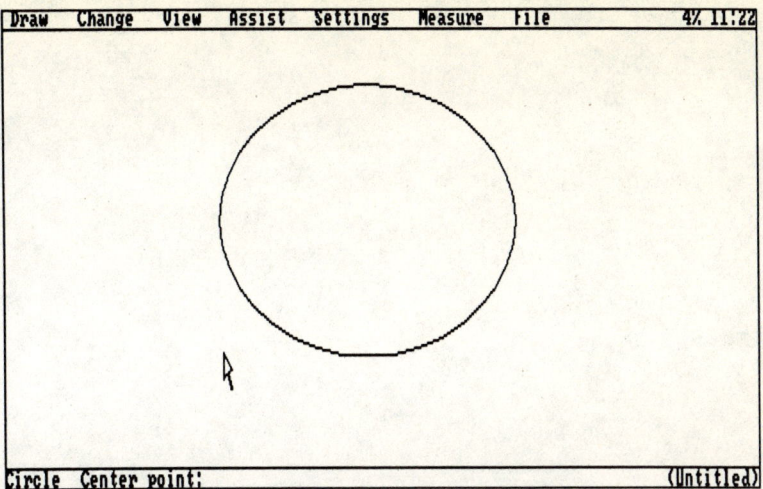

11. Pick **Quit** from the File menu and discard the drawing, or continue your work session by picking **New** from the File menu.

12. Turn to Module 40, Pan, to continue the learning sequence.

Appendix A
TERMS AND DEFINITIONS

Term	Definition
Attach	Attach is a drawing aid that lets you snap selection points to a geometric object in your drawing.
Bearing	The bearing is a direction measured in degrees. Use the following drawing to help you select the correct bearing.

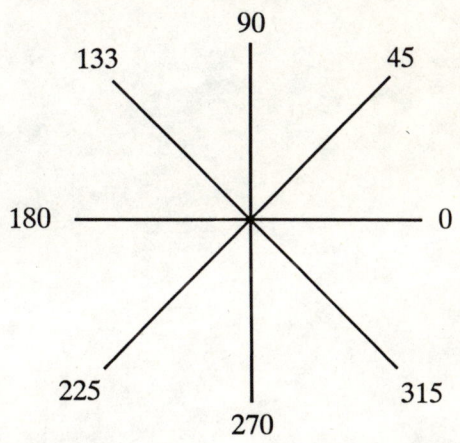

Coordinates	AutoSketch uses a Cartesian coordinate system. Each point is specified by a pair of numbers (x,y). The lower-left corner of the drawing space is (0,0). The x dimension determines the distance to the right, and the y dimension determines the distance toward the top of the drawing. For any practical purpose, there is no limit on the upper-right drawing limit.
Drag	The act of moving a geometric object across the screen dynamically. Press and hold the mouse button, move the mouse to move the object, then release the mouse button.
Drawing Units	The distance between two points in a drawing. You decide whether drawing units correspond to world units in metric, English, or other forms of representation.
Group	A collection of objects that is manipulated by a single command.

Term	Definition
Object	The elements you create in a drawing. They include arcs, boxes, circles, curves, lines, parts, points, polygons, text, groups, and dimensions.
Polar Coordinates	A system of measure defined by a distance and bearing from the last point entered.
Polygon	A sequence of connected line segments.
Snap	A drawing aid to allow selection of points only on a specified grid on a drawing.

Appendix B
EXERCISES

1. About This Book

   a. What feature is provided in this book to guide you through AutoSketch operations?

   b. If you are learning AutoSketch, follow the _____ _____ printed in the front of the book.

   c. The _____ is provided so that the book can continue serving as a convenient reference.

   d. Explain what the notation Ctrl-C means.

   e. When using a mouse, what does the word "pick" mean?

2. Sample Session

   a. Does the use of the mouse in AutoSketch mimic the Apple Macintosh environment?

   b. When picking a command to use, where does the command prompt (input request) appear on your screen?

   c. The size of the drawing sheet is set with which command?

   d. What is the default value of the Grid command?

3. Angle

   a. In what menu is the Angle command located?

   b. What is the Angle command used for?

   c. When using the Angle command, the first entry AutoSketch requests is the _____ .

   d. The resulting answer from the Angle command can be any angle between _____ and _____ degrees.

4. Arc

   a. In what menu is the Arc command located?

   b. What is the Arc command used for?

   c. What way can you use the Arc command other than using the menu?

    d. Name the three points AutoSketch prompts for when using the Arc command:

1) _____ 2) _____ and

3) _____ .

5. Area

    a. In what menu is the Area command located?

    b. The Area command works on what kind of figure?

    c. What does the Area command determine for you?

    d. When using the Area command, X's appear on the drawing screen as you are selecting points. What are these X's used for?

6. Attach

    a. In what menu is the Attach command located?

    b. The Attach command activates AutoSketch's _____ _____ mode.

    c. This mode is used for what purpose?

    d. The Attach command can be toggled on and off with the menu and what other way?

7. Bearing

    a. In what menu is the Bearing command found?

    b. In AutoSketch, a bearing is defined as what?

    c. Where is zero degrees located in AutoSketch?

    d. When the Bearing command is picked what does AutoSketch ask for first?

8. Box

    a. In what menu is the Box command?

    b. When you pick the Box command what does AutoSketch ask for first?

    c. What does AutoSketch ask for second?

    d. Explain the two ways of entering coordinates for the Box command in AutoSketch.

9. Box Array

    a. The Box Array creates a _____ group of drawing entities.

    b. A column is the _____ component of an array.

c. A row is the _____ component of an array.

d. Do you select the Array command before or after drawing the entity to be duplicated?

10. Break

    a. In what menu is the Break command located?

    b. What does the Break command do?

    c. How does the Break command differ from the Erase command?

    d. How would you call the Break command other than picking it from a menu?

    e. When using the Break command how does AutoSketch verify what entity you have picked to be broken?

    f. When breaking a circle, in what direction is the break performed?

11. Chamfer

    a. What does the Chamfer command do to a corner?

    b. If you did not have the Chamfer command, explain the sequence of operations you would have to follow to create a chamfer in your drawing.

    c. Can you chamfer a circle?

12. Circle

    a. In what menu is the Circle command located?

    b. What can you do with the Circle command?

    c. How can you call up the Circle command other than picking it from the menu?

    d. When using the Circle command what is the first point that you must pick?

    e. What effect does the Stretch command have on a circle?

13. Colour

    a. In what menu do you find the Colour command?

    b. What does the Colour command allow you to do?

14. Coords

    a. What menu contains the Coords command?

    b. When would you not want to activate the Coords command?

    c. What units are used to display the drawing coordinates?

15. Copy

    a. In what menu do you find the Copy command?

    b. What is the Copy command used for?

    c. When using the Copy command what is the first thing that must be selected after picking the command from the menu?

    d. The second and third thing you pick when using the Copy command can be thought of as the beginning and the end of a _____ _____ .

16. Curve

    a. In what menu do you find the Curve command?

    b. What kind of curve does the Curve command produce?

    c. When producing the curve, you enter a starting point and a series of control points to define a _____ .

    d. After you have completed all the control points what are the two ways of endpoint entry?

    e. What is the maximum number of points that you can enter for a curve?

17. Dimension

    a. What is the Dimensioning command used for?

    b. In what menu do you find the Dimensioning command?

    c. Name the three different types of dimensioning that are provided in AutoSketch:
        1) _____ ,
        2) _____ , and 3) _____ .

18. Distance

    a. What does the Distance command do?

    b. In what menu do you find the Distance command?

19. Erase

    a. In what menu do you find the Erase command?

    b. What method can you use to call up the Erase command, other than by using the menu?

    c. The Erase command removes what?

d. When would you need to use the Break command rather than the Erase command?

e. If you accidentally erase an object and want to bring it back, what command do you use?

20. Fill Region

   a. What color is used to fill a region?

   b. How many points can define a region for the Fill command?

   c. What disadvantages are associated with filled regions?

   d. Do any Attach modes work with filled regions?

21. Fillet

   a. Explain what the Fillet command does.

   b. How do you adjust the length of two straight lines to get them to match the radius of the fillet?

   c. What happens if you fillet two lines with a 0 radius?

   d. Does the Fillet command work with circles?

22. Frame

   a. What does the Frame command control?

   b. What menu contains the Frame command?

   c. Explain why you would need to use the Frame command.

23. Game

   a. In what menu do you find the Game command?

   b. If you want to review the rules of the game what command would you use?

   c. How do you win the game?

24. Grid

   a. Why would you select the Grid command from the Assist menu?

   b. What can you do with the Grid command?

   c. When is the Grid command most often used?

   d. Why would you select the Grid command from the Settings menu?

   e. What effect does the grid have on a drawing?

25. Group

    a. The Group command is located in the _____ menu.

    b. Other than using the menu, the Group command can be activated by using

        _____ .

    c. Give three uses for the Group command.

    d. In what ways do editing commands affect groups?

26. Information

    a. What menu contains the Information command?

    b. Name three things that the Information command informs you of in its dialogue box.

    c. What is the Information command most useful for?

27. Last Plot Box

    a. What menu contains the Last Plot Box command?

    b. What impact does the Last Plot Box have on your printed output when using the Plot command?

    c. Does the Last Plot Box change the drawing?

28. Last View

    a. What menu contains the Last view command?

    b. The Last view command toggles between what two things?

29. Layer

    a. What is the Layer command used for?

    b. To get the Layer command's dialogue box, what menu would you use?

    c. How many layers are available in AutoSketch?

    d. Give an example of why you would make a layer invisible.

    e. Give a practical example of how you might utilize the Layer command in a real-world drawing situation.

30. Limits

    a. What menu contains the Limits command?

    b. What is the Limits command used for?

    c. When may the limits of a drawing be set?

31. Line

    a. What menu contains the Line command?

    b. If not using a menu to invoke the Line command what other keystroke combination will call the command?

    c. Drawing a line in AutoSketch requires the definition of what?

    d. When the start point of a line has been selected, there is a _____ - _____ line stretching from the start point to where the screen pointer is positioned.

    e. AutoSketch treats a line as a _____ _____ and not as a series of points.

32. Line Type

    a. What menu contains the Line Type command?

    b. Name five of the ten line types available in AutoSketch.

    c. What is the Scale factor used for?

33. Make DXF

    a. Which menu contains the Make DXF command?

    b. What does DXF stand for?

    c. What is a DXF file used for?

    d. A DXF file is an _____ file.

    e. Why does the DXF file not work well when going from AutoCAD down to AutoSketch?

34. Make Slide

    a. The Make slide command is located in the _____ menu.

    b. What is the Make slide command used for?

    c. What command is used to view a slide in AutoSketch?

    d. Slides have a filename extension of _____ .

35. Mirror

    a. The Mirror command is located in the _____ menu.

    b. The Mirror command allows you to reproduce a _____ _____ .

    c. The Mirror command _____ the object over an _____ at any angle desired.

36. Move

    a. The _____ menu contains the Move command.
    b. What is the Move command used for?

37. New

    a. Which menu contains the New command?
    b. What is the New command used for?
    c. What else does the New command do besides clearing the drawing editor?

38. Open

    a. The Open command is located in the _____ menu.
    b. What is the Open command used for?

39. Ortho

    a. The Ortho command is located in the _____ menu.
    b. If not using a menu, how else would you toggle the Ortho command on and off?
    c. What does the Ortho command do when it is toggled on?
    d. It is not possible to draw a _____ line when Ortho is selected.

40. Pan

    a. What menu contains the Pan command?
    b. What does the Pan command allow you to do?
    c. What directions are allowed with the Pan command?
    d. Give an example of why you might use the Pan command?

41. Part and Part Base

    a. The Part command is located in the _____ menu.
    b. What is the Part command used for?
    c. What are part drawings normally constructed for?

42. Pen Info

    a. The Plot Info command is in the _____ menu.
    b. What has to be configured in your AutoSketch installation in order for the Pen Info command to be accessible from the menu?
    c. What is the Plot Info command used for?

43. Pick

    a. The Pick command is in the _____ menu.
    b. What is the Pick command used for?
    c. The size of the Pick target is expressed as a percentage of _____ height.
    d. How do you determine the best size of the Pick target for your needs?

44. Plot and Plot Name

    a. The Plot command is in the _____ menu.
    b. What is the Plot command used for?
    c. When you are drawing in AutoSketch what scale is used?
    d. The plot will be produced at what scale?
    e. If a plotter is not configured what happens to the Plot commands in the menu?

45. Plot Area

    a. What is the function of the Plot Area command?
    b. Can you create plotted output without using the Plot Area command?
    c. How do you control the creation of a clip box?
    d. How do you rotate the plotted area?

46. Point

    a. WHich menu contains the Point command?
    b. Define points in AutoSketch.
    c. What are the two ways of locating a point?
    d. When you plot a point, the width is controlled by the _____ of the plotter _____ .
    e. What is a point often used for?

47. Polygon

    a. Which menu contains the Polygon command?

    b. What does the Polygon command do?

    c. What are the two ways of completing the entry of points in the Polygon command?

    d. Must a polygon be open or closed?

48. Property

    a. What menu contains the Property command?

    b. What is the purpose of the Property command?

49. Quit

    a. What menu contains the Quit command?

    b. What does the Quit command do?

50. Read DXF

    a. What kinds of programs create DXF files?

    b. What is the advantage of being able to read DXF files in AutoSketch?

    c. Are there any potential problems involved in reading DXF files, such as those created by AutoCAD, Autodesk's full-featured, three-dimensional CAD package?

51. Redo

    a. The _____ menu contains the Redo command.

    b. What is the Redo command used for?

    c. When must the Redo command be used for it to have any effect?

52. Redraw

    a. What menu contains the Redraw command?

    b. What does the Redraw command do?

53. Ring Array

    a. Can AutoSketch create a polar array?

    b. What is the difference between the Box array and the Ring array?

c. What is the impact of picking the Rotate Items selection in the dialog box?

d. What is the relationship between rotating items and the pivot point?

54. Rotate

a. What menu contains the Rotate command?

b. Explain what the Rotate command does.

c. After selecting the Rotate command from its menu, what is the first step that you must complete?

d. The second step is to select the base point. Does it matter where the base point is located?

e. Explain the two ways the amount of rotation can be specified.

55. Save and Save as

a. What is the purpose of the Save command?

b. How does the Save as command differ from the Save command?

c. In what menu do you find the Save and the Save as commands?

56. Scale

a. The Scale command allows you to resize anything from an _____ to an entire _____ .

b. In what menu do you find the Scale command?

c. When the Scale command does its work, all selected points are recomputed with reference to the _____ point.

d. A scale factor of 1 does what?

e. A scale factor of less than 1 _____ the size of the drawing.

f. A scale factor of greater than 1 _____ the size of the drawing.

57. Show Properties

a. Name two thing that the Show properties command allows you to inspect concerning an entity.

b. In what menu do you find the Show properties command?

58. Snap

    a. You can select the Snap command from the _____ menu to establish the _____ spacing and the _____ spacing.
    b. What is the default value for Snap spacing?
    c. The Snap command can also be toggled on or off within the Assist menu or by pressing the key combination _____ - _____ .

59. Stretch

    a. Explain what the Stretch command allows you to do.
    b. List the three entity types that can be stretched.
    c. Explain what happens if you try to stretch a circle.

60. Text

    a. If you pick Text from the Settings menu, list the four things that you can establish concerning text.
    b. If you want to place text in your drawing, what menu do you use to select the Text command?
    c. Text height is measured in _____ units.
    d. In Text, the default angle of _____ degrees specifies _____ text.

61. Undo

    a. What does the Undo command do?
    b. What menu is used to select the Undo command?
    c. What keyboard function key will select the Undo command?
    d. What can repetitive use of the Undo command do?

62. Ungroup

    a. Explain two ways of activating the Ungroup command.
    b. Why would you need to use the Ungroup command? Give a practical example.
    c. Why might it be necessary to use the Ungroup command more than once on the same group?

63. Units

    a. What real-world units are architectural units tied to?

    b. What limitation is there on the units that you choose to use when using decimal units?

    c. How does AutoSketch tell the difference between numbers that you enter as feet and numbers that you enter as inches?

    d. What character do you use as the "fraction bar" in specifying fractional units?

64. View Slide

    a. In what menu do you find the View slide command?

    b. The View slide command is used to _____ slides created with the _____ command.

65. Zoom

    a. The Zoom command lets you _____ and _____ drawing views.

    b. In the Zoom command, what does the Last view do?

    c. Explain what the Zoom X option does.

    d. Explain how the Zoom box works and give an example of how it might be used in a practical way.

    e. Explain what the Zoom limits options does.

    f. What does the Zoom full option do to your drawing?

Index

Related Computer Books From Wordware

AutoCAD Release 10
TOM BERGHAUSER and PAUL SCHLIEVE
Create, edit, and copy a variety of drawings as easily as a word processor manipulates text. Learn to use line types, cross-hatch patterns, layer names, and text fonts/styles effectively. Define and modify screen and tablet menus, components, and shape libraries. Novice users will find that clear illustrated examples provide the key to this Computer Aided Drafting (CAD) based system. This book is an excellent reference tool for drafting design experts. It covers versions 2.17 through release 10.

1-55622-064-2 • **$23.95**
softbound • 448 pages

AutoLISP
WILLIAM M. OLIVER
Bring the power of programming to AutoCad by using this guide to the AutoLISP interpreter. Graphic examples and the alphabetical listing of commands make it easy for the beginning user to learn and a great reference tool for the seasoned user. You can simplify repetitive drawings and automate complex drawing processes to allow more time to concentrate on the design. Other features include being able to specify points and do calculations. Teachers will find this to be a great teaching aid.

1-55622-161-4 • **$21.95**
softbound • 320 pgs

Generic CADD Level 3
Version 1.1
ANN W. DUNN
Designed to accommodate the beginning and experienced user, this tutorial provides the information needed to operate the full features of this top-selling, low-cost computer design/drafting package. Functions including hatches and fills, double lines, components, dynamic drag, automatic dimensioning, and geometric snaps are thoroughly explained and illustrated with working examples and hands-on drawing activities. This example-rich reference also covers Levels 1 and 2 of this exciting, productive tool.

1-55622-153-3 • **$21.95**
softbound • 288 pages

Harvard Graphics
DAVID G. ZAHORAN
Follow the step-by-step instructions to master the variety of options of this number one selling business graphics software. Hands-on techniques are used to allow beginning users to create graphs and charts. Advanced users can use this text as a quick reference and an indepth guide to more involved graphic presentations. No matter who the user, Illustrated Harvard Graphics provides simple and effective use of the software in a non-technical and professional manner.

1-55622-164-9 • **$21.95**
1st qtr • 344 pgs

MS/PC-DOS 3.3
RUSSELL A. STULTZ
Revised to include the latest versions of MS/PC-DOS, this comprehensive tutorial/reference reveals the power of DOS utilities in brief, easy-to-understand modules. Tips on batch files, system prompts, special commands, and functions are easily found in this efficient helper. Ready-to-implement examples illustrate complex DOS functions. DOS versions 1.10 through 3.3 are detailed to help owners of IBM PC, XT, AT, PCjr, TIPC, and PC compatibles. This guide will prove indispensable to novice and expert MS/PC-DOS users.

1-55622-028-6 • **$19.95**
softbound • 232 pages

MS/PC-DOS 4.0
Sixth Edition
RUSSELL A. STULTZ
This complete, timesaving reference contains all the significant updates to the world's most popular operating system. The novice-to-expert DOS user is led keystroke-by-keystroke through a sequence of exercises designed to provide hands-on experience. Use the new text-based DOSSHELL to initiate powerful DOS utilities. Each command is detailed in brief, easy-to-understand modules which make this book an indispensable reference.

1-55622-111-8 • **$21.95**
softbound • 272 pages

Other Books from Wordware Publishing, Inc.

Call Wordware Publishing, Inc. for names of the bookstores in your area
(214) 423-0090